Also by Nina Simonds

Spices of Life

Moonbeams, Dumplings & Dragon Boats

Asian Wraps

Asian Noodles

China Express

China's Food

Chinese Seasons

Classic Chinese Cuisine

A Spoonful of Ginger

A Spoonful of Ginger

Irresistible, health-giving recipes from Asian kitchens

Nina Simonds

Full-page color photographs by Beatriz Da Costa

Black-and-white photographs by Don Rose and Michael Hodgson

Alfred A. Knopf   New York   2011

THIS IS A BORZOI BOOK
PUBLISHED BY ALFRED A. KNOPF, INC.

www.aaknopf.com

Knopf, Borzoi Books, and the colophon are registered trademarks of Random House, Inc.

Library of Congress Cataloging-in-Publication Data

   A spoonful of ginger : irresistible, health-giving recipes from Asian kitchens / Nina Simonds ; full-page color photographs by Beatriz Da Costa ; black-and-white photographs by Don Rose and Michael Hodgson.
     xii, 320 p. : ill. (some col.) ; 25 cm.
     Originally published: New York : Alfred A. Knopf, 1999.
     Includes bibliographical references (p. 301–303) and index.
     ISBN 978-0-375-71212-8
     1. Cooking, Asian. 2. Diet therapy—China. 3. Medicine, Chinese.
TX724.5.A1 S54 1999
641.595 21
                                                98075735

Manufactured in Singapore
Published April 27, 1999
First Paperback Edition, April 2011

For my mentors, Wang Lee-Tee Eng, T. C. Lai, and Chun-Han Zhu,

who taught and inspired me . . .

and for all the Asian women who generously shared their family remedies and recipes

Use the five tastes to temper the five vital organs. If these are at peace,

the vital fluid in us will flow smoothly, then our mind will find its equilibrium . . .

and the whole person will find himself in a state of supreme well-being.

—Hu Sihui, *Principles of Correct Diet* (1330)

To take medicine only when you are sick is like digging a well when you are thirsty.

Is it not already too late?

—*The Yellow Emperor's Classic of Internal Medicine* (2500 B.C.)

Let food be your medicine and medicine be your food.

—Hippocrates

Contents

Acknowledgments   xi

Introduction   3

Nourishing Soups   23

Seafood   55

Poultry: Chicken and Duck   95

Pork, Beef, and Lamb   131

Vegetables: Stir-Fries, Pickles, and Salads   155

Soybeans and Tofu   193

The Neutralizers: Rice, Breads, and Noodles   217

Sweet Flavors   253

The Kitchen Clinic and Herbal Tonics   283

Conversion Charts   299

Bibliography   301

Index   305

Acknowledgments

No book is written without the input and support of teachers, colleagues, friends, and family. This book is no different, and I sincerely thank everyone for all their help. There are, however, some whom I must mention by name.

My food-as-medicine mentors, who are featured in the pages of this book, were particularly instrumental in helping me with this work: Dr. Chun-Han Zhu, Wang Lee-Tee Eng, the chefs and Mr. Li at the Imperial Herbal restaurant, Dr. Raymond Chang, Dr. Albert Leung, Dr. Henry Lu, Dr. K. K. Tan, T. C. Lai, and Daniel Reid. Bik Ng, Dr. Chin-Chi Zhu, and the Nam Buk Hong Herb store were also especially helpful. Special thanks to Katy and Steve Luis for their generous help and hospitality.

There are others whose books inspired and guided me—most notably Paul Pitchford, author of *Healing with Whole Foods*; Cecilia Tan, author of *The Family Herbal Cookbook*; Aileen Yoh, author of *Longevity: The Tao of Eating and Healing*; Dr. Elson Haas, author of *Staying Healthy with the Seasons*; and Christopher Hobbs, author of *Medicinal Mushrooms*.

I am dearly indebted to Malla Linturi for the invaluable help and support she gave me and my family during her stay in America. Piia Kairento was indispensable in taking care of my son during my forays to Asia.

Julie Lutts, Francoise Fetchko, and Debby Richards are dear friends and tireless recipe testers.

Mat Schaffer deserves special mention for his astute editorial advice and friendship; and if not for him this book would not have its great title.

Thanks to Susan Bang, Lou Hammond Associates, the Mandarin Oriental in Hong Kong, the Oriental in Singapore, and the Oriental in Bangkok for their generous hospitality and help.

Jane Dystel, my agent, has been extraordinarily supportive and helpful to me throughout all stages of this book and beyond.

A special thank-you and a hug to Judith Jones, my editor, who has been inspirational to work with. Ken Schneider, Paul Bogaards, Sonny Mehta, Virginia Tan,

Carol Carson, Peter Andersen, and Karen Mugler at Knopf also deserve special thanks for their help and efforts.

At Ph.D, Michael Hodgson and his crew once again have toiled away and created a stunning and functional design for this book.

Thanks to Beatriz Da Costa for her exquisite photographs and Anne de Ravel, David Bonom, and Suzanne Shaker for their invaluable help in preparing and styling the food.

Roger and George Berkowitz and the staff at Legal Seafoods in Boston were extraordinarily supportive in bringing the Imperial Herbal experience to Boston for several months for a promotion, allowing me to work with the chefs and further my studies. Thank you! Thank you!

Throughout the years a number of colleagues have consistently supported me in all of my projects. I am especially grateful to Zanne Stewart and Kemp Minifie at *Gourmet,* to Jill Melton and Cynthia Lagrone at *Cooking Light,* to Fiona Luis at the *Boston Globe,* to Laurie Ochoa, Russ Parsons, and the food section staff at the *Los Angeles Times,* to Patsy Jamieson at *Eating Well,* to Anastasia Toufexis at *Psychology Today* (formerly at *Self*), to Marialisa Calta at the United Media, and to Nancy McKeon, Phyllis Richman, and all the food staff crew at the *Washington Post.*

Last but certainly not least, I'd like to thank Don and Jesse Rose, who continually bring joy, love, and balance to my life.

A Spoonful of Ginger

Introduction

It started with a stomachache—not a dull ache, but a horrible, searing pain, the kind that makes you double over in agony. That was 1972, and I had just arrived in Taipei to begin what would be a three-and-a-half-year sojourn in Asia studying Chinese language, culture, and food.

To celebrate my arrival, I had attended numerous banquets and had devoured EVERYTHING in sight with enthusiasm. Then I got a stomachache. I was immediately dispatched to my surrogate Chinese mother's favorite doctor, who, as it turned out, was trained in both Chinese and Western medicine.

Dr. Lin carefully examined my belly, gently prodding different areas. Then he asked me questions about what I had eaten in the last twenty-four hours. He made two columns, I noticed, identifying each item as either *yin* or *yang*. His frown deepened as the list of yin foods grew longer and longer. Finally, he told me that my stomachache was a result of too many yin foods. I now needed to counteract the condition with the help of herbs combined with yang dishes.

I was familiar with the yin><yang—positive versus negative—concept, but I had never before heard it applied to food. I asked him to explain, and he told me that the Chinese believed that foods—like many other things—were classified as yin or yang depending on the energy they created in the body. Yin foods were cooling to the body, while yang foods had a warming effect. Whenever there was an imbalance, certain negative conditions or illnesses were apt to develop.

In my case, he prescribed a regimen that included warm congee (rice porridge) with scallions and ginger, chicken soup with ginseng and ginger, and cinnamon lamb with garlic chives. I followed it faithfully, and within forty-eight hours my stomach was back to normal. I continued eating the foods he recommended for several more days and I began to feel healthier than I had in a long time.

That experience was my first introduction to food as medicine, and it marked the beginning—some twenty-five years ago—of my study of the Asian holistic philosophy, one that deals with the body as a whole, rather than its separate parts. For this reason, many alternative health care practitioners prefer the use of the word "wholistic" to holistic. I tend to agree.

For the Western skeptic, holistic philosophy may be difficult to grasp, but for the Chinese, the idea that balance and harmony are integral to one's well-being is a belief entrenched in their culture. And food plays a powerful role in this equation.

The practice of using food and herbs as medicine can be traced back to ancient China. The legendary Emperor Shen Nong, who is believed to have lived around 3000 B.C., and is considered by the Chinese to be the father of agriculture, was known as a student of the healing properties of various plants. He also established the theory of yin and yang, which became the foundation of Chinese culture and philosophy. Yin and yang represent the opposing yet complementary forces of the universe. Together they make up the whole. Every object or action can be classified as either yin or yang, and everything is influenced by their constant ebb and flow.

Lao Zi, the father of Taoism, who lived in the sixth century B.C., continued to promote this belief in opposing principles. Then Chinese Taoist monks began practicing herbal medicine, collecting rare plants and experimenting with them. They, too, believed that balance is the key to good health and that longevity depends on total harmony between the human body and its natural environment. Food should be consumed not only for sustenance, but also to tune up the body and fortify it against disease. *The Yellow Emperor's Classic of Internal Medicine,* which was written about 2500 B.C. and remains the bible for students of Chinese medicine, reiterated the same concept: "Diseases are thought to occur when there is an imbalance. Through their interactions and functions, yin and yang are responsible for diseases."

Foods are divided into three categories: hot, cold, and neutral, depending on their effect on the body. Yin, or cold, foods, such as fruits, vegetables, and many types of seafood, are recommended to offset too much yang. Yang, or hot, foods, which include beef, lamb, and eggs, are taken to counterbalance too much yin. Neutral foods provide balance. (At the beginning of each chapter, I discuss the role of specific foods in greater detail.)

The body's internal condition also may be classified as yin or yang, and food may play a role in balancing this condition. For example, if your internal energy at the moment is yin—you feel sluggish or tired—you can correct this condition by eating yang foods, which stimulate the body and increase energy. Conversely, when you are feeling restless and impatient, which are yang characteristics, yin foods have a cooling or calming effect.

The Chinese also believe that foods are categorized as sweet (earth), bitter (fire), sour (wood), pungent (metal), and salty (water). In turn, each of the flavors influences specific parts of the body. Sweet (earth) foods disperse stagnant energy and harmonize the stomach. Bitter (fire) foods tend to affect the heart and small intestines. Sour (wood) foods influence the liver and gallbladder, while pungent (metal) foods have an affinity for the lungs and large intestine. Salty (water) foods are associated with the kidneys and bladder. If a particular organ is weak, a Chinese doctor would suggest that you eat foods influencing that part of the body to strengthen it. Similarly, certain foods are particularly beneficial during different seasons and should be eaten at that time (see page 10).

For thousands of years, various foods have been prescribed by Chinese doctors and have been prepared by loving mothers to prevent diseases and to cure them. For the Chinese, and many Asian cultures, food is a nurturing, benevolent friend that maintains, and restores, health. We in the West tend to concentrate more on what is *not* good for us, and we are so apprehensive about what we eat that often food becomes an enemy.

The Asian holistic approach does not preach denial or impose a rigid diet but, rather, stresses a commonsense, relaxed approach to eating in which balance is key. The emphasis is on listening to your body and feeding it what it needs. Foods are appreciated and enjoyed for the pleasure they give us—for their vibrant colors, flavors, and textures. They are also respected, if not revered, for their therapeutic properties.

While the Chinese have promoted the toniclike effects of food for centuries, recent scientific and medical research in this country, Europe, and Asia is proving many of these age-old beliefs to be valid. Western doctors are now taking notice as the public has embraced a number of alternative therapies.

Western medicine too often relies on invasive procedures such as drugs and surgery, whereas Chinese medicine focuses on the whole body, particularly on the immune system, so we can fight disease and maintain long-term good health. With a holistic approach we feel more in control of our own well-being.

I have often been asked whether my diet and health have changed since I began researching this book. In fact, for many years now I have been practicing this holistic approach in the meals I prepare for myself and my family. We eat shiitake mushrooms often to bolster our immune systems. I incorporate tofu or soybean dishes into our menus on a regular basis, particularly when I am experiencing PMS. And I nurture my family with spicy and hearty dishes when we are feeling rundown and vulnerable to colds and the flu.

During the course of my research I have talked to leading doctors, researchers, and writers in the field to better understand the underlying philosophy and to benefit from the latest research, all of which I share with you on the pages of this book. But most of all, I have drawn inspiration from the many natural and home cooks I have observed in Singapore, Malaysia, China, Taiwan, Vietnam, Japan, Hong Kong, Thailand, Canada, and the United States who instinctively apply the age-old holistic principles by blending foods in the right combinations of flavors and seasonal accents that are naturally good for you. I have marveled at how quick and simple their preparations are for the most part and I have translated their techniques to our own kitchens, simplifying where necessary to make them fully accessible to Western home cooks. No one would think eating these dishes—with their fresh, vibrant flavors—that this food was meant to be "therapeutic." They are simply delicious and health-giving.

Nina Simonds
Spring 1998

Herbs, foods, and other natural remedies are not substitutes for professional medical care. For a specific health problem, consult a qualified health-care giver for guidance.

Are You Yin or Yang?

Everyone possesses both yin and yang elements that are constantly shifting depending on age, health, lifestyle, environment, and diet. We are all born, however, with a general disposition toward being yin or yang, which is hereditary as well as dependent on several other factors. Since balance is the key to good health, it is helpful to know what your disposition is. Are you yin or yang?

According to Dr. Chun-Han Zhu, a third-generation Chinese physician who practices in the Boston area, a Chinese doctor often observes general characteristics that indicate whether a person is yin or yang. They are the following:

Yin Body Types
- Listless or lacking energy
- Thin and pale-faced
- Vulnerable to infectious diseases
- Relaxed, easygoing, and quiet
- Sensitive to cold

Yang Body Types
- Usually superactive, hyper, full of energy and vitality
- Generally heavyset or overweight
- Flushed face or ruddy complexion
- Restless or impatient
- Not sensitive to cold
- Easily constipated
- Susceptible to hypertension, hyperthyroid condition, and strokes

To diagnose a patient's illness, a Chinese physician first inquires about physical symptoms such as general body pains and problems with the ears, nose, or throat. He or she also examines the patient's tongue and takes the patient's pulse, measuring the *qi,* or energy, on both wrists, which corresponds to the main organs in the body, including the heart, liver, kidney, lungs, and spleen. Usually questions will also be asked regarding:

- Diet, digestion, stools, and urination
- Intake of drugs, alcohol, and nicotine
- Perspiration and sleep patterns
- Menstrual patterns, pregnancies, and menopause

Diagnosis by a qualified Chinese doctor or physician is recommended for discerning illness and whether your body type is yin or yang.

The Seasonal Diet

The Chinese believe there are foods that correspond to each season, nourishing and balancing the body for optimum health. Each season also corresponds to one of the five basic flavors—sour, salty, pungent, sweet, and bitter—which in turn highlights a different body organ. For example:

Season	Flavor Characteristic	Corresponding Body Organ(s)
spring	sour (wood)	liver and gallbladder
summer	bitter (fire)	heart and small intestine
late summer	sweet (earth)	spleen and stomach
autumn	pungent (metal)	lungs and large intestine
winter	salty (water)	kidney and bladder

These relationships give important clues as to the best regimen to follow in each season. In any season, however, a diet that's largely based on grains, seasonal vegetables, and fruits, with some seafood and meat, is recommended. Every person should also consider his or her body's individual needs (yin><yang) in shaping a regimen for total balance.

Spring

"The forces of spring create wind in heaven and wood on Earth."
—*Naboru Muramoto,* Healing Ourselves

The spring season signifies rebirth and renewal and it is traditionally a time for cleansing. Some Chinese doctors recommend a fast, consuming only fruit and vegetable juices. Foods considered particularly appropriate for this season (apart from seasonal specialties) are:*

- grains like wheat, barley, oats, and rye
- beans like lentils, kidney beans, and green peas
- vegetables such as bean sprouts, carrots, celery, salad greens of any kind, broccoli, green peppers, shiitake mushrooms, sweet potatoes, and green beans
- all types of citrus fruits and apricots
- chicken, pork, duck, and beef

Sample Spring Menus

Spicy Stir-Fried Chicken with Fresh Vegetables
Basic Cooked White or Brown Rice
Cinnamon-Honey Orange Slices

Vegetarian Egg Drop Soup
Barbecued Pork Brown Rice
Coconut Rice Pudding with Berries

Braised Duck with Tangerine Peel and Sweet Potatoes
Flash-Cooked Bean Sprouts
Basic Cooked White or Brown Rice

*Check the index for recipes featuring these foods.

Summer

"The heart is the ruler over summer. The heart is the root of life and generates all changes in spirit."—Chinese folktale

Summer is a high energy/yang period when the fire element dominates. Some doctors recommend cutting back on coffee, alcohol, red meats, dairy products, and other fatty foods during the warmer weather. In addition to the seasonal specialties, foods that are particularly suited for summer are:*

- grains like corn and millet
- mung beans and red and green lentils
- chiles, cucumbers, cauliflower, cabbage, green peppers, kale, any bitter greens—such as endive, escarole, watercress, bitter gourd, scallions, and tomatoes
- strawberries, raspberries, apricots, grapes, and peaches
- shrimp, oysters, and clams
- pungent seasonings—such as curry, pepper, fennel, garlic, and ginger

Sample Summer Menus

Shrimp Sambal
Wilted Greens with a Spicy Garlic Dressing
Basic Cooked White or Brown Rice
Strawberries and Melon in Plum Wine

Grilled Shrimp with a Chile Dressing
Fresh Corn and Roasted Bell Pepper Salad
Steamed Rice with Toasted Pine Nuts
Fresh Mangoes and Silver Tree Ears in Syrup

Fresh Corn Chowder
Vegetarian Roll-Ups

*Check the index for recipes featuring these foods.

Late Summer

"The spleen is the ruler over the end of summer, which is a season by itself. Its condition may be read from a person's lips; if injured, whiteness will appear in the region of the mouth. It acts upon the flesh and muscles of yin, which penetrates the aura of the earth."—Chinese folktale

Late summer is a season unique to the Chinese, a transitional time between summer and fall. According to Chinese medicine, it's a time of dampness, which can penetrate the body and influence health adversely. Aromatic seasonings such as fresh mint, basil, and cilantro counteract this tendency. Along with seasonal vegetables and fruits, some of the recommended foods are:

- millet, barley, chickpeas and sesame seeds
- eggs, chicken and game
- tuna and swordfish
- all types of squash, sweet potatoes, taro, and eggplant
- apples, watermelon, cantaloupe, and honeydew melons
- fresh herbs such as basil, cilantro, and mint

Sample Late Summer Menus

Grilled Ginger Teriyaki Tuna
Curried Pumpkin or Squash
Basic Cooked White or Brown Rice
Baked Apples with Honey, Cinnamon, and Jujubes

Chicken Salad with Fresh Mint
Spicy Stir-Fried Sweet Potatoes
Japanese Wild Mushrooms with Soba

Spicy Stir-Fried Tempeh with Basil
Basic Cooked White or Brown Rice
Almond Soy Jelly with Litchees and Melon

Autumn

"The lungs are the rulers over autumn. Since the lungs correspond to the large intestine, both organs are treated together. The lungs are the stronghold and the root of breath."—Chinese folktale

Autumn is the season of the harvest, when the earth slowly but inexorably moves toward winter. Pungent foods are best eaten in this period and include the following:

- rice, wild rice, barley, and wheat
- soybeans, tofu, tempeh, and other soybean products
- cabbage, bamboo shoots, cauliflower, celery, cucumber, eggplant, lettuce and green leafy vegetables, pumpkin, winter squash, spinach, and water chestnuts
- apples, bananas, kumquats, mangoes, litchees, pears, and strawberries
- flounder, cod, salmon, turkey, and chicken

Sample Fall Menus

Stuffed Cabbage Pot
Saucy Ground Turkey Wrapped in Lettuce Leaves

Black Mushroom and Leek Soup
Rainbow Salad with Spicy Peanut Dressing
Banana-Coconut Pudding

Hot and Sour Salmon with Greens
Cinnamon Curry Rice
Pumpkin Caramel Custard

Winter

"The kidneys are the rulers over winter. The kidney and bladder are related and have to be treated together. Within the kidneys, 'essence' is stored, and they govern all that is secluded and dormant and that is hoarded up."—Chinese folktale

Winter is the season when the yin element controls the climate; darkness and cold are the pervasive influences. Foods that are particularly suited to this time of year are:

- brown rice, wheat, barley, millet, and oats
- kidney beans, adzuki beans, black beans, and pinto beans
- carrots, onions, potatoes, seaweeds such as kelp and nori, lettuce, and bitter vegetables, including endive and escarole
- cranberries
- halibut, bluefish, salmon, swordfish, clams, crab, chicken, beef, and lamb
- garlic, ginger, pepper, and other pungent spices

Sample Winter Menus

Wilted Spinach and Mushroom Salad
Katy Luis's Vindaloo Lamb
Basic Cooked White or Brown Rice

Spicy Fish Stew
Scallion Pancakes
Two-Spice Vanilla Tapioca Pudding

Chinese Cinnamon Barley Soup
Hot and Sour Cabbage Slaw
Curried Tofu
Basic Cooked White or Brown Rice

Life Passages—Foods for Growth and Good Health

Life, like the seasons of the year, evolves in a series of stages or passages from infancy to old age. Cecilia Tan, author of *The Family Herbal Cookbook* (Times Books International, 1989), and many Chinese doctors divide these stages into five distinct periods:

- Babies and Toddlers
- Growing Years: twelve years and under
- Adolescence
- Adulthood and Motherhood
- Fifties and Beyond

The Chinese believe that there are foods particularly beneficial to growth and health at these stages. Accordingly:

Babies and Toddlers

Once an infant is ready for solid food, the Asian mother concocts a variety of porridges (congees), soups, and simple noodle dishes. Mothers are careful to prepare a balanced diet, emphasizing a selection of meats, seafood, vegetables, fruits, and eggs. Lean meats, which digest more easily, are favored, and the amount of sugar and salt is restricted.

Growing Years

During the years after infancy and up to about twelve, a good diet is essential to a child's health and often determines his well-being in the years to come. Children are particularly vulnerable to illness such as colds, earaches, and the flu during this period, so a balanced diet of stimulating and calming foods with an accent on tonics is stressed. (See the list of tonic foods described on page 19.)

Hyperactivity is easily exacerbated by what the child eats. Asians believe that an excess of yang foods, such as chocolate, fried foods, and animal fats, should be avoided. Foods such as peanuts (which aid growth) and sesame seeds or oil (which lubricate the system), green vegetables (which prevent illness), and soybean products (which are rich in calcium, iron, and potassium) are recommended.

Adolescence

Rapid and sometimes sporadic growth, moodiness, mood swings, and uncertainty are common traits of adolescence. Diet is particularly important as girls reach puberty. Ice-cold foods or drinks should be avoided during their menstrual cycle, as should the consumption of many yin foods—such as cabbage, bananas, grapefruits, and lemons, which can cause cramps.

Boys in adolescence should concentrate on energy-giving foods that will stimulate growth and fuel energy, and a mix of grains, meats, seafood, and vegetables is recommended.

Adulthood

Balance and moderation are the most important considerations in the adult diet. Immune-bolstering foods such as vegetables, soy products (especially tofu), seafood, and fruits should be in generous supply. The regimen of the young and middle adult years is especially significant in terms of preventing disease in later years. Seasonings like garlic, ginger, chile peppers, and onions are particularly therapeutic as the body ages. The Asian diet, with its emphasis on staple foods such as rice and noodles garnished with vegetables, seafood, and smaller portions of meat, is exemplary.

Motherhood

Diet is especially important for expectant mothers. The Chinese have developed a meticulously evolved calendar of the best foods to eat during pregnancy. Here is a summary:

First Trimester: In the earliest weeks of pregnancy, the Chinese believe that women favor "sour" food as the baby's nervous system is formed. Mothers-to-be are encouraged to eat more meats and chicken and to consume lots of chicken soup.

Second Trimester: As the mother's appetite improves and the movement of the baby is felt, she is encouraged to eat more rice, poultry, and fish. Beans and meat are recommended to boost vitality and improve circulation.

Third Trimester: In general, moderation is recommended, but foods that are too yin, or cold, should be avoided since they are believed to harm the development of the baby's bones. Clear soups and soybean milk, which are believed to ensure a baby's smooth complexion, are suggested. As the mother nears the end of her pregnancy, foods that restore energy for the delivery should be consumed.

After childbirth, a new mother's health is considered particularly vulnerable. She usually enters a period of confinement that traditionally lasts from a month to 44 days. During this time, Chinese women stay indoors and avoid drafts and dampness. They adhere to a strict diet composed of mainly yang foods, including chicken, meat, fish, and eggs with lots of soups and stews. These dishes are believed to replenish the new mother's energy, stamina, and blood supply.

Fifties and Beyond

As the body begins to show signs of aging and life's pace usually slows down a bit, there are certain foods that are especially beneficial. A balanced diet is still extremely important, with an emphasis on seafood, lean meats, and tonic soups, which strengthen the body and ease digestion. Seasonings such as garlic (which is antibacterial), cinnamon (which improves circulation), and basil (which is a spiritual tonic), ginseng (which promotes longevity through strengthening the immune system and improving blood pressure), and cordyceps, a Chinese herb otherwise known as dried winter worm grass (which restores energy and stimulates nerve centers) are all recommended.

Women during menopause are given special attention. Foods such as tofu, tempeh, soybean milk, and other soybean products are recommended because they contain phytoestrogens. Yang tonics, like chicken, oxtail, shrimp, and eggs, are also favored. Chinese herbs such as *dang gui,* or angelica, a highly prized root that is considered to be the ultimate woman's tonic, and *bai shao* (dried white peony), which is recommended for hot flashes, are cooked with dishes to relieve distressing menopausal symptoms.

Common Conditions and Ailments

Below are common conditions or ailments with page references to discussions of foods that help relieve symptoms or address the condition:

acne, pimples: 295

anemia: 152

arthritis: 77

blood pressure, hypertension: 73, 78, 83, 127, 181, 208, 221, 278, 279, 293

burns: 179, 238

canker sores, boils: 159, 161

cholesterol: 78, 171, 178, 212, 233

complexion: 153, 186, 265, 272

colds, congestion, coughs, sore throat: 72, 84, 85, 122, 146, 149, 169, 172, 175, 185, 190, 221, 233, 258, 261, 269, 272, 278, 280, 292

constipation: 169, 175, 265, 269, 276, 294

depression: 75, 160, 229, 263

diarrhea: 163, 174, 215, 229, 233, 275

dizziness: 88, 127, 233, 273

energy depletion, exhaustion: 146, 171, 233

eye inflammation, conjunctivitis: 162, 163, 173, 187

frostbite: 168

gastric ulcer: 63

goiter: 88

hangover: 44, 160, 275, 298

hemorrhoids: 41, 42, 85, 136, 160, 169, 267

immune system: 166, 212, 226, 233, 265

impotence: 77, 152

indigestion, heartburn: 49, 71, 73, 82, 120, 122, 134, 149, 153, 188, 197, 233, 236, 256, 258, 279, 281, 297

laxative: 185, 186, 187, 263

longevity: 290

loss of appetite: 37, 92, 118, 257, 263, 273

menopausal symptoms: 202

menstrual problems, PMS: 181, 265, 272, 291

motion sickness: 67, 122

nausea: 229, 233, 243

poison ivy or oak: 275

recovery from illness: 32

stress, ulcers: 243

toothache: 296

urinary problems: 166, 189, 269

How to Use the Recipes in This Book

The recipes in this book are inspired by the Asian holistic philosophy of eating foods that are good for you, that are seasonally appropriate, and that taste good. Some cooks may be intimidated by preparing Asian dishes that call for unfamiliar ingredients and cooking techniques. Relax. I've simplified many of the recipes to make them more accessible. Stir-frying, which requires intense heat and fast cooking, may be frightening at first, but if you organize all your ingredients and line them up before you start, you'll find this kind of cooking quite easy. Here are some other suggestions to keep in mind as you use this book:

- Read the recipes completely before preparing the dishes.
- Cut up and marinate meats, poultry, and/or seafood, as well as the prepared vegetables with the seasonings, and set them out with any sauces, all neatly organized by your stove before you start cooking. Particularly with stir-fried dishes, having everything lined up in advance makes last-minute execution of the dishes easy.
- Use fresh, seasonal, and top-quality (and preferably organic) ingredients. Don't be afraid to substitute foods available in your market or to improvise with new foods.
- You may improvise a Chinese steamer by placing a small rack or a tunafish can with both ends removed in a large pot with a tight-fitting lid.
- Use the highest heat when stir-frying and heat the pan until it is very hot before adding anything to it. The delicious seared taste and exquisite *al dente* textures in stir-fried dishes come from cooking food quickly over high heat.
- Plan each meal with balance. As you can see from the sample menus in the Seasonal Diet section, you don't need to prepare a number of different dishes and multiple courses. Often the simplest, freshest meals are the best—like a steamed fish with rice and a stir-fried freshly picked vegetable. Usually you start with a staple such as rice, noodles, or bread and choose one or two dishes with contrasting flavors, textures, colors, and cooking techniques to garnish or flavor the staple.

- When water chestnuts are called for in the recipes, use whole, canned water chestnuts. They should be blanched in boiling water for ten seconds, refreshed in cold water, drained on paper towels, and used as directed. Of course, you can use fresh water chestnuts, but they must be peeled and cooked for five minutes in boiling water, then refreshed in cold water and drained.

Nourishing Soups

Nourishing Soups and the Imperial Herbal Restaurant

I was seated in front of Mr. Li Lian Xing, a Chinese herbalist who was trying to diagnose my malady. I complained that I had no appetite and that I was constantly cold. He checked the pulse of my right hand; it was weak and slow. He inspected my tongue and noticed that it was pale and slightly white. He made his diagnosis. "You are too yin," he solemnly pronounced, and prescribed an order of baked lamb with Chinese wolfberries and a pot of "double-boiled" chicken soup (two yang dishes).

This was no ordinary herbalist's office, although I was surrounded by Chinese herbs. We were seated at the front of the Imperial Herbal restaurant in Singapore, where Mr. Li is the resident herbalist. From the day it first opened eleven years ago, the Imperial Herbal has drawn praise from its local and international clientele for its masterful marriage of herbs and Chinese haute cuisine. And Mr. Li has acquired a devoted following of customers who come to the restaurant for treatment. I had come to be treated for a minor ailment and to sample the legendary food.

The idea of treating illness and disease with food and herbs is not new to Asians: Different foods have long been prescribed and eaten as a form of preventative therapy. Ginger is believed to stimulate the stomach and intestines. It is also reputed to have warming properties. Bean curd, or tofu, is eaten to increase body energy, produce fluids, and lubricate the system. It is said to have yin, or cooling, properties.

Fresh Corn Chowder

Disease occurs, Chinese doctors believe, when there is an imbalance in the system. All foods are classified as yin, yang, or neutral, depending on their effect on the body. Yin foods have a calming effect, while too much yang can trigger hyperactivity. Generally, yang foods—which include eggs, fatty meats, and pungent spices—are strong, rich, and spicy, while yin foods, such as raw fruits and vegetables, and many types of seafood, are bitter, salty, and light. Neutral foods, such as rice, peanuts, and bread, provide balance.

At first glance, the menu of the Imperial Herbal looks like that of any other Chinese restaurant. The offerings include braised cod with spicy sauce, sautéed chile prawns with walnuts, and orange-peel beef. Then you notice the little notes on the menu next to the dishes' names. The cod—so the menu informs you—is cooked with *dang shen* and *huang qi,* two Chinese herbs that increase body energy and aid digestion. The walnuts, which garnish the chile prawns, are believed to strengthen the kidneys and nourish the brain. The orange peel with the beef inhibits coughing and the orange pith is beneficial to the lungs.

For many years, Chinese herbal cuisine has been confined to the home kitchen, and the dishes have tended to be hearty, unrefined, and bitter-tasting. Some Cantonese restaurants, however, have offered delicacies that are relished for their flavor and pharmacological benefits. For instance, shark's fin is believed to maintain youth, while abalone soothes the lungs and improves eyesight.

The Imperial Herbal restaurant offers dishes that are both delicious and beneficial. It is the brainchild of Mrs. Wang-Lee Tee Eng, a forty-four-year-old Singaporean businesswoman, who visited an herbal restaurant in China in the mid-1980s and became fascinated with the concept. She was determined to refine herbal dishes and elevate them to haute cuisine, broadening their appeal. She brought in from northern China two gold-medal master chefs and an herbalist.

Mrs. Wang felt that with today's pressing concerns about health and the widespread appreciation for fine food, a marriage between a Chinese doctor and a master chef was a natural.

The menu has broadened and diversified greatly since the restaurant first opened. The chefs not only create their own specialties but also adapt classic dishes to make them even healthier: Beggar's Chicken—an eastern specialty where a whole chicken is first stuffed and wrapped in a lotus leaf, then surrounded by clay and baked for several hours before the clay is cracked open at the table—is embellished further with the addition of four yin herbs and four yang herbs to reinforce blood and energy. Lacquered Peking Duck is served with paper-thin homemade Mandarin pancakes enriched with a flavorless herb that reduces cholesterol.

The list of soups is especially impressive: Double-boiled Soft-Shell River Turtle Soup is a yin energy tonic that, according to the menu, strengthens the body's immune system and helps to prevent cancer. Chicken Soup with Wolfberry promotes blood circulation, and Freshwater Fish with American Ginseng promotes the energy to offset fatigue and "shortness of breath."

Soups, according to Mrs. Wang, are a vital and important way of dispensing herbs and tonics, second only to teas. "Traditionally, Asians adore soups, and when we are making herbal tonics one of the most popular cooking methods is 'double-boiling,' where the soup is steamed inside a container so that the broth is very clear and intense. It's the most effective way of extracting the pure essence of the herb into the soup," she told me.

One of the most spectacular soups, which has become a house specialty, is

"Buddha Jumping over the Wall." It is a clear soup with many types of seafood, fresh and dried, poached in a "superior" stock, a rich broth made with chicken and pork bones and seasoned with scallions and ginger. Customers are equally enthusiastic about the Turtle Soup. It is believed to be especially good for the immune system and it's excellent for strengthening *qi,* or energy. The restaurant also makes a special crocodile meat soup that's excellent for asthma.

Exotic or mundane, humble or pretentious, soups are guaranteed to satisfy even the most demanding palate. The following chapter offers a varied selection of refined, homespun, and tonic soups.

Classic Chicken Broth

This delicate chicken broth is used as a base for many soups and sauces. It freezes beautifully and can be prepared in advance. If you are not making a very delicate soup or need broth for a sauce, you may use a simple broth made with equal parts of a small can (about 2 cups) of a good-quality low-salt chicken broth and water, $^1/_3$ cup rice wine or sake, and three slices of fresh ginger, smashed lightly. Put all these ingredients in a saucepan and cook for about 10 minutes over medium-low heat.

9 cups water

2$^1/_2$ pounds chicken backs, necks, bones, and/or pieces

1 cup rice wine or sake

6 slices fresh ginger, each the size of a quarter, smashed lightly with the flat side of a knife

6 whole scallions, ends trimmed, smashed lightly with the flat side of a knife

MAKES ABOUT SIX CUPS

1. Put the water with the chicken bones, rice wine or sake, ginger slices, and scallions in a large pot and bring to a boil. Reduce the heat to low and simmer uncovered for 1$^1/_2$ hours, skimming the surface to remove any impurities.
2. Strain the broth through a fine-meshed strainer, removing the bones or chicken pieces, and skim to remove any fat. Use the broth as directed in the recipe.

Clear-Steamed Chicken Soup with Ginger

Clear-steaming, otherwise known as double-boiling, is a simple technique used by Chinese cooks where a food is cooked slowly within a closed container. The result is a very clear, intense broth.

SIX SERVINGS

1 whole chicken, about 3 to 3 1/2 pounds	10 whole scallions, ends trimmed and smashed lightly with the flat side of a knife
Soup Broth	10 slices fresh ginger, the size of a quarter, smashed with the flat side of a knife
6 cups boiling water	1 teaspoon salt, or to taste
1 3/4 cups rice wine, preferably Shaoxing wine (available at Asian markets)	

☯ As do other cultures, the Chinese consider chicken soup a universal panacea for many illnesses and conditions. Chicken soup with ginger is often eaten by new mothers every day for a month after they have given birth. It is believed to restore and renew the body's energy.

1. Remove any fat from the cavity opening and around the neck of the chicken. Rinse lightly and drain. Using a heavy knife or a cleaver, cut the chicken, through the bones, into 10 to 12 pieces. Heat 2 quarts water until boiling and blanch the chicken pieces for 1 minute after the water reaches a boil to clean them. Drain the chicken, discarding the water, then rinse in cold water and drain again.

2. Place the chicken pieces and the Soup Broth ingredients, except the salt, in a heat-proof pot or 2-quart soufflé dish. Cover tightly with heavy-duty aluminum foil and place on a steamer tray or small rack. Fill a wok with enough water to just reach the bottom of the steamer tray or rack and heat until boiling. Place the food on the steamer tray or rack over the boiling water, cover, and steam 2 hours over high heat, replacing the boiling water in the wok as necessary. Alternatively, you may steam the soup in the oven: Pre-heat the oven to 425°F. Place the ingredients in a Dutch oven or casserole with a lid and, before putting on the cover, wrap the top tightly with heavy-duty aluminum foil; then cover. Place the pot in a lasagna pan or a casserole and fill with 1 1/2 inches boiling water. Bake for 2 hours, replenishing the boiling water as necessary.

3. Skim the top of the broth to remove any impurities and fat. Add the salt. Remove the ginger and scallions, ladle the soup and pieces of the chicken into serving bowls, and serve. To reheat and retain a clear broth, steam or bake in a closed pot for 10 to 15 minutes, or until piping hot.

Clear-Steamed Chicken Soup with Chinese Black Mushrooms: Soften 10 dried Chinese black mushrooms in hot water to cover for 20 minutes. Drain, remove and discard stems, and cut the caps, holding the knife on the diagonal, into quarters or thirds, depending on the size. Add to the soup ingredients and prepare as directed.

Clear-Steamed Chicken Soup with Prosciutto in Melons: Delete salt from the ingredients. Trim 1/4 pound paper-thin prosciutto slices of any fat and cut into 1 1/2-inch squares. Add to the soup ingredients and prepare the soup as directed. Once cooked, discard the ginger and scallions.

Using a sharp knife, cut a very thin wedge from the bottom of 6 slightly underripe cantaloupe or honeydew melons, so that they will stand upright. Cut off the top quarter of each melon, reserving the quarters for lids, and scoop out the seeds and some of the flesh, creating a bowl for the soup. Place 2 or 3 melons upright on a circular rack in a large pot, add 4 inches boiling water, and steam 12 to 15 minutes, until somewhat tender. Remove the melons and place each in a bowl. When all are ready, portion some of the soup into each melon. Reposition the lids on top of the melons and serve. Alternatively, if small melons are not available, you may scoop balls from 2 to 3 melons, add to the hot soup, and simmer for 5 minutes. Ladle into soup bowls and serve.

Clear-Steamed Chicken Soup with Chinese Ginseng: Put 1 ounce high-quality Chinese ginseng and 2 cups water in a pot. Bring to a boil and cook over medium-low heat for 30 minutes. Cut ginseng into 1/2-inch pieces. Add the ginseng and its cooking water to the soup ingredients, using only 4 cups (instead of 6) and prepare as directed. Discard the scallions and fresh ginger and serve the chicken and soup with the ginseng pulp.

Clear-Steamed Chicken Soup with Angelica and Chinese Dates: Soften 25 Chinese dates, or jujubes (available at Asian markets), in hot water to cover for 20 minutes. Drain and remove the pits. Prepare the Clear-Steamed Chicken Soup recipe as directed, adding 6 to 7 wafer-thin slices angelica (*dang gui*) and the pitted dates. Clear-steam the ingredients for 3 1/2 to 4 hours. Remove and serve as directed.

☯ Chinese ginseng is reputed to promote the secretion of hormones, like an aphrodisiac. It is also believed to retard aging.

☯ Angelica and Chinese dates are especially good for PMS and menopausal distresses such as hot flashes. Cecilia Tan, author of *The Family Herbal Cookbook,* says they're also excellent for the entire family. *Dang gui,* a Chinese herb, is believed to be one of the most effective medicines for numerous gynecological disorders or ailments.

Clear-Steamed Drunken Chicken Soup

This is the soup I dream about when I feel my resistance is low. I love its pure, mellow flavor. It soothes and warms up the body at the same time. It is called "drunken" because of the generous quantity of rice wine in the recipe. For optimum flavor, use a good quality Shaoxing rice wine and a free-range, natural chicken.

1 whole chicken, about 3 to 3^1/2 pounds

Soup Broth

4 cups water

2 cups rice wine, preferably Shaoxing
  (available at Asian markets)

10 to 12 slices fresh ginger, about the size of a quarter, smashed lightly with the flat side of a knife or a cleaver

1 teaspoon salt, or to taste

SIX SERVINGS

1. Remove any fat from the cavity opening and around the neck of the chicken. Rinse the chicken lightly and drain; then, using a heavy knife or a cleaver, cut it through the bones into 10 to 12 pieces. Heat 2 quarts water until boiling and blanch the chicken pieces for 1 minute, then return to a boil to clean them. Remove the pieces, rinse in cold water, and drain.

2. Put the chicken pieces and Soup Broth ingredients, except the salt, in a heatproof pot or 2-quart soufflé dish. Cover tightly with heavy-duty aluminum foil and place in the bottom of a steamer tray or on a circular rack. Put into a wok, fill with enough water to reach the bottom edge of the tray or the top of the rack, and heat until boiling. Cover and steam 1^1/2 hours over high heat, replacing the boiling water in the wok as necessary. Alternatively, you may steam the soup in the oven: Preheat the oven to 425°F. Put the ingredients in a Dutch oven or casserole with a lid and, before placing cover, wrap the top tightly with heavy-duty aluminum foil, then cover. Place the pot in a lasagna pan or a casserole and pour in 1^1/2 inches boiling water. Bake for 1^1/2 hours, replenishing the boiling water as necessary.

3. Skim the soup to remove any impurities and fat. Add the salt. Remove the ginger, ladle the soup into serving bowls, and serve. To reheat and retain a clear broth, steam or bake in a closed pot for 10 to 15 minutes, or until piping hot.

Clear-Steamed Drunken Chicken Soup with Cordyceps: Soak 10 pieces of cordyceps in cold water to cover for 20 minutes. Remove from water and rub away any dirt. Add the cordyceps to the ingredients of the soup broth and prepare as directed. Serve each bowl of soup with several cordyceps.

☯ Cordyceps: The Chinese name literally translated is "winter worm grass," since this herb/vegetable is believed to be a worm in the winter that undergoes a metamorphosis throughout spring to become a leaf in the summer. Once it dries up in the fall, it is collected and is sold in small bundles at Chinese herbal shops. Cordyceps enrich the bone marrow and build *qi* in the body. It is often prescribed as a tonic to patients recovering from serious injuries or illnesses. Chicken and duck are believed to further enhance its tonic properties.

Homey Chicken Soup

I love to make this humble but hearty soup in the cooler weather, when my body craves its warmth and goodness. It is also one of those soups that gains flavor with reheating.

1 recipe Classic Chicken Broth (page 27), replacing backs and necks with 1 whole 3- to 3 1/2-pound chicken, fat trimmed and cut into 10 or 12 pieces

1 small head Chinese cabbage (preferably Napa) (about 1 1/2 pounds)

1 teaspoon canola or corn oil

6 cloves garlic, peeled and smashed lightly with the flat side of a knife

2 tablespoons rice wine or sake

1/2 pound fresh shiitake mushrooms, stems trimmed, and cut in quarters

2 ounces bean threads (cellophane noodles), softened in hot water to cover (if unavailable, substitute 1/3 pound thin rice stick noodles or vermicelli, softened in warm water to cover)

2 teaspoons salt

1. Prepare the Classic Chicken Broth as directed. Remove the chicken pieces and skim the broth to remove any impurities.

2. Using a sharp knife, cut away the stem of the cabbage and discard. Cut the cabbage in half and cut the leaves into 2-inch squares, separating the leafy sections from the tough ones. Place the cabbage sections in a bowl. Set by the stove with the shiitake mushrooms.

3. Heat a Dutch oven or casserole, add the oil, and heat until very hot. Add the garlic cloves and the harder sections of the cabbage and stir-fry over high heat about 1 minute. Add the rice wine, cover, and continue cooking about 5 minutes, until tender. Add the leafier sections, the shiitake mushrooms, and the chicken broth, and bring to a boil. Reduce the heat to low and simmer 20 minutes uncovered.

3. Drain the bean threads and cut them into 4-inch lengths. Add them to the soup and cook for another 2 to 3 minutes. Return the chicken pieces to the soup and stir in the salt. Ladle into soup bowls and serve.

Miso Chicken Soup with Snow Peas and Tofu

Miso soup has always been one of my favorites; it is so soothing and satisfying. Here I offer a variation of the most traditional recipe, using a chicken broth as the base rather than the classic dashi (bonito tuna stock). Shredded chicken, tofu, and snow peas round out the flavor, making it a meal in itself.

SIX SERVINGS

1 whole chicken, about 3 pounds, trimmed of fat

12 cups water

8 slices fresh ginger, about the size of a quarter, smashed lightly with the flat side of a knife

1/2 to 2/3 cup medium-colored miso paste (*chu miso* or *shinsu ichi miso*), or to taste

1 pound firm tofu, cut into thin slices about 1/4 inch thick and 11/2 inches long

3/4 pound snow or snap peas, ends snapped and veiny strings removed

3 tablespoons minced scallion greens

☯ Miso paste is made from fermented soybeans and is chock-full of protein and health. For further information on miso see page 66.

1. Cut the chicken through the bones into 10 to 12 pieces. Put the chicken pieces, water, and ginger in a heavy pot and bring to a boil. Lower the heat so that the liquid is at a simmer and cook about 1¹/₂ hours, skimming the broth to remove any impurities. Remove the chicken pieces and let them cool. Remove the ginger slices and discard. Skim the broth to remove any fat. Scoop out ¹/₂ cup broth and reserve it.

2. Using your hands or a knife, remove the skin and bones from the chicken and cut or shred the meat into thin julienne shreds. Add the chicken shreds to the skimmed broth. In a small bowl mix the reserved chicken broth with the miso paste and stir until smooth.

3. Add the tofu slices and snow peas to the soup and bring it to a boil. Reduce the heat, add the miso mixture, and stir to blend. Heat the soup until near boiling; then ladle it into serving bowls. Sprinkle the top of each bowl with some minced scallion greens and serve.

Spicy Kimchee Soup

Kimchee is a potent pickle made by Korean cooks with cabbage and all types of vegetables. Most of us know it as a garnish with rice and other dishes, but it is also used as a seasoning in stir-fried dishes and soups. I love this pungent soup, particularly in cold weather, when the spicy kimchee and hearty broth warm my entire system.

1 small Chinese (Napa) cabbage, about 1/2
   pound
1 teaspoon canola or corn oil
4 cloves garlic, smashed lightly
1/3 cup rice wine or sake
5 cups Classic Chicken Broth (page 27)
1/4 pound Korean cabbage pickle, or
   kimchee, cut into 1-inch squares
1 pound center-cut pork loin, fat or gristle
   removed

Marinade
1 1/2 tablespoons soy sauce
1 1/2 tablespoons rice wine or sake
1/2 teaspoon toasted sesame oil

1 1/2 cups scallion greens, cut on the diagonal into 1/4-inch sections
Salt to taste
3 teaspoons toasted sesame seeds for garnish

1. Cut away the stem of the cabbage and discard. Cut the cabbage in half and cut the leaves into 2-inch squares, separating the leafy sections from the tough ones. Place the cabbage sections in two bowls and set by the stove.
2. Heat a Dutch oven or a covered casserole, add the oil, and heat until hot, about 30 seconds. Add the garlic cloves and harder cabbage pieces and stir-fry for a minute over medium-high heat. Add the rice wine or sake and toss lightly, cover, and cook for $1^1/_2$ minutes. Uncover, and add the remaining cabbage pieces, chicken broth, and kimchee. Partially cover and, once the liquid reaches a boil, uncover and simmer for 30 minutes.
3. While the soup is cooking, cut the pork across the grain into thin slices about $^1/_4$ inch thick. Cut the slices into $1^1/_2$-inch squares and place them in a bowl. Add the Marinade to the pork, stir to coat the pieces, and let them sit 20 minutes.
4. Add the pork and scallions to the soup and cook for about $1^1/_2$ to 2 minutes, or until the pork is cooked. Skim the surface to remove any impurities. Taste for seasoning, adding salt if necessary. Ladle the soup into serving bowls and sprinkle the top with the sesame seeds. Serve immediately.

Chicken and Shark's Fin Soup

The Chinese find the slippery texture of the shark's fin appealing, and before it is added to a dish, any fishy flavor is removed by cooking it with fresh ginger, scallions, and rice wine. Fake shark's fin is rampant in Chinese markets, so make certain to buy the fin from a reputable source.

SIX SERVINGS

4 ounces shark's fin needles (available at a Chinese herbal shop or market)

Shark's Fin Seasonings
1/4 cup rice wine or sake
8 whole scallions, ends trimmed, and smashed lightly with the flat side of a knife
8 slices fresh ginger, the size of a quarter, smashed with the flat side of a knife

1 whole chicken, about 31/2 to 4 pounds, trimmed of fat

Braising Mixture
6 cups Classic Chicken Broth (page 27)
1/2 cup rice wine or sake
5 tablespoons soy sauce

4 scallions, ends trimmed, and smashed lightly with the flat side of a knife
4 slices fresh ginger, the size of a quarter, smashed with the flat side of a knife

Chicken Seasonings
8 dried Chinese black mushrooms, softened in hot water to cover for 20 minutes
3 ounces matchstick-size shreds prosciutto or Chinese ham
3 tablespoons finely shredded scallion greens
11/2 tablespoons finely shredded fresh ginger

11/2 tablespoons cornstarch mixed with 3 tablespoons water

1. Soften the shark's fin needles in hot water to cover for 15 minutes and drain. Put in a saucepan with the Shark's Fin Seasonings and water to cover. Bring to a boil, reduce the heat to low, and simmer uncovered for 30 minutes. Let cool and strain in a colander, discarding the liquid and seasonings.
2. With a sharp knife or cleaver, cut the chicken into 10 to 12 pieces.
3. Put the chicken and the Braising Mixture ingredients in a heavy casserole or a Dutch oven with a lid and bring to a boil. Reduce the heat to low, cover, and cook for 45 minutes. Skim the broth to remove impurities. Discard the scallions and ginger slices.

36   A SPOONFUL OF GINGER

4. Drain the mushrooms, remove the stems, and cut the caps into matchstick-size shreds.

5. Add the shark's fin needles and the Chicken Seasonings to the chicken and continue cooking for 20 minutes, partially covered. Using a slotted spoon, arrange the chicken pieces in a serving bowl. Bring the chicken broth to a boil and slowly add the cornstarch and water, stirring to prevent lumps. Pour over the chicken pieces and serve.

☯ Shark's fin is considered an expensive delicacy in China, but it is also revered as a tonic for enriching *qi,* or the body's energy, and restoring the appetite. The most costly part of the fin is the cartilage, which requires more precooking, whereas the needles are held in slightly lower regard but take less time to cook.

Vietnamese Chicken Noodle Soup

For many Asians, particularly the Vietnamese, who consume this soup daily for breakfast or lunch, it is the ultimate comfort food. The broth, infused with the pungent seasonings of fresh ginger, cinnamon, star anise, and shallots, is a feast by itself. In northern Vietnam, where beef is popular, the soup is commonly made with meat (which heats the body), but in the south, where the climate is generally hotter, chicken is often used.

SIX SERVINGS

1 whole chicken, about 3 1/2 to 4 pounds, trimmed of fat

12 cups water

Seasonings

4 shallots, cut into thin slices

6 slices fresh ginger, about the size of a quarter, smashed lightly with the flat side of a knife

4 whole star anise

2 sticks cinnamon

1/3 cup fish sauce

1/4 teaspoon freshly ground black pepper

6 ounces flat rice stick noodles or vermicelli, softened in hot water to cover for 20 minutes

2 cups bean sprouts, rinsed and drained

Accompaniments

1/4 cup minced scallion greens

1/4 cup minced fresh cilantro leaves

1 cup Thai holy basil or sweet basil leaves, stems removed, rinsed, drained, and shredded

1 lime, cut into 6 wedges

1 fresh hot red pepper, cut into thin slices

1. Using a heavy knife or a cleaver, cut the chicken through the bones into 10 to 12 pieces. Put the chicken, water, and Seasonings in a large, heavy pot and bring to a boil. Turn the heat to low and simmer uncovered for 1 1/2 hours, skimming the impurities from the broth. Strain the seasonings and chicken into a bowl, then return the broth to the pot, skimming it again. Add the fish sauce and black pepper, and reduce the heat to a bare simmer to keep warm.

2. In a large pot, bring 4 quarts water to a boil. Drop the noodles into the water and stir to prevent them from sticking together. Heat until boiling and cook for a minute, or until just tender. Drain in a colander and rinse under warm, running water to remove the starch. Drain again.

3. Using your hands or a knife, remove the skin and bones from the chicken and cut or shred the meat into thin strips. Ladle equal portions of the cooked noodles into 6 serving bowls. Add the bean sprouts to the hot soup, turn the heat to high, and cook about $1^{1}/_{2}$ to 2 minutes. Skim the surface to remove any impurities.

4. Ladle the chicken, bean sprouts, and broth over the noodles in the bowls. Sprinkle the scallions, cilantro, and basil on top. Serve with the lime wedges and hot pepper slices for extra seasoning.

Healthy Hot and Sour Soup

Try this sumptuous soup as a light lunch or dinner. This adapted, lighter version is made with chicken rather than pork, as in the classic recipe.

1 whole chicken, about 3 pounds, trimmed of fat

12 cups water

1/2 cup rice wine or sake

8 slices fresh ginger, about the size of a quarter, smashed lightly with the flat side of a knife

8 whole scallions, ends trimmed, smashed lightly with the flat side of a knife

1 pound firm tofu, cut into slabs about 1 inch thick

2 1/2 tablespoons cornstarch

1/4 cup water

6 dried Chinese black mushrooms, softened in hot water to cover for 20 minutes, stems removed and caps cut into thin julienne strips

1/4 cup dried wood ears, softened in hot water to cover for 20 minutes, drained, hard ends trimmed, and cut into thin julienne strips

2 cups julienned leeks (edges and green leaves trimmed, white part rinsed, drained, and cut into thin julienne strips)

Seasonings

4 1/2 tablespoons Chinese black vinegar or Worcestershire sauce, or more to taste

3 tablespoons soy sauce

2 1/2 to 3 tablespoons minced fresh ginger, or to taste

3/4 teaspoon freshly ground black pepper

1 teaspoon toasted sesame oil

1 teaspoon salt, or to taste

1 large egg white, lightly beaten with 2 tablespoons water

1. Cut the chicken through the bones into 10 to 12 pieces. Put the chicken pieces in a large pot with the water, rice wine, ginger, and scallions, and bring to a boil. Lower the heat so that the liquid is at a simmer and cook about 1 1/2 hours, skimming the surface to remove any impurities.

2. Wrap the tofu in paper towels, and place a heavy object such as a skillet on top. Let stand for 30 minutes to press out the excess water; then cut into thin julienne strips about 3 inches long and 1/6 inch thick.

3. Remove the ginger and scallions from the broth and skim the surface to remove any

fat. Remove the chicken pieces with a slotted spoon, remove and discard the skin, and take out the bones. Using a knife or your hands, tear the chicken meat into thin julienne strips. Mix the cornstarch with the water.

4. Strain the chicken broth into a large, heavy pot. Add the chicken shreds, julienned tofu, black mushrooms, wood ears, and leeks, and heat until boiling. Boil for about 2 minutes, skimming the surface to remove any impurities.

5. Slowly add the cornstarch thickener, stirring constantly to prevent lumps, and cook until the broth has thickened. Add the Seasonings and stir. Taste and adjust the seasonings if needed. Remove the soup from the heat and slowly add the beaten egg white, pouring it in a thin stream around the edge of the pot. Stir the soup several times in a circular motion so that the egg forms streamers. Ladle the soup into bowls and serve immediately.

☯ Wood ears, or black "herbal" fungus, have been used by the Chinese for thousands of years as a stomach tonic and for hemorrhoids. Once softened in water, they have a crunchy consistency. According to Chinese doctors, they activate the blood and act as an anticoagulant. They are also reputed to increase physical and mental energy.

Hot and Sour Seafood Soup

This seafood rendition of Hot and Sour Soup is a wonderful variation on the classic recipe. You may substitute or add scallops, shrimp, or any type of seafood to replace or embellish the fish.

1 1/2 pounds firm-fleshed fish fillets, such as haddock, red snapper, or lake trout, rinsed and drained

Marinade
1/3 cup rice wine or sake
1 1/2 tablespoons minced fresh ginger
1 teaspoon toasted sesame oil
1 teaspoon salt

5 cups Classic Chicken Broth (page 27)
1 1/2 cups scallion greens, cut into 1-inch sections
1/4 cup dried wood ears, softened in hot water to cover for 20 minutes, drained, hard ends trimmed, and cut into thin julienne strips
3/4 pound snow peas, ends snapped and veiny strings removed

2 1/2 tablespoons cornstarch mixed with 1/4 cup water

Seasonings
4 1/2 tablespoons Chinese black vinegar or Worcestershire sauce, or more to taste
3 tablespoons soy sauce
2 1/2 to 3 tablespoons minced fresh ginger, or to taste
3/4 teaspoon freshly ground black pepper
1 teaspoon toasted sesame oil
1 teaspoon salt, or to taste

1 large egg white, lightly beaten with 2 tablespoons water
2 tablespoons minced scallion greens for garnish

1. Cut the fish fillets into 1-inch chunks and place them in a bowl. Add the Marinade, toss lightly to coat, and let the fish marinate for 30 minutes.

2. Put the chicken broth in a casserole or a Dutch oven. Add the fish, scallions, and wood ears. Bring to a boil, reduce the heat to medium, and simmer about 4 to 5 minutes, or until the fish is just about cooked, skimming the surface to remove any impurities. Add the snow peas and stir.

3. Slowly add the cornstarch thickener, stirring constantly to prevent lumps, and cook until the broth has thickened. Add the Seasonings and stir; taste and adjust seasonings as needed. Remove the soup from the heat and slowly add the beaten egg white, pouring it in a thin stream around the edge of the pot. Stir the soup several times in a circular motion so that the egg forms streamers. Ladle the soup into bowls and serve immediately.

The beneficial properties of wood ears are described on page 41.

Korean Clampot with Garlic Chives

The fragrant broth of this soup is served in Korea to alleviate hangovers. I like the flavor so much that I serve it with fried rice for an easy dinner. It is traditionally made with the fresh miniature clams sold in Asian markets. If they are unavailable, use the smallest clams you can find.

SIX SERVINGS

3 pounds littleneck clams, preferably small
2 cups fresh garlic chives, ends trimmed,
   cut into 1-inch sections

4 cups water

1. Scrub the clams lightly to remove any sand and soak in cold water to cover for 1 hour. Drain the clams.
2. Put the clams, garlic chives, and water in a large, heavy pot and bring to a boil. Reduce the heat to low and simmer for 10 minutes. Serve the soup immediately.

Fresh Fish Fillet and Pea Shoot Soup

I was introduced to a version of this soup many years ago by a Hunanese chef in Taipei, Taiwan. I was struck by its subtlety and delicacy. The chef used watercress, but I feel that tender pea shoots give the soup additional dimension. If pea shoots aren't available, substitute watercress or spinach.

11/2 pounds firm white fish fillets, such as haddock, red snapper, or lake trout, skin removed

Marinade
31/2 tablespoons rice wine or sake
1 tablespoon minced fresh ginger

1 teaspoon canola or corn oil
1 tablespoon minced scallions, white part only

2 teaspoons minced garlic
1/2 pound fresh pea shoots, stems removed and wilted leaves discarded, cut into 2-inch lengths
1/4 cup rice wine or sake
51/2 cups Classic Chicken Broth (page 27)
11/2 teaspoons salt, or to taste
3 tablespoons chopped fresh cilantro

1. Holding your knife at a slight angle to the cutting board, cut the fish across the grain into 1/4-inch-thick slices. Put the slices in a bowl, add the Marinade, and mix with your hands to coat. Let marinate briefly.

2. Heat the oil in a heavy pot until hot, about 30 seconds. Add the scallions and garlic and stir-fry 15 seconds, until fragrant, over medium-high heat. Add the pea shoots and rice wine and stir-fry over high heat for 30 seconds, then add the chicken broth and salt. Bring to a boil, then add the fish slices and cook for about 1 minute, until the fish is done, skimming the surface to remove any impurities. Add the cilantro, stir gently, and ladle the soup and fish slices into serving bowls. Serve immediately.

This simple fresh soup is delightful in warm weather, when the seafood and vegetable will cool the body.

Stuffed Cabbage Pot

The original version of this dish, which is made with ground pork and called Lion's Head casserole, originated in the charming and scenic city of Hangzhou located in eastern China. It is so named because the four cabbage leaves, once braised to a golden brown tenderness, are said to resemble the mane of a lion. This soup is particularly delicious in the winter or cooler weather. It reheats beautifully.

SIX SERVINGS

1 medium head Chinese (Napa) cabbage, about 1/2 to 3/4 pound	Seasonings
	2 tablespoons minced scallions, white part only
2 teaspoons canola or corn oil	1 1/2 tablespoons minced fresh ginger
4 cloves garlic, smashed lightly with the flat side of a knife	2 tablespoons soy sauce
1/3 cup rice wine or sake	2 tablespoons rice wine or sake
5 cups Classic Chicken Broth (page 27)	1 1/2 teaspoons toasted sesame oil
1 pound ground turkey	1/2 teaspoon freshly ground black pepper
6 dried Chinese black mushrooms, softened in hot water for about 20 minutes, stems removed, and caps finely chopped	1 tablespoon cornstarch
	2 tablespoons soy sauce
	3/4 teaspoon salt

1. Cut away the stem of the cabbage and discard. Remove and reserve four of the outermost leaves. Cut the remaining cabbage in half and cut the leaves into 2-inch squares, separating the leafy sections from the stem pieces. Set aside in 2 bowls.
2. Heat a Dutch oven or a covered casserole, add half the oil and heat until hot, about 30 seconds. Add the garlic cloves and tougher cabbage sections and stir-fry for a minute over medium-high heat. Add the rice wine and toss lightly; cover and cook for 1 1/2 minutes. Uncover and add the remaining cabbage pieces and the chicken broth. Partially cover, and once the soup reaches a boil, uncover and simmer for 30 minutes.
3. While the soup is cooking, put the ground turkey, minced Chinese black mushrooms, and Seasonings in a bowl. Mix with your hands to combine the ingredients evenly, then shape into 4 oval-shaped balls.

4. Preheat the oven to 350°F. Heat a wok or skillet, add the remaining teaspoon of oil, and heat until very hot. Place the meatballs in the pan and sear until golden over high heat; then turn them over and sear on the other side. Remove with a slotted spoon and place the meatballs in the center of the cabbage soup. Cover with the four reserved leaves. Replace the lid and put the casserole in the middle shelf of the oven. Bake for 45 minutes. Add the soy sauce and salt to taste and ladle into soup bowls. Serve immediately.

Chinese Cinnamon Barley Soup

This hearty, warming soup-stew is perfect for a raw, blustery day. I often serve it over cooked rice noodles or wheat noodles for a simple but totally satisfying meal. The meat is luscious and the flavor seems to improve with reheating.

SIX SERVINGS

☯ Barley is a nutritious grain blessed with vitamins. Some health food authorities claim that when the outer hulls are removed, the remaining grain is nutritionally sound, but further processing, or pearling, removes the nutrients. So buy the hulled whole barley grains found at health food stores. Barley harmonizes the stomach and aids digestion. It is often given to the sick, since it encourages appetite. The Chinese drink barley water on a hot day to cool their constitution.

Seasonings

8 whole scallions, ends trimmed, cut into $1^1/_2$-inch sections, and smashed lightly with the flat side of a cleaver or knife

8 cloves garlic, smashed lightly with the flat side of a knife, then sliced thinly

8 slices fresh ginger, about the size of a quarter, smashed lightly with the flat side of a knife

2 sticks cinnamon

1 teaspoon anise seeds

$1/_2$ cup soy sauce

$1/_2$ cup rice wine or sake

7 cups water

2 pounds chuck or beef stew meat, trimmed of fat and gristle and cut into $1^1/_2$-inch cubes

1 cup barley

$1^1/_2$ pounds spinach, trimmed, rinsed, and drained

3 tablespoons minced scallions, white part only

1. Put the Seasonings and water in a large pot or casserole. Bring to a boil.

2. Add the beef and the barley, and boil again. Reduce the heat to low, cover, and simmer, skimming the surface to remove impurities and fat. Cook for $1^1/_2$ hours, until the beef is very tender. Scoop out the ginger slices, cinnamon sticks, and anise seeds, and discard.

3. Add the spinach to the beef, cover, and heat until boiling. Ladle the meat with broth and spinach into serving bowls, sprinkling the top with scallions. Serve immediately.

Thai Beef with Mint Soup

I love to make this soup in the dead of winter; the beef warms up my body and the mint imparts a fresh and lively flavor.

3 pounds beef shin bones or oxtails, preferably with meat and marrow

Seasonings

6 slices fresh ginger, about the size of a quarter, smashed lightly with the flat side of a knife

6 whole scallions, ends trimmed, smashed lightly with the flat side of a knife

1 cinnamon stick

2 whole star anise

12 cups water

Soup Flavorings

4 1/2 tablespoons fish sauce

3 tablespoons soy sauce

1 teaspoon sugar

1/4 teaspoon freshly ground black pepper

3 1/2 cups fresh bean sprouts, rinsed and drained

1 cup mint leaves, stems removed, rinsed, drained, and cut into fine shreds

2 whole eggs, lightly beaten with 2 tablespoons water

1. Put the beef bones, Seasonings, and water in a large pot and bring to a boil. Turn the heat to low, and simmer uncovered for 1 1/2 hours, skimming the surface to remove fat and impurities.

2. Remove the meat with a slotted spoon. Pull away the bones and discard them; cut the meat into thin slices, trimming away the fat. Discard the seasonings and mix the broth with the Soup Flavorings. Return the meat to the pot and reduce the heat.

3. Add the bean sprouts and mint leaves, turn up the heat briefly, bring to a near boil, then remove from the heat. Skim the surface to remove any impurities. Slowly pour the eggs in a thin stream around the outer edge of the soup and carefully stir once or twice in a circular motion so that the eggs form thin streamers. Taste for seasoning, adding a tiny bit of soy sauce, if necessary, and serve.

Asian cooks make a simple egg and mint leaf soup to relieve an upset stomach or heartburn. This soup is particularly beneficial for the elderly, although I like to make it for my family during the colder weather, when the beef heats up the body.

Vegetarian Egg Drop Soup

Sometimes your body craves a simple soup that can be prepared with just a few ingredients. This is such a dish. Egg drop soup is one of the first foods children are fed in China. We used to make it with fried rice for a Sunday lunch or dinner, a habit I continue to this day.

SIX SERVINGS

1 1/2 teaspoons canola or corn oil

2 medium tomatoes, cored and cut into
   1/4-inch dice

1/2 cup minced scallions, white part only

3 tablespoons soy sauce

3/4 cup rice wine or sake

5 cups water

1 teaspoon salt, or to taste

1/2 pound snow peas, ends snapped and
   veiny strings removed

2 1/2 tablespoons cornstarch mixed with 6
   tablespoons water

2 large eggs, lightly beaten with 2 tablespoons water

1. Heat a heavy soup pot over high heat, add the oil, and heat until hot, about 20 seconds. Add the tomatoes and scallions, and stir-fry until fragrant, about 15 seconds. Add the soy sauce and rice wine or sake, and stir-fry over high heat for 20 seconds. Add the water and salt, and bring to a boil. Reduce the heat to medium-low and cook for 2 minutes, skimming the surface to remove any impurities. Add the snow peas and stir.

2. Slowly add the cornstarch mixture and bring the liquid to a boil, stirring to prevent lumps from forming. Once slightly thickened, remove from the heat and slowly add the beaten eggs, pouring them in a thin stream around the edge of the pot. Carefully stir once or twice so that the eggs form thin streamers. Taste for seasoning and ladle into serving bowls. Serve.

Black Mushroom and Leek Soup

I nicknamed this dish "winter" soup since I make it frequently during the winter when colds and flu threaten my family.

12 dried Chinese black mushrooms, softened in 4 cups hot water about 20 minutes

2 large leeks, ends trimmed, cleaned thoroughly (enough for 2 cups julienned)

3 small carrots, peeled, ends trimmed (enough for 2 cups julienned)

1 tablespoon canola or corn oil

1 teaspoon toasted sesame oil

2 1/2 tablespoons minced garlic

2 1/2 tablespoons minced fresh ginger

1/3 cup rice wine or sake

Broth

2 cups black-mushroom soaking liquid

4 cups Classic Chicken Broth (page 27) or water

4 1/2 tablespoons soy sauce

3 1/2 tablespoons oyster sauce

1/4 teaspoon freshly ground black pepper

1 tablespoon cornstarch

1. Cut the stems from the soaked black mushrooms and discard them. Cut the caps into very thin julienne shreds. Reserve the soaking liquid for the broth. Cut the leeks into thin, matchstick-size shreds about 2 inches long. Cut the carrots into thin, matchstick-size shreds.

2. Heat a heavy soup pot or Dutch oven, add the oils, and heat until hot, about 20 seconds. Add the garlic and ginger, and stir-fry until fragrant. Add the leeks and carrots, and stir-fry lightly over high heat for about 2 1/2 minutes. Add the rice wine and cook for another minute. Add the Broth ingredients and stir until thickened to prevent lumps. Toss lightly to blend and ladle into serving bowls. Serve.

☯ The dried black mushrooms in this soup bolster the immune system, and the pungent seasonings, like leeks and garlic, fight infection. Best of all, the soup just tastes delicious.

Fresh Corn Chowder

This lovely soup accentuates the essence of fresh corn and red peppers.

5 1/2 cups low-sodium canned chicken broth	Garnish
1/2 cup dry white wine	3 red peppers
4 or 5 ears fresh corn	1 teaspoon salt
1 teaspoon salt	1/2 teaspoon freshly ground black pepper
1/4 teaspoon freshly ground black pepper	1 1/2 teaspoons red wine vinegar
	2 tablespoons minced scallion greens (optional)

☯ Corn is particularly beneficial for the kidneys, and a tea made from brewing 1 cup dried kernels with 2 cups water is prescribed for kidney disease.

1. Put the chicken broth, white wine, and corn in a heavy non-aluminum pot. Bring the liquid to a boil and skim the surface to remove any impurities. Reduce the heat to medium and cook for 25 to 30 minutes. Using a pair of tongs, remove the corn and set aside to cool.

2. While the corn is cooking, preheat the broiler and arrange the peppers on a cookie sheet. Place about 3 inches under the broiler and broil, turning them occasionally, until their skins char and blister on all sides. Remove and place them in a paper bag, closing the bag. After 15 minutes, using a paring knife, peel away the skin. Cut open the peppers; core and seed them.

3. Cut the kernels from the corn cobs (there should be about 3 cups) and puree with some of the chicken broth in a blender or a food processor fitted with a steel blade. Add the corn puree to the chicken broth and season with salt and pepper. Heat until hot over medium heat.

4. In a blender or a food processor fitted with a steel blade, puree the peppers until smooth and foamy, about 5 minutes. Add salt, pepper, and wine vinegar to taste.

5. When the corn soup is piping hot, ladle it into soup bowls. Spoon 2 tablespoons of the pepper puree on top of each serving. Using the tip of a knife, make points at equal intervals drawing out points like a star. Sprinkle the top with the scallion greens, if using them, and serve.

THE
Sea food
INTERNATIONAL
MARKET & RESTAURANT
"IF IT SWIMS WE HAVE IT"

Seafood

Seafood and Dr. Chun-Han Zhu

Seafood, oddly enough, was the common bond that first drew me and Dr. Chun-Han Zhu together in 1992. At the time, I was working on a project with Legal Seafoods restaurant to bring Chinese master chefs and an herbalist from the Imperial Herbal restaurant in Asia to Boston. Dr. Zhu, a highly regarded Chinese doctor, herbalist, and acupuncturist, and his younger brother, who also practices Chinese medicine, were hired to create herbal brews that could be used in cocktails and alcoholic drinks.

Their herbal infusions were masterful and it was not long before I regularly consulted Dr. Zhu as a patient.

Dr. Zhu, who grew up in Beijing, is a third-generation Chinese doctor. Both his father and grandfather were distinguished authorities in the field. Dr. Zhu studied and worked with his father, as well as other doctors, for years before starting his own practice, as was the custom in China.

"Before schools teaching traditional Chinese medicine opened in China in the 1950s," he explained one night as we sat in his office in Newton, Massachusetts, "students would study with different elderly doctors for about ten years to get experience with a wide range of diseases and treatments." These days Chinese doctors can receive their training in a six-year school program.

He first began practicing at Tianqiao Hospital in Beijing. In 1981 he immigrated to the United States, where he began a three-year program as a research fellow at Children's Hospital, a Harvard University teaching hospital, in Boston. Today he has a thriving private practice and is in great demand as a speaker.

One of the first tenets of Chinese medicine, according to Dr. Zhu, is the vital importance of the kidneys and the spleen. The kidneys contain congenital "essence" (*qi,* or life energy), inherited from the mother. (Essence, according to Daniel Reid, in *The Complete Book of Health & Healing* [Shambhala Publications, 1986] refers to the vital fluids in the human organism.)

Once the child is born, however, the spleen becomes even more important, because it produces the body's essence from outside forces (such as food), with the help of the rest of the body.

"The Chinese concept of the spleen is different from the Western," Dr. Zhu told me. "We believe that the spleen controls your entire body's gastric system. As *The Yellow Emperor's Classic of Internal Medicine* [the bible of Traditional Chinese Medicine] states, 'When essence is deficient, replenish it with food.' "

Accordingly, food and herbs, which are often interchangeable, are critical to a person's health. They also are a primary form of medicine, and seafood figures prominently in this area. Some claim that fish is second only to tofu as an important source of protein. And it's easy to digest, so it doesn't tax the body's energy and strength.

China is a country with a long coastline, and its land is liberally threaded with rivers, streams, and ponds, so it is not surprising to find that fresh and saltwater fish play an important role in the Chinese diet. Shellfish—shrimp, crab, lobster, clams, scallops, and mussels—though popular, is considered slightly less healthful than fish, since it is not as easily digested and often imparts cooler energy to the body.

Most seafood, because it comes from water, is coolish in nature, yet there are some exceptions—like shrimp. The degree of cold can be adjusted with the ingredients the seafood is cooked with. For instance, not only do ginger, scallions, rice wine, cilantro, black pepper, and vinegar complement the flavor of seafood and remove any strong fishy flavors but also they are warming. Accordingly, they balance the effect that seafood has on the body.

The cooking technique can also influence the seafood's effects: Stir-frying, roasting, and grilling are considered the most warming cooking methods. Since much of the seafood we eat in North America is from very cold waters, these techniques are perfect for neutralizing the coolish effects of the seafood.

Seafood is relished in China in all its prepared forms—fresh, dried, salted, and pickled. It is particularly savored when it's freshly killed. In many Chinese restaurants, fish, shrimp, clams, and lobsters are picked live from a tank just minutes before being cooked. It is not unusual for a customer to personally select his or her dinner before it is brought to the kitchen. This is one way of insuring that the seafood is absolutely fresh, and it is believed that the energizing vitality of the creature will then be transferred directly to the diner.

Steamed Scallion-Ginger Fillets

Seafood is usually steamed to accentuate and highlight its sweet flavors, but only the freshest fillets should be used. If very fresh sole or flounder is unavailable, substitute a local, fresh fish.

SIX SERVINGS

2 pounds firm-fleshed fillets, such as flounder, sole, pickerel, or lake trout, skin removed

Ginger Marinade
2 tablespoons rice wine or sake
1 1/2 tablespoons soy sauce

1 tablespoon minced fresh ginger
1 teaspoon toasted sesame oil

2 tablespoons chicken broth
3 tablespoons finely shredded scallions, white part only
1/4 teaspoon freshly ground black pepper

☯ Flounder and sole, because they are from cold waters, are cooler in nature than other fish and are often cooked with pungent and warm seasonings, such as ginger and scallions, to balance.

1. Rinse the fish fillets lightly under cold water and drain thoroughly in a colander. Place the fillets in a bowl.

2. Add the Ginger Marinade to the fillets and toss lightly to coat. Cover with plastic wrap and let the fillets marinate in the refrigerator for 10 minutes.

3. Arrange the fillets, skinned side down, on a heatproof plate and place in a steamer tray or on a rack.

4. Pour enough water for steaming into a wok or large pot and heat until boiling. Carefully place the steamer tray or rack containing the fish over the boiling water and steam until the fish flakes when prodded with a knife, about 6 or 7 minutes for flounder or sole, 10 to 12 minutes for pickerel or lake trout. Just before the fish is done, heat the chicken broth until boiling.

5. Sprinkle the steamed fillets with the scallions and pepper; then slowly pour the hot chicken broth over the surface. Serve with steamed rice and a vegetable.

To round out the meal, serve with Flash-Cooked Greens with Garlic (page 159) or Saucy Braised Eggplant (page 169).

Steamed Fish with a Fresh Cilantro Sauce

In the classic rendition of this dish, hot oil is poured over the steamed fish and seasonings. The oil sears the seasonings. I have substituted chicken broth, which creates a lighter, cleaner flavor that underscores the sweetness of the seafood.

2 pounds meaty, firm-fleshed fillets, such as haddock, lake trout, sole, or flounder, skin removed

Ginger Marinade
2 tablespoons rice wine or sake
1½ tablespoons minced fresh ginger
1 tablespoons soy sauce
1 teaspoon toasted sesame oil

Cilantro Sauce (mixed together)
6 tablespoons Classic Chicken Broth (page 27)
3 tablespoons soy sauce
2 teaspoons sugar
1/4 teaspoon freshly ground black pepper
1/4 cup coarsely chopped fresh cilantro

SIX SERVINGS

1. Rinse the fish fillets lightly under cold water and drain thoroughly in a colander. Place them in a bowl.
2. Stir the ingredients of the Ginger Marinade, pour over the fillets, and toss lightly to coat. Cover with plastic wrap and let the fillets marinate in the refrigerator for 10 minutes.
3. Arrange the fillets, skinned side down, on a heatproof plate and place in a steamer tray or on a rack over an empty tunafish can.
4. Pour enough water for steaming into a wok or large pot and heat until boiling. Place the steamer tray or rack into the wok or pot and steam until the fish flakes when prodded with a knife, about 6 or 7 minutes for flounder or sole, 10 to 12 minutes for pickerel or lake trout. (Alternatively, you may grill the fish or sear it in a hot nonstick pan brushed lightly with oil. Cook for the prescribed cooking time.)
5. While the fish is steaming, mix the Cilantro Sauce and then heat until boiling in a small saucepan. Stir and turn off the heat. Pour the heated sauce over the steamed fillets and serve immediately with steamed rice and a vegetable.

Cilantro has a pungent, musky flavor that marries perfectly with seafood. It is warming, and reinforces the stomach as well as regulates *qi,* or body energy.

To round out the meal, serve with Grilled Leeks in a Garlic-Soy Dressing (page 174) or Roasted Asparagus with a Sesame Vinaigrette (page 175).

Steamed Fish with Black Mushrooms and Prosciutto

The pairing of pungent black mushrooms and smoky Chinese ham is a classic one in traditional Chinese cooking. Since prosciutto has a flavor similar to Chinese ham, I think it makes a great substitute; just a little gives the dish an appealing richness.

SIX SERVINGS

2 pounds firm-fleshed fillets, such as flounder, sole, pickerel, or lake trout, skinned

Ginger Marinade
2 tablespoons rice wine or sake
1 tablespoon minced fresh ginger

8 dried Chinese black mushrooms, softened in hot water to cover about 20 minutes
1/4 pound Italian prosciutto, fat removed, and cut into thin, julienne strips about 3 inches long

Steaming Sauce (mixed together)
4 tablespoons chicken broth
1 tablespoon soy sauce
1/2 teaspoon toasted sesame oil
1/4 teaspoon freshly ground black pepper

2 tablespoons minced scallions, white part only

1. Rinse the fish lightly under cold water, drain thoroughly, and put in a bowl.
2. Add the Ginger Marinade to the fillets, and toss lightly to coat. Cover with plastic wrap and marinate in the refrigerator for 10 minutes.
3. Remove and discard the stems from the soaked mushrooms and cut the caps into fine julienne strips.
4. Arrange the fillets, skinned side down, on a heatproof plate and place in a steamer tray or on a rack over an empty tunafish can.
5. Sprinkle the shredded black mushrooms and prosciutto over the fish.

6. Pour enough water into a wok or large pot for steaming and heat until boiling. Place the steamer tray or rack containing the fish over the boiling water and steam until the fish flakes when prodded with a knife, about 6 or 7 minutes for flounder or sole, 10 to 12 minutes for pickerel or lake trout. Just before the fish is done, pour the premixed Steaming Sauce into a pan and heat until boiling.

7. Sprinkle the scallions over the steamed fillets; then slowly pour the hot fish sauce over the surface. Serve immediately with steamed rice and a vegetable.

To round out the meal, serve with Flash-Cooked Greens with Garlic (page 159) or Flash-Cooked Bean Sprouts (page 161).

Baked Fish Packages
with Wild Mushroom Sauce

Here a stir-fried mushroom mixture becomes a flavored topping for the fish. I generally use whatever fresh wild varieties are available in the market, being on the lookout for the more medicinal types, such as shiitake, maitake, oyster mushrooms, and cèpes.

SIX SERVINGS

6 firm-fleshed fish fillets, such as sole, flounder, or lake trout (3 to 4 ounces apiece), skin removed

Ginger Marinade
3 tablespoons rice wine or sake
2 teaspoons minced fresh ginger

2 teaspoons canola or corn oil
12 cloves garlic, smashed with the flat side of a knife, and sliced very thinly
1/2 pound fresh shiitake mushrooms, rinsed lightly, drained, stem ends trimmed, and cut into thin slices

1/2 pound fresh maitake mushrooms, rinsed lightly, drained, stem ends trimmed, and cut into thin slices
1/3 pound oyster mushrooms, rinsed lightly, drained, stem ends trimmed, and cut into thin slices
31/2 tablespoons rice wine or sake
11/2 cups minced scallion greens
31/2 tablespoons soy sauce

6 12-inch squares parchment paper or aluminum foil

1. Rinse the fish fillets under cold water and drain thoroughly in a colander. Place the fillets in a bowl, add the Ginger Marinade, and toss lightly to coat. Cover with plastic wrap and let the fillets marinate for 10 minutes.

2. Preheat the oven to 450°F. Heat a wok or skillet, add the oil, and heat until very hot. Add the garlic slices and stir-fry over high heat, turning with a slotted spoon or spatula, for 15 seconds or until fragrant.

3. Add the fresh mushrooms and stir-fry over high heat briefly, about 1 minute. Lower the heat slightly and add the rice wine. Partially cover and cook for about 3^{1}/$_2$ minutes, until the mushrooms are cooked. Uncover and add the scallion greens. Cook to reduce the liquid slightly. Add the soy sauce and toss thoroughly. Remove the pan from the heat.

4. Fold each square of parchment paper or aluminum foil in half on the diagonal to create a crease; unfold. Arrange 1 fish fillet just below the fold. Spoon the mushroom mixture over the fish, and fold the paper or foil over to enclose the fish completely. Fold and crimp the edges of the packages to seal.

5. Arrange the packages on a cookie sheet and bake for 8 to 9 minutes on the middle shelf, or until the packages puff up (the fish should flake when prodded with a fork). To serve, cut open the packages with scissors, trimming the paper around the fish, or let everyone open the packages at the table. Serve immediately.

To round out the meal, serve with Flash-Cooked Greens with Garlic (page 159) or Broccoli or Cauliflower with a Soy-Lemon Dressing (page 173).

☯ For a simple remedy to soothe a gastric ulcer, cook $^1/_2$ pound roughly chopped bok choy in 4 cups boiling water about 30 minutes, until it is soft. Stir in some honey, drain off the bok choy, and drink the broth.

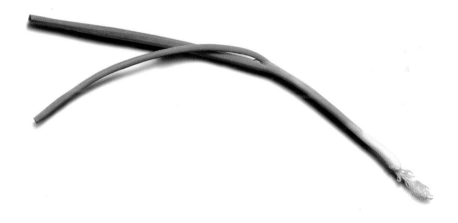

Hot and Sour Salmon with Greens

Since salmon is a slightly oily fish, it plays beautifully against the clean flavors of ginger, scallion, and bok choy. For me, there's nothing more soothing than tender, cooked cabbage; it is often prescribed in China for relieving stomach pain.

SIX SERVINGS

2 1/2 pounds baby bok choy or bok choy, stem ends and leaf tips trimmed

8 to 9 whole scallions, ends trimmed, cut into thin julienne slices on the diagonal

3 heaping tablespoons fresh ginger cut into very thin julienne shreds

Dressing

6 tablespoons soy sauce

3 1/2 tablespoons Chinese black vinegar or Worcestershire sauce

1/4 cup sugar, or to taste

2 tablespoons minced garlic

6 salmon steaks, about 6 ounces each

1. Trim the tough outer leaves from the bok choy and discard. Rinse the stalks and leaves and drain. Cut the stalks in half lengthwise. Cut the halves diagonally into 2-inch sections. In a bowl, toss the scallions and ginger with the bok choy sections. Arrange on a heatproof platter.

2. Mix the ingredients of the Dressing, and pour into a serving bowl.

3. Preheat the oven to 450°F. Place the salmon steaks on top of the greens. Pour into a roasting pan several inches of water and heat until boiling. Carefully place the platter of salmon and vegetables on top of a rack or steamer tray in the roasting pan. Cover the top of the pan tightly with aluminum foil. Bake 7 to 9 minutes, or until the fish is cooked.

4. Serve the salmon from the heatproof platter or arrange the steamed vegetables and salmon on serving plates. Spoon some of the dressing on top and serve with steamed rice.

Grilled Miso Fish Fillets

Miso is a bean paste that begins with the fermentation of rice and barley and to which soybeans and sea salt are added. It is then left to age from 3 to 36 months, depending on the variety. In this country, the most available varieties are light or sweet white, mellow white or light yellow (*shinshu miso,* the most popular), and sweet red.

SIX SERVINGS

2 pounds halibut steaks, about 1 inch thick (to be cut into 6-ounce serving portions)

Miso Marinade

1/2 cup sweet white miso *(shiro miso)*

1/3 cup sweetened rice wine *(mirin)*

1¹/2 tablespoons minced fresh ginger

2 tablespoons minced scallion greens

☯ Miso not only provides a rich, subtle flavor, but also is extremely healthful. Because it is made from soybeans, it lowers the risk of heart disease, reduces menopausal symptoms, and prevents cancer. It also aids digestion.

1. Rinse the fish steaks under cold water and drain thoroughly in a colander. Cut the steaks into six pieces and place in a bowl.

2. Add the Miso Marinade to the fish steaks and toss lightly to coat the entire surface of the fish. Cover with plastic wrap, and refrigerate. Let the halibut marinate for at least 1 hour, or for several hours.

3. Prepare a medium-hot fire for grilling and place the grill about 3 inches above the coals. Remove the fish from the marinade, spreading the marinade on with your hands so there is a light coating. Arrange the fish steaks on the grill and cook about 5 to 6 minutes on each side, or until the flesh is opaque all the way through. Alternatively, you may broil the fish about 7 to 9 minutes on each side, or until the fish flakes when prodded with a knife. The miso glaze should bubble and brown at the edges. Remove and serve with steamed rice and stir-fried or steamed vegetables.

To round out the meal, serve with Hot and Sour Cabbage Slaw (page 186) or Sweet and Sour Cucumber Slices (page 185).

Grilled Ginger Teriyaki Tuna

This multipurpose teriyaki sauce is an excellent marinade for any grilled or pan-seared seafood, including swordfish, cusk, shrimp, and scallops.

2 pounds sushi-quality tuna

Ginger Teriyaki Marinade
1/3 cup soy sauce
1/3 cup rice wine or sake
41/2 tablespoons sugar
11/2 tablespoons minced fresh ginger

1/2 teaspoon crushed dried red chiles (optional)
11/2 tablespoons cornstarch
1/3 cup water

2 teaspoons canola or corn oil
3 tablespoons minced scallions

1. Rinse the tuna under cold water and drain thoroughly in a colander. Cut the steaks into six pieces and place in a bowl.

2. Mix the Ginger Teriyaki Marinade in a medium-size saucepan, and heat until thickened, stirring constantly over medium heat with a wooden spoon to prevent lumps. Remove and let cool. Pour the marinade over the tuna and rub the mixture all over with your hands. Cover with plastic wrap and let the tuna marinate at room temperature for 1 hour, if possible.

3. Prepare a medium-hot fire for grilling, and brush the grill lightly with the oil. Place the grill about 3 inches above the coals. Arrange the tuna on the grill and cook for about 3 to 4 minutes on each side for rare and 5 to 6 minutes for medium-rare. Alternatively, you may sear the fish in a heavy frying pan, heating the pan until it is very hot, brushing it with oil and searing the tuna on both sides, covered, over very high heat. Distribute the cooked tuna on plates, sprinkle the scallion greens on top, and serve immediately.

To round out the meal, serve with Curried Coconut Green Beans (page 163) or Spicy Stir-Fried Sweet Potatoes (page 168).

Just as Westerners use lemon with seafood, the Chinese believe that ginger removes fishy odors. Medicinally, it is used to prevent motion sickness and to sweat out colds or the flu.

A Meal with a Chinese Gastronome

"The eyes and nose are neighbors to the mouth and act as a middleman. A good dish strikes the nose and eyes first. Sometimes, it is clear like the autumn clouds and beautiful like amber. Its flowery flavor tells the secret before being tasted by the mouth and tongue."
—*translated by T. C. Lai, from* Cookery Book, *by Yuan Mei, an eighteenth-century Chinese poet and essayist*

T. C. Lai was born to the role of scholar and gastronome. His father, who was a Hanlin, the highest rank of an Imperial scholar, fled his native Guangdong for Hong Kong on the eve of the fall of the Ch'ing dynasty and then became the head of the Chinese department at the University of Hong Kong. He also was a renowned gastronome. As his son and heir, T. C. inherited that knowledge.

I first became familiar with T. C. Lai through his anecdotal writings on food in his book *Chinese Food for Thought*. I discovered he had also written over thirty books on different aspects of Chinese culture. In 1984, Oxford University Press published *At the Chinese Table*, which contains more of T. C. Lai's musings on food. The concept of food as medicine is a recurring theme in both of these food books.

T. C. and I were introduced by a mutual friend in the early 1980s. As our friendship deepened through the years over a series of memorable meals, our discussions widened, and we delved deeper into the topic of food as medicine. The concept is so ingrained in the Cantonese culture that in addition to the hot and cold properties normally ascribed to food, the Cantonese believe that there is also a quality they call *bu*.

"*Bu* is a term we use to describe food that is invigorating or mending," he explained recently over dinner at one of his favorite seafood restaurants. "Northerners may laugh at us, but we Cantonese believe that there are many foods that replenish the body and restore what is lacking. At times *bu* may even have a connotation similar to an aphrodisiac."

"Mutton or lamb is *bu*," he explained. "Ginger is *bu,* but it's more than just warming. For instance, brandy is considered to be *bu,* whereas whisky is the opposite. The opposite of *bu* is *xue* (damaging)."

Despite this one difference, the Cantonese, like all other Asians, believe strongly in the idea of harmony and completeness in planning a meal. After enjoying countless superb meals in T. C.'s company, I've realized that he is a true master of this art.

"You should aim at a balance of tastes and textures, as well as dietary variety," he said as we began to eat steamed shrimp that were lightly flecked with bits of garlic. "A meal should begin with dishes that are delicate both in taste and texture and that will not fail to whet the appetite. For a Cantonese meal, a light stir-fried dish of seafood or chicken might do for a start."

Dishes with soup should come before those without, he suggests. For other tips he quotes Yuan Mei, one of his "mentors": "Of course, there are other tastes than mere saltiness. When your guests show signs of satiety, you may stimulate their appetite with something hot or pepperish. When they have had too many drinks, you may revive their appetite with sweet and sour."

That evening, we dined at what has become one of T. C.'s favorite haunts, and from the entrance it is apparent why. The restaurant is very modest, with a simple decor, but huge fish tanks brimming with all types of seafood dominate the space and it is here that each meal begins—with the ritual of selecting the seafood. T. C. believes, as many Chinese do, that a steamed fish is one of the greatest delicacies of the Chinese table.

"One of the best tests of culinary skill is the steaming of freshly killed fish," he said as he directed the fishman to snag the selected prey for our meal. "The timing must be precise, so that, when served piping hot, the fish is succulent and smooth, and not, as when overcooked, powdery, or dead."

T. C.'s total enjoyment of seafood was apparent from the way he consumed the steamed shrimp. With his chopsticks, he would pluck a whole shrimp (including the head) and pop it into his mouth. Then, using a combination of nibbling and sucking, he would meticulously withdraw all the meat and juices from the shrimp, neatly spitting the whole shell back onto his plate. "The teeth and the tongue are instruments that all work together," he explained.

"You should always consider the number of persons, the style of the restaurant, and the ingredients in season," he advised. "In a Cantonese restaurant, the guiding principle is to order one dish per person. Northern restaurants often tend to serve larger portions, so fewer dishes may be ordered. A proper meal should include some foods that are cooling, like vegetables, and some that are warming, such as meat, to be consumed with a good amount of neutral food, such as rice."

Once again, his words stressed the monumental importance of balance and harmony.

Pan-Seared Halibut
with a Garlicky Black Bean Sauce

While a black bean sauce might be considered strong and pungent on its own, it is superb paired with fresh seafood and vegetables. Serve with plenty of rice.

1 1/2 pounds halibut steaks, haddock
    fillets, or some other firm-fleshed fish
    about 1 inch thick

Garlic Marinade
3 tablespoons soy sauce
2 tablespoons minced garlic
1 teaspoon toasted sesame oil

1 1/2 tablespoons canola or corn oil

Seasonings
3 tablespoons fermented or salted black
    beans, rinsed, drained, and minced
2 tablespoons minced garlic

2 tablespoons minced fresh ginger
3/4 teaspoon dried chile flakes (optional)

2 red onions, thinly sliced
2 red bell peppers, cored, seeded, and cut
    into julienne slices
3/4 pound snow peas, ends snapped and
    veiny strings removed

Sauce (mixed together)
2 cups Classic Chicken Broth (page 27)
3 1/2 tablespoons soy sauce
3 tablespoons rice wine or sake
1 tablespoon sugar
1 1/2 teaspoons cornstarch

1. Rinse the fish under cold water and drain. Cut into 6 pieces and put in a bowl.
2. Mix the Garlic Marinade and pour over the fish pieces. Toss lightly to coat, cover with plastic wrap, and let the fish sit at room temperature for 30 minutes.
3. Heat a heavy skillet and brush lightly with the oil. Arrange some of the fish in the pan and sear over very high heat for 5 to 6 minutes on each side, or until the fish is opaque. Arrange the cooked fish on a platter, reheat the pan, and repeat with the remaining fish.
4. Heat a heavy skillet or a wok, add the remaining oil, heat until hot, about 30 seconds, and add the Seasonings, sliced onions, and julienned peppers. Toss lightly with a slotted spoon or spatula over high heat and cook about 2 minutes, until the onions and peppers are slightly tender. Add the snow peas and the premixed Sauce, and toss lightly until the sauce has thickened. Spoon the mixture over the cooked fish and serve.

◐ Fermented soybeans are among the earliest Chinese seasonings, even predating soy sauce. Black soybeans (there are yellow ones as well) have been used by the Chinese for medicinal purposes for over 2,000 years. They are generally prescribed for illnesses that affect the lungs and digestive system.

Braised Garlic Fish Fillets

This dish was inspired by one of my favorite Eastern specialties—a whole fish braised with garlic cloves and dried black mushrooms. I've streamlined and modernized the dish by using fillets, lots of sliced garlic, and fresh shiitake mushrooms.

SIX SERVINGS

2 pounds meaty, firm-fleshed fish fillets, such as haddock, scrod, red snapper, or lake trout, skin removed

Ginger Marinade
3 tablespoons rice wine or sake
1 tablespoon minced fresh ginger

Braising Liquid (mixed together)
1 3/4 cups Classic Chicken Broth (page 27)
1/4 cup soy sauce
3 1/2 tablespoons rice wine or sake
1/2 tablespoon sugar

1 teaspoon toasted sesame oil
1 tablespoon cornstarch mixed with 2 tablespoons water

1/2 pound fresh shiitake mushroom caps, thinly sliced
1 tablespoon canola or corn oil
16 cloves whole garlic, smashed with the flat side of a knife and cut into thin slices
1 cup minced scallions, ends trimmed
2 tablespoons minced scallion greens

☯ This sumptuous dish, with its generous use of garlic and shiitake mushrooms, will fortify the body against colds and the flu.

To round out the meal, serve with Fresh Ginger Fennel (page 188) or Flash-Cooked Bean Sprouts (page 161).

1. Rinse the fish fillets under cold water and drain thoroughly in a colander. Cut into 2- to 3-inch-long sections. Place the fillets in a bowl and add the Ginger Marinade. Toss lightly to coat the fillets, cover with plastic wrap, and let them marinate for 10 minutes.

2. Heat a casserole or Dutch oven with a lid, add the oil, and heat until very hot. Add the garlic and scallions and stir-fry over high heat with a slotted spoon or spatula, until fragrant, about 15 seconds. Add the shiitake mushrooms and sauté over medium heat for 15 seconds, then cover and cook for 2 to 3 minutes.

3. Add the braising liquid and bring the mixture to a boil. (You may prepare this dish at any time up to this point.)

4. Carefully arrange the fish pieces in the casserole, cover, and place over medium heat. Cook covered for about 6 to 8 minutes, or until the fish flakes when prodded with a fork. Carefully spoon the fillets into a serving bowl. Spoon the thickened sauce over the fillets. Sprinkle the minced scallion greens on top. Serve with rice and a vegetable.

Spicy Fish Stew

I adore seafood stews chock-full of fresh seafood in a spicy sauce. This dish is one of the best. Make the base at your convenience, then reheat it and add the seafood at the last minute.

1 1/2 tablespoons canola or corn oil

1 1/2 tablespoons minced garlic

3 medium red onions, coarsely chopped (about 3 cups)

1 teaspoon crushed red chiles (optional)

1 1/4 cups chopped green peppers (about 2)

2 1/2 cups peeled, seeded, and coarsely chopped tomatoes

1 1/2 cups rice wine or sake

1 1/2 cups clam juice or water

1 1/2 teaspoons salt

1/4 teaspoon freshly ground black pepper

1 1/2 pounds cod fillets, skin removed, cut into chunks about 1 inch thick and 3 inches long

2 tablespoons minced scallion greens

1. In a 6-quart casserole or Dutch oven, heat the oil over medium-high heat until hot. Add the garlic, onions, optional crushed red chiles, then the green peppers. Sauté about 5 to 7 minutes, until the onions are slightly transparent and the peppers are tender.

2. Add the tomatoes, rice wine, clam juice, salt, and pepper, and bring to a boil. Reduce the heat to low and simmer uncovered for 10 to 15 minutes.

3. Add the fish pieces to the tomato mixture, toss to coat, cover, and simmer for about 10 to 12 minutes, or until the fish flakes when prodded with a fork. Taste for seasoning (adding more salt if necessary) and sprinkle the top with the minced scallion greens. Serve with a vegetable and crusty bread or steamed rice.

To round out the meal, serve with Black Bean Acorn Squash (page 179) or Spicy Garlic Broccoli with Pine Nuts (page 162).

Tomatoes are cooling in nature. They relieve dryness, tone the stomach, cleanse the liver, and aid digestion. Chinese doctors prescribe one or two tomatoes each day to relieve hypertension.

Steamed Ginger Shrimp

Chinese seafood dishes are often the simplest. The Chinese believe that if ingredients are top grade, the flavors should stand on their own. Use only the best-quality shrimp for this delicious dish.

SIX SERVINGS

2 pounds large shrimp in shell (16 to 20 per pound)

Shrimp Marinade
3 1/2 tablespoons rice wine or sake
2 tablespoons minced fresh ginger
1 1/2 tablespoons minced scallions, white part only

1 tablespoon soy sauce
1 1/2 teaspoons toasted sesame oil

5 to 6 Chinese or American cabbage leaves
1/2 cup chicken broth or water
3 tablespoons coarsely chopped fresh cilantro

☯ Chinese cooks generally prefer freshwater shrimp to the saltwater varieties because they are sweeter. Shrimp are one of the few types of seafood that are warmer in nature. They nourish the kidneys.

1. Rinse the shrimp and pat dry. Using a sharp knife, carefully cut along the back and open each shrimp to butterfly it. Place them in a bowl. Add the Shrimp Marinade and toss lightly to coat the shrimp. Cover with plastic wrap, and refrigerate for 20 minutes.
2. Blanch the cabbage leaves in boiling water for 10 seconds, remove, and refresh in cold water. Line a steamer tray with the blanched leaves, making certain that there are no holes, and arrange the butterflied shrimp flat, shell side down, with the flaps open in the steamer. (You may substitute an aluminum pie plate for the steamer tray.)
3. Fill a wok or a large pot with enough water to reach the bottom of the steamer tray or pie plate, bring to a boil, then carefully lower the tray or plate, anchored by a tunafish can with ends removed, into the pot. Cover and steam 5 to 6 minutes, until the shrimp are cooked and change color. (Alternatively, you may arrange the shrimp in a dish, cover with aluminum foil, and bake on the top rack of a preheated 450°F. oven for 7 to 8 minutes, or until cooked.) When the shrimp are almost done, heat the chicken broth and cilantro in a small saucepan until boiling. Uncover the shrimp and carefully pour the hot broth over them. Serve from the steamer or pie plate.

To round out the meal, serve with Flash-Cooked Greens with Garlic (page 159) or Stir-Fried Wild Mushrooms with Snap Peas in Oyster Sauce (page 166).

Baked Black Bean Shrimp

Traditionally this dish is done in a Chinese steamer, but I find that if wrapped tightly and baked in a hot oven, shrimp steam in their own juices, creating the same effect.

2 pounds large shrimp (16 to 20 per pound), shelled and deveined

Shrimp Marinade
3 1/2 tablespoons rice wine or sake
2 tablespoons minced fresh ginger

1 tablespoon canola or corn oil

Seasonings
2 tablespoons fermented black beans, rinsed and drained
2 tablespoons minced scallions, white part only

1 tablespoon minced fresh ginger
1 tablespoon minced garlic
1 teaspoon dried chile flakes

Sauce (mixed together)
3/4 cup Classic Chicken Broth (page 27)
2 1/2 tablespoons soy sauce
2 tablespoons rice wine or sake
1 tablespoon sugar
1 1/2 teaspoons cornstarch

2 tablespoons minced scallion greens

SIX SERVINGS

◐ According to Dr. Henry Lu, author of *The Chinese System of Food Cures,* a regular diet of fermented black beans can relieve depression and stress and counteract any toxins.

1. Rinse the shrimp, drain, and pat dry. Using a sharp knife, carefully cut along the back and open each shrimp to butterfly it. Put the shrimp in a bowl and add the Marinade. Toss lightly to coat, cover with plastic wrap, and refrigerate for 20 minutes.

2. Preheat the oven to 450°F. Arrange the butterflied shrimp shell side down, with the flaps open, in 1 or 2 heatproof quiche or pie pans.

3. Heat a wok or heavy skillet over high heat, add the oil, and heat until very hot. Add the Seasonings and stir-fry for about 10 seconds with a slotted spoon or spatula until fragrant. Add the premixed Sauce and cook, stirring, to prevent lumps, until it has thickened. Then spoon the sauce over the butterflied shrimp and cover with aluminum foil. (Alternatively, you may place the fish pan in a steamer over boiling water.)

4. Bake the shrimp on the middle rack for about 8 to 9 minutes, or until they have become opaque. (Steam for 10 to 12 minutes.) Uncover the pan and sprinkle the minced scallion greens over the shrimp. Serve immediately with steamed rice and a vegetable.

To round out the meal, serve with Hot and Sour Cabbage Slaw (page 186) or Curried Pumpkin or Squash (page 180).

Grilled Shrimp with a Chile Dressing

Chiles were introduced to China only in the last hundred years. They were originally known as the "barbarian spice." Today, however, they are used widely in dishes and in folk remedies. The spicy dressing will keep unrefrigerated for up to a month. (For more on chiles see page 110.)

(For more on chiles see page 110.)

SIX SERVINGS

2 pounds large shrimp (16 to 20 per pound), shelled and deveined

6 cloves garlic, peeled and smashed with the flat edge of a knife

3 small, fresh red Thai chiles, ends trimmed, seeds removed, and cut into thin slices (or substitute dried *pequín* or red Thai chiles and reconstitute in hot water for 15 minutes)

1/4 cup rice wine or sake

11/2 teaspoons toasted sesame oil

6 skewers for grilling (if bamboo, soak in cold water 1 hour)

Chile Dressing

3 to 4 small, fresh red Thai chiles or cherry peppers, or dried *pequín* or red Thai chiles (if using dried chiles, reconstitute in hot water for 15 minutes)

1/2 cup clear rice vinegar

1/4 cup virgin olive oil

11/2 teaspoons toasted sesame oil

1/2 teaspoon salt

1. Using a sharp knife, cut along the back of the shrimp to butterfly them. Place them in a bowl.

2. Add the garlic, chiles, rice wine or sake, and sesame oil to the shrimp. Toss lightly, cover with plastic wrap, and let the shrimp marinate for at least 3 hours at room temperature, or overnight in the refrigerator. Before grilling, thread the shrimp loosely through the skewers so that they lie flat.

3. Meanwhile, prepare the Chile Dressing. Trim the ends and stems from the chiles, remove the seeds, and coarsely chop by hand or in a food processor, pulsing the machine by turning it on and off. Place the chopped chiles in a clean jar and add the vinegar, olive oil, sesame oil, and salt. Seal tightly and shake the dressing. Store at room temperature for several hours or overnight before using it.

☯ Freshwater shrimp stir-fried with garlic chives are a common remedy prescribed for impotence due to a kidney deficiency. Prawns, which are a large version of shrimp, are considered even more nourishing.

For medicinal purposes, chiles are normally used in their dried form. They are often prescribed to treat arthritis and rheumatism, and are used as a pain reliever and in anti-inflammatory balms.

4. Prepare a medium-hot fire for grilling, and place the grill about 3 inches above the coals. Arrange the shrimp on the grill and cook for about 5 to 7 minutes on each side or until cooked through, basting with the marinade.

5. Remove the cooked shrimp from the skewers, put them in a serving bowl, and toss with the chile dressing, or serve the dressing on the side for dipping.

To round out the meal, serve with Wilted Greens with a Spicy Garlic Dressing (page 160) or Broccoli or Cauliflower with a Soy-Lemon Dressing (page 173).

Yin-Yang Shrimp with Hawthorn Dipping Sauce

This was one of the most popular specialties of the chefs from the Imperial Herbal restaurant during their stay in Boston. You can fry the shrimp in advance and reheat them just before serving.

SIX SERVINGS

2 1/4 pounds medium shrimp, peeled and deveined

Shrimp Marinade
3 tablespoons rice wine or sake
4 whole scallions, smashed lightly with the flat side of a knife
4 slices fresh ginger, smashed lightly with the flat side of a knife
1 teaspoon salt
1 teaspoon toasted sesame oil

Sweet and Sour Hawthorn Sauce
8 packages hawthorn wafers (12.5 grams apiece), softened in 1/2 cup boiling water for about 15 minutes, then mashed through a sieve*
3 1/2 tablespoons ketchup
2 tablespoons clear rice vinegar
2 teaspoons soy sauce
1 teaspoon salt
2 tablespoons water
1 teaspoon cornstarch dissolved in 1 tablespoon water

1 egg, lightly beaten
14 6-inch bamboo skewers
1/2 cup white sesame seeds
1/2 cup black sesame seeds
1/2 cup canola or corn oil

☯ Hawthorn promotes digestion by increasing the secretion of digestive juices, dissolves cholesterol deposits in the lining of blood vessels, and lowers blood pressure.

1. Holding a sharp knife or a cleaver parallel to the cutting board, score each shrimp along the back. (The scoring will allow the shrimp to curl when cooked.) Place the shrimp in a bowl and add the Shrimp Marinade. Toss lightly to coat the shrimp and let them marinate for at least 30 minutes, or longer if possible.

2. Mix the Sweet and Sour Hawthorn Sauce in a saucepan and heat until thickened, stirring constantly to prevent lumps. Keep warm and, before serving, pour it into a small serving dish.

3. Add the egg to the marinated shrimp and thread four shrimp per skewer. Place the white and black sesame seeds on separate plates.

*Hawthorn is the fruit of a Chinese plant related to the Western hawthorn. The dried fruit is sold in Chinese herbal stores, but the wafers used in this recipe may be purchased at an Asian market.

Yin-Yang Shrimp (continued)

◐ Black sesame seeds, which are from a black variety of sesame plant, are used extensively in Chinese medicine. They share the qualities of the white seeds and are believed to vitalize the internal organs of the body.

4. Dip one side of the skewered shrimp in the white sesame seeds, turn over, and dip the other side in the black. Arrange on a cookie sheet.

5. Heat a large skillet, add the olive oil, and heat to about 375°F. Lay 3 or 4 of the skewers in the pan and fry until the white sesame seeds are golden brown, about 3 minutes; then turn and fry the black seeds, about 3 minutes. Remove with a pair of tongs, and drain briefly in a colander; then drain on absorbent paper. Reheat the oil when necessary before adding the next batch and skim the loose sesame seeds from the oil between batches. Arrange the drained shrimp on a serving platter, alternating white and black sides. Serve with the Sweet and Sour Hawthorn Sauce.

To round out the meal, serve with Hot and Sour Cabbage Slaw (page 186) or Fresh Corn and Roasted Bell Pepper Salad (page 189).

Stir-Fried Saucy Shrimp

Sweet bean sauce, or *tian mian jiang,* is one of the earliest forms of Chinese seasonings and was the predecessor to soy sauce. Each region in China has its own variation, but all are made with fermented soybeans. Sweet bean sauce is the northern version. Its most familiar role is with Peking Duck, but it may be used as the base for sauces for cold noodles and assorted stir-fried dishes.

2 pounds medium shrimp in the shell, rinsed and drained

Shrimp Marinade
3 1/2 tablespoons rice wine or sake
2 tablespoons minced fresh ginger
1 1/2 tablespoons minced scallions, white part only
1 teaspoon toasted sesame oil

1 tablespoon canola or corn oil
1 tablespoon minced garlic

2 red peppers, cored, seeded, and cut into 1/4-inch dice

Sweet Bean Sauce (mixed together)
1/4 cup sweet bean sauce (if unavailable, substitute hoisin sauce)
3 tablespoons soy sauce
3 tablespoons rice wine or sake
2 1/2 teaspoons sugar
1/3 cup water

2 tablespoons minced scallion greens

1. Rinse the shrimp and pat dry. With a sharp knife, carefully cut along the back through the shell and open each shrimp to butterfly it. Place the shrimp in a bowl, add the Shrimp Marinade, and toss lightly to coat. Cover with plastic wrap and refrigerate for 20 minutes.
2. Heat a wok or heavy skillet over high heat, add the oil, and heat until hot. Add the garlic and red peppers, and stir-fry about 15 seconds, until fragrant. Add the premixed Sweet Bean Sauce and heat until boiling. Add the shrimp and toss lightly with a slotted spoon or spatula to coat them with the sauce. Cover, reduce the heat to medium, and cook for about 3 minutes. Then uncover and cook another minute to reduce the sauce slightly. Spoon the shrimp and sauce onto a serving platter and sprinkle with the scallion greens. Serve with rice and cooked greens arranged around the shrimp.

To round out the meal, serve with Broccoli or Cauliflower with a Soy-Lemon Dressing (page 173) or Flash-Cooked Bean Sprouts (page 161).

Shrimp Sambal

This sumptuous dish epitomizes Malaysian cooking, with its intoxicating blend of Chinese, Malay, Thai, and European influences.

SIX SERVINGS

1 1/2 pounds medium shrimp, peeled and
    deveined

Seasonings

3 dried red chiles, seeds removed, or 1 1/2
    teaspoons dried chile flakes

2 1/2-inch slices fresh ginger, peeled

6 cloves garlic

1 1/2 teaspoons ground cumin

1/2 teaspoon ground turmeric

3/4 pound snow peas, ends trimmed and
    strings removed

2 tablespoons canola or corn oil

1 1/2 red onions, cut into thin julienne
    slices

Coconut Sauce (mixed together)

1 cup light coconut milk

1 tablespoon light-brown sugar

1 teaspoon salt

2 tablespoons fresh lime juice (or to taste)

☯ Cumin is a seasoning savored by Indian cooks and Ayurvedic doctors. It is extremely effective in dispelling gas from the stomach and intestines. In India, a cup of tamarind water mixed with cumin seeds is drunk to aid digestion.

1. With a sharp knife, score the shrimp along the back, then rinse and drain thoroughly.

2. Drop the Seasonings in descending order into a blender or the feed tube of a food processor while the machine is running and process to a paste. Turn the machine on and off several times to get a smooth mixture. Blanch the snow peas in boiling water for 15 seconds, drain in a colander, refresh under cold water, and drain again.

3. Heat a wok or skillet, add the oil, and heat until hot. Add the seasonings and cook over medium-low heat, stirring with a wooden spoon for about 2 to 3 minutes until fragrant.

4. Add the red onions and toss over medium heat until soft, about 1 1/2 minutes. Add the premixed Coconut Sauce, and heat until boiling. Add the shrimp and lime juice and cook for about 2 1/2 minutes, then add the snow peas and cook another minute. Remove and serve with steamed rice.

To round out the meal, serve with Wilted Greens with a Spicy Garlic Dressing (page160) or Flash-Cooked Bean Sprouts (page 161).

Grilled Hoisin Scallops

Grilled scallops are one of my favorite foods, and these taste extra sweet marinated in the delectable sauce. Serve the scallops on top of any green vegetable, for contrast, or just by themselves.

1 1/2 pounds sea scallops, rinsed and drained

Hoisin Marinade
1/2 cup hoisin sauce
2 tablespoons rice wine or sake
2 tablespoons soy sauce
1 tablespoon sugar
1 1/2 tablespoons minced ginger

Ten 10-inch bamboo or metal skewers (if bamboo, soak in water to cover for 1 hour)

Broccoli Dressing
1/4 cup soy sauce
2 tablespoons freshly squeezed lemon juice
1 1/2 teaspoons sugar

1 1/2 pounds broccoli, stems peeled, stem and florets separated, and stems cut on the diagonal into 1 1/2-inch lengths

SIX SERVINGS

Dried scallops have been considered a delicacy by the Chinese for centuries. They are not only revered for their pungent flavor (and are used as a seasoning), but they strengthen the yin element in the body, making them ideal for those who suffer from high blood pressure. Fresh scallops, which were introduced to China only in the last ten years, are now widely available.

To round out the meal, serve with Sweet and Sour Cucumber Slices (page 185) or Hot and Sour Cabbage Slaw (page 186).

1. Put the scallops in a bowl and add the Hoisin Marinade. Toss lightly to coat, cover with plastic wrap, and marinate in the refrigerator for 1 hour. Thread the marinated scallops onto the bamboo or metal skewers and reserve the marinade.

2. Stir the Broccoli Dressing in a bowl to dissolve the sugar.

3. Bring 3 quarts water to a rolling boil. Add the broccoli and cook for about 3 minutes, or until crisp-tender. Drain in a colander, refresh in cold water, and drain again. Put the broccoli in a bowl, add the dressing, and toss lightly to coat with a spoon.

4. Heat the broiler or prepare a fire for grilling and arrange the scallops about 3 inches from the source of heat. Broil or grill about 4 to 5 minutes on each side, turning once and brushing with the marinade. Remove and set aside.

5. Arrange the cooked broccoli in a serving bowl, leaving a slight indentation in the center for the scallops. Spoon the dressing on top. Remove the scallops from the skewers and arrange them on top of the broccoli. Serve immediately with crusty bread or a side of noodles.

Five-Spice Scallops with Lemon Sauce

Five-spice powder is a fragrant spice blend of star anise, powdered licorice root, cinnamon, Sichuan peppercorns, cloves, and fennel. (The blends vary depending on the manufacturer.) Used sparingly, it will underscore rather than overpower the seafood.

SIX SERVINGS

☯ Chinese doctors credit the lemon with securing the fetus in pregnant women, and preserved lemons are eaten to relieve indigestion. A common remedy used to relieve a cough or whooping cough in children is a fresh lemon cut into pieces and steamed with several tablespoons of rock sugar.

To round out the meal, serve with Flash-Cooked Greens with Garlic (page 159) or Flash-Cooked Bean Sprouts (page 161).

2 pounds sea scallops, rinsed and drained

Five-Spice Marinade

3 tablespoons soy sauce

3 tablespoons rice wine or sake

1 teaspoon five-spice powder

1/4 teaspoon freshly ground black pepper

2 tablespoons minced fresh ginger

2 tablespoons minced garlic

3/4 cup flour

1/3 cup canola or corn oil

Lemon Sauce (mixed together)

6 tablespoons chicken broth (preferably Classic Chicken Broth, page 27)

3 tablespoons freshly squeezed lemon juice

1 teaspoon toasted sesame oil

1 tablespoon sugar

1 teaspoon salt

1/2 teaspoon cornstarch

1. Place the scallops in a bowl, add the Five-Spice Marinade, and toss lightly to coat. Cover with plastic wrap and marinate at room temperature for 30 minutes.

2. Sprinkle the flour on a plate and lightly dredge several scallops at a time in the flour coating. Gently squeeze the scallops so that the flour adheres to them and arrange on a tray to air-dry for 20 minutes.

3. Heat a large nonstick skillet, add 2 to 3 tablespoons of the oil, and heat over high heat until very hot, about 400°F. Add as many scallops as will fit without crowding and fry over medium-high heat about 3 to 4 minutes, until golden brown and crisp on all sides. Remove with a slotted spatula and drain on paper towels. Reheat the pan, add a little more oil, and reheat. Continue frying the scallops and draining them on paper towels. Remove the pan and wipe it out with paper towels.

4. Reheat the pan, add the premixed Lemon Sauce, and heat over high heat, stirring with a wooden spoon. Cook until the sauce thickens slightly, then add the scallops and toss lightly in the sauce to coat. Spoon the glazed scallops onto a serving platter and serve immediately with steamed rice and a vegetable.

Clams with Basil and Garlic

When I lived in Taiwan as a student, this was one of my favorite late-night snacks. These days, I make it for a light lunch or dinner accompanied by crusty bread or thin noodles.

3 pounds littlenecks or steamers (preferably small), scrubbed and soaked in cold water to cover for 1 hour
1 teaspoon canola or corn oil

Seasonings
1 teaspoon dried chile flakes
8 cloves garlic, smashed and thinly sliced
8 whole scallions, ends trimmed, cut into 11/2-inch lengths and smashed lightly with the flat edge of a knife

3/4 cup good-quality rice wine or sake
11/2 cups water
1/2 cup Thai holy basil or sweet basil leaves, rinsed, drained, and cut into thin julienne shreds
2 tablespoons soy sauce

SIX SERVINGS

1. Drain the clams.
2. Heat a large heavy pot, add the oil, and heat until hot, about 30 seconds. Add the Seasonings, and stir-fry about 10 seconds, until fragrant, then add the rice wine and water. Cover and bring to a boil. Add the clams, cover, and once the liquid reaches a boil, reduce the heat to medium and cook, shaking the pot from time to time to allow the clams to cook evenly. Cook for 8 minutes, or until the clams are just open.
3. Add the basil, and fold the shreds into the clams and their liquid. Cover and cook briefly. Uncover and add the soy sauce; taste and add more if necessary. Stir carefully to combine the flavors and serve the clams from the pot or scoop them and their broth into serving bowls. Serve immediately.

To round out the meal, serve with Mu Shu Vegetable Rolls (page 170) or Stir-Fried Wild Mushrooms with Snap Peas in Oyster Sauce (page 166).

Clams, like most other types of seafood, are cooling in nature. They are prescribed to rid the body of excess mucus. Some Chinese doctors also use them in treating hemorrhoids and swelling of the thyroid.

Spicy Grilled Squid with Warm Greens

With its mild, sweet taste and tender texture, squid is the perfect contrast to the spicy hoisin sauce marinade and garlic greens.

2 pounds squid

Hoisin Marinade
1/2 cup hoisin sauce
2 tablespoons rice wine or sake
2 tablespoons soy sauce
1 tablespoon sugar
1 1/2 tablespoons minced fresh ginger
1 teaspoon hot chile paste or 3/4 teaspoon
    dried chile flakes

1 1/4 pounds (or 2 10-ounce packages)
    fresh spinach, watercress, or other leafy
    green vegetable
1 1/2 teaspoons canola or corn oil

Garlic Dressing (mixed together)
3 tablespoons soy sauce
2 tablespoons rice wine or sake
1 tablespoon minced garlic
1 teaspoon sugar

1. Either buy already cleaned squid or do it yourself: Pull the head away from the body of each squid. Cut off the tentacles, just below the eyes, reserving the tentacles and body sac and discarding the rest. Pull out the transparent quill from inside the body sac and discard. Gently pull back the flaps from the body sac, reserving them, and peel off and discard the purple membrane. Rinse the body under cold water and drain. Place the cleaned squid and tentacles in a bowl.

2. Add the Hoisin Marinade to the squid. Toss lightly to coat, cover with plastic wrap, and marinate the squid in the refrigerator for 1 hour.

3. Tear the stems from the spinach and toss the leaves into a colander. Rinse thoroughly under cold water, drain, and place near the stove.

4. Heat a large wok or skillet, add the oil, and heat until near smoking. Add the spinach, and toss lightly over high heat with a spatula or slotted spoon for about 1 minute. Add the Garlic Dressing and continue stir-frying about 30 seconds, until the leaves are slightly wilted, but still bright green. Scoop out the greens and the sauce to a serving plate and make a well in the center for the squid.

5. Heat the broiler or prepare a medium-hot fire for grilling and arrange the squid about 3 inches from the source of heat. Broil or grill about 2 minutes on each side, turning once and brushing with the marinade. Remove and set aside.

6. Cut the squid into thin slices about $1/2$ inch wide. Arrange the slices on top of the greens. Serve immediately with crusty bread.

To round out the meal, serve with Grilled Wild Mushrooms with a Teriyaki Dressing (page 178) or Black Bean Acorn Squash (page 179).

Steamed Mussels with Cilantro

SIX SERVINGS

1 1/2 teaspoons canola or corn oil

8 cloves garlic, smashed with the flat edge
  of a knife and cut into thin slices

1 1/2 cups water

3/4 cup rice wine or sake

6 1/2 pounds mussels, scrubbed and rinsed

lightly to remove any sand and placed in
cold water to cover for several hours (if
unavailable, use littleneck clams or
steamers)

1/4 teaspoon freshly ground black pepper

1 cup coarsely chopped fresh cilantro

1. In a large casserole or Dutch oven, add the oil and heat until hot. Add the garlic, toss lightly until fragrant, about 10 seconds, and add the water and wine. Heat until boiling.
2. Drain the mussels and add them to the boiling liquid. Cover and cook about 4 to 5 minutes, shaking and stirring from time to time so that they will cook evenly. When they are just opening, sprinkle in the black pepper and cilantro. Toss lightly and cover, cooking for another minute. Uncover and serve from the pot, scooping the mussels and some of the broth into individual soup bowls.

To round out the meal, serve with Curried Coconut Green Beans (page 163) or Roasted Asparagus with a Sesame Vinaigrette (page 175).

Mussels strengthen the liver and kidneys and improve the body's *qi,* or energy. Like clams, they are used in the treatment of goiter and abdominal swelling. An old remedy—a pot of mussels cooked with several preserved eggs—is sometimes prescribed for dizziness and headaches due to deficiencies in the liver and kidneys.

Warm Crab Salad with Garlic Pea Shoots

In China, crab is a food celebrated during the autumn, when the roe is at its plumpest. In southern China, Hong Kong, and Taiwan, crab is widely available throughout the year and may be stir-fried, steamed, or boiled.

1 pound fresh lump crabmeat (if unavailable, substitute medium peeled, deveined cooked shrimp)

1 pound fresh snow pea shoots, tough stem and leafy ends removed (if unavailable, use fresh spinach, stems removed, rinsed thoroughly, drained, and torn into pieces)

Seasonings
3 tablespoons minced scallion greens
1 1/2 tablespoons minced fresh ginger
1 1/2 tablespoons minced garlic

Dressing
6 tablespoons soy sauce
1 1/2 tablespoons sugar
3 1/2 tablespoons clear rice vinegar

1 tablespoon canola or corn oil
2 tablespoons rice wine or sake
2 red bell peppers, cored, seeded, and cut into 1/4-inch dice

1. Put the crabmeat in a bowl and, with your fingers, pick through it to remove any shells or cartilage. Trim and discard any tough stems or wilted leaves from the snow pea shoots. Cut shoots into 4-inch-long sections. Mix the Seasonings in a small bowl, mix the Dressing ingredients in another, and set both by the stove.

2. Heat a wok or skillet, add 1 teaspoon of the oil, and heat to near smoking. Add the snow pea shoots and toss lightly over high heat for 30 seconds, then add 1 tablespoon of the rice wine. Continue cooking for another half minute, stir-frying until the leaves are slightly wilted but still bright green. Scoop out the greens with a slotted spoon, draining off the liquid, and arrange on a serving plate.

3. Reheat the pan, add the remaining oil, and heat until very hot. Add the seasonings and toss lightly over high heat until fragrant, about 15 seconds. Add the red peppers and remaining rice wine and toss lightly over high heat until crisp-tender, about 1 minute.

4. Add the dressing and heat until boiling, then add the crabmeat and toss lightly over high heat for 30 seconds to a minute. Arrange the crab mixture over the snow pea shoots and serve hot or at room temperature.

Although crab is nutritious, it is usually not recommended for pregnant or postpartum women because of its cooling nature.

Steamed Crabs with a Ginger Dipping Sauce

6 live blue crabs (about 5 to 7 ounces each), preferably female (check the underside of the crab—the apron should be an oval)

Ginger Marinade
1/3 cup rice wine or sake
2 tablespoons minced fresh ginger
2 tablespoons minced scallions, white part only

Ginger Dipping Sauce
1/2 cup soy sauce
2 1/2 to 3 tablespoons clear rice vinegar
3 tablespoons water
1 1/2 tablespoons very finely shredded fresh ginger

☯ Crab is considered very cooling, but it is especially effective in activating blood circulation. Some doctors recommend crab steeped in millet wine or rice wine to help heal traumatic injuries or bone fractures.

1. Heat 4 quarts water until boiling in a large pot. Add the live crabs one at a time and cook about 1 minute. Strain the crabs in a colander, rinse under cold water, and drain. Cut away the first two hairy joints of each leg. Twist off and discard the apron from the underside of the crab. Pry off and discard the top shell. Remove and discard the spongy tissue (the gills) that covers the cartilage. Cut the bodies in half to expose the meat. Lightly tap the claws with a mallet or the blunt edge of a heavy knife to crack the shell. Place the crab halves in a bowl. Mix the ingredients of the Ginger Marinade and add to the crab halves, tossing lightly to coat them. Cover with plastic wrap and let the crabs sit for 1 hour, or refrigerate for several hours. Mix the ingredients of the Ginger Dipping Sauce and transfer to a serving bowl.

2. Arrange the crabs in a steamer tray or on a heatproof plate that will sit on a tray, on a rack, or in a steamer. Fill a pot or wok with several inches of water and heat until boiling. Arrange the steamer tray or rack over the boiling water and steam the crabs about 12 to 15 minutes, or until they are cooked. Alternatively, you may arrange the crabs on a tray, cover with aluminum foil, and bake on the middle shelf in a preheated 450°F. oven for 30 minutes, or until they are cooked.

3. Arrange the cooked crabs on serving plates or a platter and serve with the dipping sauce on the side. Guests may pick up the crab and eat with their fingers. Serve with small individual bowls of water containing slices of lemon to remove the seafood smell from everyone's hands.

Ginger-Scallion Lobster

Lobster is a delicacy in China. One of the simplest, and the most delicious, methods of preparation is stir-frying with bunches of scallions and fresh ginger so that the sweet flavor of the meat is accentuated.

3 live lobsters, each about 1³/4 to 2 pounds	12 whole scallions, ends trimmed, smashed lightly with the flat side of a knife	SIX SERVINGS
1 tablespoon canola or corn oil		
12 thin slices fresh ginger, smashed lightly with the flat side of a knife	¹/4 cup rice wine or sake	

1. Heat about 4 quarts water until boiling in a large stockpot. Drop the lobsters into the boiling water one at a time and cook about 1 to 1¹/₂ minutes. Drain in a colander and rinse under cold water. Drain again.

2. Using a heavy knife or a cleaver, cut each lobster in half lengthwise. Cut crosswise near the head and discard the head and antennae. Cut off the pincer claws and cut at the joints to divide into serving-size pieces. Using the flat side of a knife or a mallet, crack the claws slightly. Cut the legs away from the body and save. Cut each half of the lobster crosswise in half, cutting through the shell. Split the tails in half lengthwise, removing the intestinal tract that runs along the back. Then cut the tails crosswise in half. Remove the coral and tomalley from the lobster and reserve. Place the cut lobster pieces in a bowl.

3. Cut the scallions into 2-inch sections.

4. Heat a large skillet or a wok until hot. Add the oil and heat until near smoking. Toss in the ginger and scallions, and stir-fry with a spatula or slotted spoon over high heat about 15 seconds, until fragrant. Add the lobster pieces and toss lightly over high heat for about a minute. Add the rice wine or sake and flame if the heat is hot enough; then toss again. Partially cover and cook about 4 to 5 minutes. Add the reserved tomalley and coral and cook for an additional minute. Scoop the lobster, seasonings, and juice onto a serving platter. Serve immediately with a vegetable and rice.

To round out the meal, serve with Fresh Corn and Roasted Bell Pepper Salad (page 189) or Black Bean Acorn Squash (page 179).

Saucy Garlic Lobster

SIX SERVINGS

3 live lobsters, each about 1³/4 to 2
   pounds
1 tablespoon canola or corn oil

Seasonings
2 tablespoons fermented black beans, rinsed,
   drained, and lightly chopped
2 tablespoons minced scallions, white part only
1¹/2 tablespoons minced garlic
2 tablespoon minced fresh ginger

1¹/2 tablespoons rice wine or sake

Sauce (mixed together)
³/4 cup Classic Chicken Broth (page 27)
2¹/2 tablespoons soy sauce
1 tablespoon sugar
1¹/2 teaspoons cornstarch

2 tablespoons minced scallion greens

1. Prepare the lobster as directed in steps 1 and 2 of Ginger-Scallion Lobster (page 91).
2. Heat a wok or a heavy skillet over high heat, add the oil, and heat until very hot. Add the minced Seasonings and stir-fry about 10 seconds with a slotted spoon or spatula, until fragrant. Add the lobster pieces and rice wine, and flame if possible. Add the pre-mixed Sauce and cook, stirring to prevent lumps, until the sauce has thickened. Reduce the heat to medium-high, cover, and cook about 5 to 6 minutes. Add the reserved tomal-ley and coral, if using them, and cook for an additional minute. Scoop the lobster, sea-sonings, and sauce out of the pan onto a serving platter. Sprinkle the top with the minced scallion greens. Serve with a vegetable and steamed rice.

To round out the meal, serve with Roasted Asparagus with a Sesame Vinaigrette (page 175) or Fresh Corn and Roasted Bell Pepper Salad (page 189).

☯ While most seafood is cooling, lobster is warm. According to Dr. Henry Lu, it tones the kidneys and can improve the appetite. Dr. Lu recommends lobster for impotence and pain in the tendons and bones.

Poultry: Chicken and Duck

Poultry/Duck and Dr. Henry Lu

Dr. Henry Lu, author of the groundbreaking book *Chinese System of Food Cures* (Sterling Publishing, 1986) and one of the leading authorities of the "food as medicine" movement, was not always a believer. Although he was born in Taiwan, he was quite skeptical of Traditional Chinese Medicine.

But during his late twenties he developed an ailment that was resistant to every form of Western medical treatment. In desperation, he traveled to Taiwan and Hong Kong to consult with Chinese specialists. The outcome changed his life.

"After so many visits to Western doctors in Canada and the United States, no one could help me," he told me in an interview from his office in Vancouver, Canada, where he now lives. "Finally, I saw a Chinese doctor whose treatment cured me in a few months. I started studying the *Nei Jing—The Yellow Emperor's Classic of Internal Medicine*—a classic Chinese medical text, and I realized that there might be something there. I was thirty-two, but I decided to change my field." (Dr. Lu already held a Ph.D. in education and philosophy from the University of Alberta.)

He began by translating the *Nei Jing* from Chinese to English. He then went on to translate twenty-five other Chinese medical books, including seven books on acupuncture that are now listed by the Board of Acupuncture Examiners as required texts for the study of acupuncture. He first began practicing Chinese medicine and acupuncture in 1972.

Katy Luis's Ambila Chicken

In 1986, he founded the Academy of Oriental Heritage in Vancouver, which now has fifteen full-time teachers and more than a hundred students. Since then, he has written five books on food and Chinese medicine; the latest, *Chinese Herbs with Common Foods,* was published in 1997 by Kodansha International.

Balance, Dr. Lu maintains, is the key to the maintenance of good health. A yin person should eat more yang foods and a yang person should eat more yin foods.

"Since we now live in an environment full of potential enemies," says Dr. Lu, "it is essential to enhance the immune system to resist disease. Food as tonics plays a critical role in strengthening the system. And the main types of food tonics are energy, blood, yin, yang."

Briefly, *energy tonics* are for individuals with a low level of energy or inefficient functioning of their internal organs. Energy tonics include foods like beef, chicken, ginkgo nuts, shiitake mushrooms, and string beans.

Blood tonics are for people who may be suffering from a poor absorption of nutrients or excessive bleeding. Among the foods in this category are beef, liver, eggs, oysters, and pig's feet.

Yin tonics are often prescribed for those with a shortage of fluid resulting from chronic illness or excessive sex. Yin tonics include asparagus, tofu, tropical fruits, pork, shrimp, and tomatoes.

Yang tonics are for those who lack yang energy in the kidneys, which is essential to body warmth. This may result from old age, chronic illness, or excessive sex. Among the more prominent yang tonics are beef kidney, cinnamon, lobster, oxtail, and eggs.

One of the most important of the energy tonics, according to Dr. Lu, is chicken. "Chicken warms up the internal region, rejuvenating the spleen and strengthening the stomach," he says. "There are so many uses: in children, it is very effective against malnutrition; in women, chicken is especially helpful after childbirth to replenish energy and increase milk secretion for lactating mothers."

Duck, says Dr. Lu, is a yin tonic. It affects the lungs and kidneys and heals swelling. Dr. Lu recommends duck as an antidote for insomnia.

"There are many yang tonics," says Dr. Lu, who also showed his appreciation of fine food by taking me to a superb Cantonese restaurant in Vancouver's booming Chinatown. As we sat and talked, we munched on pieces of succulently crisp chicken dipped in a pepper-salt. "Among all the meats," he said, polishing off another piece of chicken, "I like chicken the best."

Malay Barbecued Chicken

This simple barbecued chicken, with its eclectic mixture of seasonings, illustrates well the diverse influences of China, Portugal, India, and Thailand found in Malaysian cooking. Like the Chinese, Malay cooks hold the chicken in high esteem for its nutritional and toniclike properties. A whole chicken is often served on auspicious occasions such as holidays and birthdays.

SIX SERVINGS

1 whole roasting chicken, about 4¹/2 to 5 pounds, trimmed of excess fat

Roasting Sauce
4¹/2 tablespoons oyster sauce
2 tablespoons soy sauce
1¹/2 tablespoons ketchup
1¹/2 tablespoons light-brown sugar
2 tablespoons minced garlic
1¹/2 tablespoons minced fresh ginger
5 small shallots, peeled and minced
1¹/2 teaspoons hot chile paste

1. The day before or several hours before cooking, prick the skin of the chicken thoroughly with a fork so that the seasonings can penetrate. Whisk the Roasting Sauce ingredients in a bowl, then rub the sauce all over the chicken and inside the cavity. Cover with plastic wrap, refrigerate, and let the chicken marinate overnight, if possible.

2. Preheat the oven to 425°F. Arrange the chicken, with its sauce, breast side down in a roasting pan or on a cookie sheet lined with aluminum foil. Roast for 30 minutes, then turn the chicken over and baste the breast with the sauce. Continue roasting for another 40 minutes, or until the chicken is cooked and has turned a deep golden brown. Remove from the oven and let it cool slightly before cutting it into serving pieces. Serve with steamed rice and a side vegetable.

To round out the meal, serve with Spicy Stir-Fried Sweet Potatoes (page 168) or Black Bean Acorn Squash (page 179).

Vietnamese Lemon Chicken

For me, traveling in Vietnam and tasting the food there was a revelation. I loved the clean flavors of the fresh herbs contrasted with the salty fish sauce and tart limes. This simple roasted chicken dish combines all of these elements. I often serve the chicken meat cold or at room temperature with a Vietnamese sweet and sour dipping sauce.

1 whole roasting chicken, about 4 to 4 1/2 pounds, excess fat trimmed away

Vietnamese Seasonings
1 lime
1 stalk lemon grass, ends trimmed, tough outer husks removed, and cut into 1-inch lengths

3 to 4 garlic cloves, peeled
3 slices fresh ginger, about the size of a quarter, peeled
1 teaspoon crushed dried chiles or dried chile flakes (optional)
1 1/2 tablespoons fish sauce
1/4 teaspoon freshly ground black pepper

SIX SERVINGS

1. Preheat the oven to 400°F. Rinse the chicken, drain, and pat dry inside and out.
2. Remove the peel from the lime and drop the peelings along with the remaining ingredients of the Vietnamese Seasonings in descending order into the feed tube of a food processor fitted with a steel blade, while the machine is running, or into a blender. Blend to a paste and rub the mixture inside the chicken and all over the skin.
3. Working carefully with your fingers, make a small pocket under the skin at the breast. Slip some of the seasonings into the pocket, and use your fingers to spread it out evenly over the breast. Cut the peeled lime and squeeze the juice inside the cavity as well as over the chicken. Put the lime halves in the cavity.
4. Place the chicken in a shallow roasting pan, breast side up, and roast 1 1/2 hours, or until the juices run clear when the thigh is pierced with a knife. Remove from the oven and cool slightly. To serve, remove the lime from the cavity, and carve the chicken into serving pieces.

To round out the meal, serve with Flash-Cooked Bean Sprouts (page 161) or Grilled Leeks in a Garlic-Soy Dressing (page 174).

☽ Like lemon, lemon grass is cooling and aids digestion.

A Malaysian Chicken Tale: Penang, Katy Luis, and Chicken Ambila

I was in Penang, a beautiful little island northwest of Kuala Lumpur in the Malay Peninsula, watching Katy Luis, a Malaysian cook, prepare one of her intoxicating spice mixtures for Ambila Chicken, a chicken stew with Chinese long beans. She was making a huge batch of the seasoning to send back to her daughter in the United States. (It can be made in large quantities, refrigerated in a tightly closed jar, and used several tablespoons at a time for weeks.)

"This spice mixture, which is called a *rempeh*, is the heart and soul of Malaysian curries and sauces," Katy explained. "It is of the utmost importance that the *rempeh* is properly prepared, and it cannot be hurried."

Traditionally, *rempeh* is made with a mortar and pestle to form a paste. The wet and dry ingredients are mashed separately and then combined. The paste is then cooked slowly over medium heat until it is very fragrant. *Rempeh* can be used with chicken, beef, lamb, seafood, or vegetables—virtually any food. It's a brilliant Malaysian-style "shake-and-bake," and I think she should market it.

First she soaked a mountain of dried red chiles until they were soft and pliable. Next she gathered stalks of lemon grass and another mountain of shallots, garlic cloves, turmeric, dried shrimp paste, and candlenuts (a type of buttery nut used as a thickener), and threw them into a food processor, spinning them around until they were ground to a paste. Finally, she heated some oil and fried the paste slowly, cooking and stirring it the way you would a New Orleans roux.

The spice mixture—like Katy Luis herself—reflects the diverse, multicultural roots of Malaysian cooking. Katy Luis's family is Hakka Chinese (from the southern region), but they are Malaysian born. Her husband, Steve, is Indian-Portuguese and many of the dishes that Katy has incorporated into her repertory are those of Steve's mother, who was 100 percent Portuguese.

Perhaps more than any other place in Asia, Malaysia is at the crossroads of East and West. Penang is nicknamed the "Pearl of the Orient" and is famous for its outstanding scenery and food. Here, as in the rest of Malaysia, Chinese, Indian, European, Thai, Indonesian, Muslim, and local influences converge to produce an almost overwhelming number of culinary styles, including Malay, Nonyan (a marriage of Chinese and Malay), Eurasian, Chinese, and Indian.

When the Ambila Chicken spice paste was ready, Katy Luis heated a wok with some oil, added three heaping tablespoons of paste, mixed it briefly, and then added the chicken pieces, which she stirred for a bit in the spices. She then poured in some water and braised the chicken until it was just tender. Finally, she added the Chinese long beans and some tamarind water. Once the beans were cooked, we ladled up the stew and served it over mounds of steaming jasmine rice.

I was almost speechless at how delicious the chicken was with its overlapping sensations of spicy, sour, salty, and sweet flavors. Steve, Katy's husband, helped himself to another serving. "Katy not only learned the dishes from my mother, but she also improved them," he confessed. "My mother would be proud."

Katy Luis's Ambila Chicken

Several years ago, I had the pleasure of visiting Penang, a little island northwest of the Malay Peninsula. For four days, I cooked, visited markets, and memorized the dishes made by Katy Luis, a talented home cook, whom I describe on the preceding pages. This delicious dish is a revised version of one of her classic specialties. It is not for timid souls; the seasoning is quite fiery, but rice, which goes well with it, absorbs some of the heat.

Seasonings

8 cloves garlic, peeled

15 small fresh cherry peppers or 4 3-inch-long fresh red chiles, stems trimmed and seeds removed

2 fresh jalapeño chiles, ends trimmed, seeds removed, and cut into strips

3 stalks lemon grass, outer leaves removed, ends trimmed, and cut into thin slices

2 1-inch pieces fresh ginger, peeled and cut into 1/4-inch sections

1/2 pound or about 8 shallots, peeled and cut in half

1 teaspoon ground turmeric

1 whole chicken, about 3 3/4 to 4 pounds, fat trimmed

3 tablespoons canola or corn oil

2 red onions, peeled and cut into thin julienne slices

1 3/4 cups water

1 1/2 pounds Chinese long beans or green beans, ends trimmed and cut into 2-inch lengths

2 tablespoons freshly squeezed lemon juice

1 1/2 teaspoons sugar

1 teaspoon salt, or to taste

2 1/2 tablespoons soy sauce

1. Put the Seasonings in descending order into the tube of a food processor or in a blender with the machine running. Process or blend to a paste.

2. With a sharp knife, cut the chicken through the bones into 12 serving-size pieces: First cut the chicken in half lengthwise, then separate the wings and legs from each half, and cut each breast half into three pieces. Separate the leg and thigh.

3. Heat a large pan or Dutch oven, add the oil, and heat until medium hot. Add the seasonings paste and cook over medium heat, stirring frequently, for 20 minutes, until dry and very fragrant. Add the red onions and cook over medium heat for several minutes, then add the chicken pieces and turn them in the paste. Cook 4 to 5 minutes. Pour in the water and bring to a boil. Reduce the heat slightly and cook covered for 10 minutes. Turn

the chicken over in the sauce and continue simmering another 20 minutes, or until the chicken is cooked. Skim any fat or oil from the surface.

4. Add the beans, stir, cover, and continue cooking for 5 minutes, until the beans are almost tender. Stir in the lemon juice, sugar, salt, and soy sauce, cover, and continue cooking for several more minutes. Serve the chicken and sauce over rice.

☯ Ground turmeric is a popular Indian seasoning and beauty aid. It increases the mucus content in gastric juices and is prescribed for stomach disorders. Indian women mix ground turmeric with water to make a paste that they rub on their faces to clear up blemishes.

Scallion-Ginger Chicken

When I was a student in Taiwan, a whole steamed chicken flavored with ginger and scallions was one of the dishes reserved for special occasions. We often served it at Chinese New Year and when we had special guests. Today, I often prepare the steamed chicken for dinner and use the leftover meat in chicken salad or with vegetables served over cold noodle dishes.

SIX SERVINGS

1 whole roasting chicken, about 4 to 4 1/2 pounds, trimmed of excess fat

Chicken Marinade
3 1/2 tablespoons rice wine or sake
3 tablespoons minced scallions, white part only

2 1/2 tablespoons minced fresh ginger
2 tablespoons soy sauce
1 1/2 teaspoons toasted sesame oil

3 tablespoons coarsely chopped fresh cilantro (optional)

To round out the meal, serve with Stir-Fried Wild Mushrooms with Snap Peas in Oyster Sauce (page 166) or Broccoli or Cauliflower with a Soy-Lemon Dressing (page 173).

1. Several hours before cooking, prick the skin of the chicken thoroughly with a fork so the Chicken Marinade can penetrate. With a sharp chef's knife or cleaver, cut the chicken through the bones into about 12 serving pieces. First cut the chicken in half lengthwise. Remove the wings from each half, and the leg and thigh sections. Cut each breast half into three pieces. Separate the legs from the thighs. Put all the pieces in a bowl. Add the marinade and rub it all over the chicken. Cover with plastic wrap and marinate for an hour refrigerated, or several hours, if possible.

2. Arrange the chicken pieces snugly in a heatproof quiche pan or pie plate.

3. Fill a wok or a large pot with enough water to reach the bottom of a steamer tray, a rack, or a tunafish can with ends removed. Place the dish of chicken on top. Cover and steam 30 to 35 minutes, until cooked. (Prick the chicken through the thigh to check for clear juices.) Or you may arrange the chicken in a dish, cover with aluminum foil, and bake on the middle rack of a preheated 450°F. oven for 40 to 45 minutes, or until cooked.

4. Drain the liquid from the chicken into a saucepan. Skim the fat from the top, and add the cilantro. Heat until boiling. Arrange the chicken on a serving platter or serve the chicken right from the steaming dish. Pour the hot broth over the chicken and serve with a vegetable and steamed rice.

Dad's Chinese Chicken Wings

My father, who in his later years has become a superb cook, always longed to make at home the chicken wings he ordered in Asian restaurants. This is the recipe I developed to satisfy his cravings. Many Chinese restaurants deep-fry the wings, but the high-heat roasted method used here is far healthier and the taste is delicious.

Chinese Marinade

1 1/4 cups soy sauce

1 1/4 cups rice wine or sake

1 cup water

12 whole scallions, ends trimmed, smashed with the flat side of a knife

10 cloves garlic, smashed with the flat side of a knife

2 1/2-inch chunk fresh ginger, peeled, then cut into **10** slices about the size of a quarter, each smashed with the flat side of a knife

3 1/2 to 4 pounds chicken wings (about 20), rinsed and drained

SIX SERVINGS

1. Stir the Chinese Marinade ingredients in a saucepan and heat until boiling. Reduce the heat to low and simmer for 10 minutes. Let the marinade cool slightly.

2. With a sharp knife separate the drumettes from the wing tips at the joint. Place all the pieces in a bowl or a deep pan and add the still-warm marinade. Stir to coat, cover with plastic wrap, and let the wings marinate for several hours, or overnight if possible, in the refrigerator.

3. Preheat the oven to 500°F. Line a cookie sheet with aluminum foil and arrange the wings on the cookie sheets. Brush liberally with the marinade. Roast for about 40 minutes, turning once, until the wings are cooked and crispy brown at the edges. Serve hot, at room temperature, or cold as an appetizer or an entrée with a vegetable and steamed rice.

Clay-Pot Chicken in Oyster Sauce

Traditionally, this braised chicken is prepared in a heatproof clay pot with rice. I use a heavy Dutch oven or casserole with the same pleasing results. This is one of those dishes that just get better with reheating.

SIX SERVINGS

Marinade

2 tablespoons soy sauce

2 tablespoons rice wine or sake

1 teaspoon toasted sesame oil

4 whole scallions, ends trimmed, cut into 1-inch lengths

2-inch chunk fresh ginger, peeled, then cut into 6 slices

3 1/2 to 4 pounds chicken legs, thighs, wings, or assorted chicken parts, rinsed and drained

10 dried Chinese black mushrooms, steeped in hot water for 20 minutes until soft, stems removed, caps cut into thirds (optional)

Braising Sauce (mixed together)

1 1/2 cups Classic Chicken Broth (page 27)

3 tablespoons oyster sauce

3 tablespoons rice wine or sake

1 1/2 teaspoons sugar (rock sugar, if available)

About 1 teaspoon cornstarch dissolved in 1 tablespoon water (optional)

This is another of my favorite fighting-the-flu remedies.

To round out the meal, serve with Flash-Cooked Greens with Garlic (page 159).

1. Mix the Marinade ingredients in a large bowl, add the chicken pieces, and turn to coat them with the marinade. Cover with plastic wrap and let the chicken marinate for 30 minutes or longer in the refrigerator. Preheat the oven to 475°F.

2. Arrange the chicken pieces, with the marinade, and the drained black mushrooms on cookie sheets lined with aluminum foil. Roast for 15 minutes, turning once, until the skin is golden. Remove.

3. Transfer the browned chicken and mushrooms to a clay pot, Dutch oven, or a casserole with a lid. Add the Braising Sauce and heat until the liquid is boiling. Reduce the heat to medium, partially cover, and cook for 45 minutes, until the meat is very tender. Skim any fat from the surface. The sauce should be slightly thick. If it hasn't thickened sufficiently, heat until boiling, add a little cornstarch dissolved in water, and cook, stirring, until the sauce has a smooth coating consistency. Scoop the chicken and sauce onto a serving platter or serve from the pot. Accompany the dish with a vegetable and rice.

Tandoori Chicken

Tandoori chicken is so named because of the clay oven, or *tandoor,* in which the chicken is traditionally cooked. But you can cook it successfully on a grill or in a hot oven. Here is my version of this venerable Indian classic.

6 to 7 chicken legs and thighs (about 2 1/2 pounds), trimmed of fat

Tandoori Marinade
1 1/2 cups plain or low-fat yogurt
2 tablespoons minced fresh ginger
1 1/2 tablespoons minced garlic

1 teaspoon dried chile flakes (or to taste)
1 1/4 teaspoons ground cumin
1 1/4 teaspoons dried oregano
3/4 teaspoon ground turmeric
1 teaspoon salt
1/2 teaspoon freshly ground black pepper

SIX SERVINGS

1. Several hours or the day before cooking, prick the skin of the chicken thoroughly with a fork so that the Tandoori Marinade can penetrate.
2. Mix the marinade ingredients in a bowl, add the chicken legs, and turn them in the marinade. Cover with plastic wrap and let the chicken marinate for several hours, or overnight if possible.
3. Prepare a medium-hot fire for grilling or preheat the oven to 400°F. Arrange the meat 3 inches from the source of heat, cover, and grill about 8 to 10 minutes per side, until cooked through. Alternatively, roast 45 minutes, turning once, until crispy brown and cooked. Remove, let cool slightly, and serve with a vegetable and rice.

To round out the meal, serve with Spicy Stir-Fried Sweet Potatoes (page 168) or Celery Hearts in a Spicy Sesame Dressing (page 181).

Spicy Stir-Fried Chicken with Fresh Vegetables

This simple yet delicious chicken dish, when served with some steamed rice, is virtually a meal in itself. I vary the vegetables depending on the season, using asparagus, broccoli, or even baby corn shoots to create a colorful contrast of flavors and textures.

SIX SERVINGS

1¹/₂ pounds boned chicken breast, skin removed

Marinade
2 tablespoons soy sauce
1¹/₂ tablespoons rice wine or sake
1 teaspoon toasted sesame oil
1 teaspoon cornstarch

1 pound oyster or button mushrooms, stem ends trimmed
³/₄ pound snap or snow peas, ends snapped off and veiny strings removed
3¹/₂ tablespoons canola or corn oil

Seasonings
3 tablespoons minced scallions, white part only

2 tablespoons minced garlic
2 tablespoons minced fresh ginger
1 teaspoon hot chile paste (or to taste)

1 red bell pepper, cored, seeded, and cut into ¹/₂-inch squares
1 orange bell pepper, cored, seeded, and cut into ¹/₂-inch squares

Chicken Sauce
³/₄ cup Classic Chicken Broth (page 27)
3 tablespoons soy sauce
2 tablespoons rice wine or sake
2 teaspoons sugar
1 teaspoon salt
1 teaspoon toasted sesame oil
1 tablespoon cornstarch

1. Trim the chicken of any fat or gristle. Cut it into ¹/₂-inch cubes and place them in a bowl. Add the premixed Marinade and turn the chicken cubes in it to coat them. Cover with plastic wrap, and let the chicken marinate for 30 minutes.

2. Cut the mushrooms in half or into thirds, if large.

3. Blanch the snap or snow peas in boiling water for 10 seconds. Refresh immediately in cold water and drain.

4. Heat a wok or large skillet, add 2 tablespoons of the oil, heat until very hot, and add the chicken. Cook over high heat, stirring, until the chicken changes color and separates—about 3 to 4 minutes. Remove the chicken cubes with a slotted spoon and drain. Wipe out the pan.

5. Reheat the pan, add the remaining $1^1/_2$ tablespoons oil, heat, and add the Seasonings. Stir-fry briefly, about 15 seconds, then add the red and orange peppers and mushrooms; toss them with the seasonings and stir-fry for $1^1/_2$ minutes. Add the snow peas and Chicken Sauce, and cook, stirring continuously, to prevent lumps, until the sauce is thickened. Return the cooked chicken to the pan, and toss lightly to heat through and coat the pieces. Scoop onto a platter and serve immediately.

☯ In India, women like to dissolve dried turmeric in water to make a paste that they rub on their faces as a beauty mask. They believe it clears the complexion.

An Ode to Hot Chiles

Hot chiles were first introduced to Asia by Spanish and Portuguese traders during the seventeenth century. The Chinese called them *fan jiao,* or "barbarian's spice" (later the name was changed to *la jiao,* or "hot pepper"). In spite of the derogatory term, chiles were quickly embraced and became a predominant seasoning in the cooking of Sichuan and Hunan in China, as well as in Thailand, Vietnam, Korea, Indonesia, and India.

Chiles were not only widely used as a seasoning, but also used in folk remedies to increase appetite, aid digestion, and treat arthritis and rheumatism. A hot pepper poultice, made by boiling chiles in water for several minutes, was often used for chilblains and frostbite. In a recent paper published in the *Quarterly Review of Biology,* Dr. Paul Sherman theorized that many people traditionally used chiles in the belief that they contained powerful antibiotic chemicals capable of killing poisonous bacteria or fungi.

Capsaicin, which is the component in the chile responsible for the heat, can also clear sinuses and relieve congestion, says Dr. Irwin Ziment, a professor of medicine at the University of California at Los Angeles. In addition, hot peppers clear blocked arteries, cut blood cholesterol, and shield the stomach lining from ulcer-causing acids. (For years, ulcer patients were advised *not* to eat spicy foods; now doctors suggest the opposite.)

There are many different types of hot chiles used in Asian cooking. Generally, the smaller the chile, the more intense the heat; the larger the chile, the milder and sweeter it is. You might want to taste a tiny bit to judge the heat. Since the capsaicin runs through the length, cut a tiny slice across the chile, and remove the seeds and membrane before tasting. Some cooks recommend wearing rubber gloves when handling chiles. Make certain to scrub your knife and cutting board with soap after cutting chiles and don't touch any sensitive areas, such as your eyes. The following are some of the main types of chiles, with their individual characteristics, that Asian cooks use frequently. Substitutions are given whenever possible.

Fresh chiles:

Thai chile is probably one of the most widely used hot peppers in Asian cooking since it became available in this country. It is about 1 1/2 inches long and can range from dark green to red. The green ones seem to have a more intense initial punch than the red, which are subtle but no less lethal. The heat may be tempered by removing the seeds and membrane. If unavailable, you may substitute 2 fresh serrano or jalapeño chiles for each Thai chile.

Korean chile is related to the Thai chile, but usually you find only the green variety. It generally measures about 3 to 4 inches long and has a hot green vegetable flavor. This is the pepper that gives kimchee its fiery edge. You may substitute 2 jalapeños for each Korean pepper.

Kashmiri chiles are large, mild in flavor, and have a deep red color. They are similar in taste and appearance to California and Anaheim chiles. I sometimes substitute hot cherry peppers, which are a bit hotter but just as sweet.

Cayenne chiles are used frequently in Indian and Malaysian cooking and are related to the fiesta chiles. They are usually cylindrical, slightly tapered, and measure about 2 to 3 inches long. These chiles vary in flavor from mild to sweet and intense. They are used both fresh and dried. If they are unavailable, substitute *serrano* or *fiesta* chiles.

Dried peppers:

Pequín chile is oval and orangy-red. It usually measures about 1/2 to 3/4 inch long. The flavor is sweet and smoky, but very intense. If unavailable, substitute the dried Thai or *de arbol* pepper.

De arbol pepper is closely related to the cayenne chile. It is usually brick-red and measures about 2 to 3 inches long. Generally, *de arbol* peppers have a searing heat. You may substitute dried Thai or *pequín* chiles.

Chile Chicken with Cashews

For the Chinese, nuts, like watermelon seeds, are a popular snack. They are also added to stir-fried dishes, where they impart a rich flavor and appealingly crisp texture. They are usually sold in bulk in Asian markets at a cheaper price than in supermarkets.

SIX SERVINGS

1 1/2 pounds boned chicken breast, skin removed

Marinade
2 tablespoons soy sauce
1 1/2 tablespoons rice wine or sake
1 teaspoon toasted sesame oil
1 tablespoon minced fresh ginger
1 teaspoon cornstarch

4 1/2 tablespoons canola or corn oil

Seasonings
1 1/2 tablespoons minced scallions, white part only
2 tablespoons minced garlic
1 teaspoon hot chile paste or dried chile flakes (or to taste)

1 1/2 cups thinly sliced canned water chestnuts, blanched for 10 seconds, then refreshed in cold water and drained (see page 21)

Sauce (mixed together)
3/4 cup Classic Chicken Broth (page 27)
3 tablespoons soy sauce
2 1/2 tablespoons rice wine or sake
1 1/2 tablespoons sugar
1 teaspoon toasted sesame oil
2 teaspoons Chinese black vinegar or Worcestershire sauce
1 1/4 tablespoons cornstarch

1 1/4 cups dry-roasted cashews

1. Trim the chicken of any fat or gristle. Cut it into 1/2-inch cubes and place in a bowl. Add the premixed Marinade ingredients, and toss the chicken cubes to coat them. Cover with plastic wrap, and let the chicken marinate for 30 minutes.

2. Heat a wok or large skillet, add 2 1/2 tablespoons of the oil, heat until very hot, and add the chicken. Cook over high heat until the chicken cubes become opaque and are cooked, about 3 to 4 minutes. Remove with a slotted spoon to a plate. Wipe out the pan.

3. Reheat the pan, add the remaining 2 tablespoons oil, heat, and add the Seasonings. Stir-fry briefly, about 15 seconds, then add the water chestnuts, and stir-fry over high heat for about 1¹/₂ minutes to heat them through. Add the premixed Sauce, and cook, stirring continuously, to prevent lumps, until thickened. Return the cooked chicken and add the cashews. Toss lightly to coat and heat through. Scoop everything onto a platter. Serve with a vegetable and steamed rice.

> To round out the meal, serve with Flash-Cooked Greens with Garlic (page 159) or Flash-Cooked Bean Sprouts (page 161).

☯ **Generally, nuts are neutral in nature; if eaten on a regular basis, they are a common remedy in China for quenching excessive thirst.**

Stir-Fried Chicken with Basil

I have always loved this simple Thai stir-fried dish, especially with steamed basmati rice. Feel free to add some blanched vegetables if you want to create a one-dish meal.

SIX SERVINGS

1 1/2 pounds boned chicken breast, skin removed

Marinade

3 tablespoons fish sauce

1 1/2 tablespoons rice wine or sake

1 1/2 tablespoons minced shallots

3 1/2 tablespoons canola or corn oil

Seasonings

1 1/2 tablespoons chopped fresh red chile (seeds removed)

2 tablespoons chopped garlic

3 medium red onions, peeled and cut into thin julienne slices

Sauce (mixed together)

2 tablespoons fish sauce

1 1/2 tablespoons soy sauce

1 tablespoon sugar

1 1/2 tablespoons water

1 1/2 cups fresh Thai holy basil or sweet basil leaves, stems removed, leaves rinsed, drained, and coarsely shredded

1. Arrange the chicken breast flat on a cutting board. Holding the blade of your knife horizontal with the board, cut the chicken into thin slices on the diagonal and put them in a bowl. Add the Marinade ingredients and toss the chicken lightly to coat.

2. Heat a wok or large skillet, add 2 tablespoons of the oil, and heat until very hot, about 30 seconds. Add the Seasonings, and stir-fry over high heat about 1 1/2 to 2 minutes, or until the onions are tender. Push to the side of the pan.

3. Add the remaining 1 1/2 tablespoons oil, and heat until very hot. Add the chicken, stir-frying over high heat about 2 minutes, or until the meat changes color and is cooked. Give the premixed Sauce another stir and pour it into the pan. Bring to a boil. Add the fresh basil and mix. Scoop the chicken onto a serving platter and serve with rice and a vegetable, if desired.

To round out the meal, serve with Wilted Greens with a Spicy Garlic Dressing (page 160).

🌀 Basil, which many might consider foreign to China, has, in fact, been used in Chinese medicine since the sixth century A.D. Basil tea (1 cup fresh basil leaves brewed with 1 cup water) is often drunk for indigestion.

Flash-Cooked Chicken with Leeks

Traditionally, meats or seafood pieces are often first deep-fried or flash-cooked in a lot of hot oil. But I find that if you cook them in a small amount of very hot oil, maintaining the heat as you stir-fry, you get the same effect and the foods are tender and juicy.

1 1/2 pounds boned chicken breast, skin removed

Marinade

3 tablespoons soy sauce

2 tablespoons rice wine or sake

1 teaspoon toasted sesame oil

2 teaspoons cornstarch

4 1/2 tablespoons canola or corn oil

Seasonings

10 cloves garlic, sliced very thin

8 cups shredded leeks (about 3), ends trimmed, and rinsed thoroughly

2 tablespoons rice wine or sake

Sauce (mixed together)

2 tablespoons soy sauce

2 teaspoons toasted sesame oil

2 teaspoons Chinese black vinegar or Worcestershire sauce

1. Arrange the chicken breast flat on a cutting board. Holding the blade of your knife horizontal with the board, cut the chicken crosswise into thin slices and place in a bowl. Stir the Marinade ingredients, then add to chicken and toss lightly to coat the slices.
2. Heat a wok or large skillet, add 1 1/2 tablespoons of the oil and heat until very hot. Add half the chicken, and stir-fry over high heat about 2 minutes, or until the meat changes color and is cooked. Drain in a colander. Reheat the pan, add 1 1/2 tablespoons of the oil, heat, and cook the remaining chicken. Drain in a colander and clean the pan.
3. Reheat the pan, add the remaining 1 1/2 tablespoons of oil, and heat until very hot. Add the Seasonings and stir-fry about 1 minute, tossing over high heat. Add the rice wine and continue cooking, until the leeks are tender, about 1 minute. Add the Sauce and the cooked chicken, and stir to combine the ingredients evenly. Scoop the mixture onto a serving platter. Serve with rice and a vegetable, if desired.

☯ Chinese cooks consider leeks pungent and astringent, making them ideal for counteracting diarrhea.

Grilled Lemon Grass Chicken

Lemon grass is one of the most widely used seasonings in Vietnamese and Thai cooking. Happily, it is now widely available here in Asian markets and in some well-stocked supermarkets. The lower part of the stem, up to the point where the leaves start branching out, is the edible portion. Trim both ends and remove any tough outer husks before using. If unavailable, substitute the dried variety and soak 1 hour in hot water.

SIX SERVINGS

1 1/2 pounds boned chicken breasts, skin removed

Marinade
4 cloves garlic, peeled
3 shallots, trimmed and peeled
1 stalk lemon grass, tough outer husks removed, ends trimmed, and cut into 1 1/2-inch lengths
2 tablespoons rice wine or sake
1 1/2 tablespoons sugar
3 tablespoons fish sauce
1 tablespoon canola or corn oil

Vietnamese Dressing
1 teaspoon crushed dried red chiles or dried chile flakes
Juice of 5 limes or 3 lemons
1 1/2 tablespoons minced garlic
1/4 cup sugar
5 tablespoons fish sauce, or to taste

3 cups leafy lettuce, cut into thin julienne strips
2 cups julienned carrots (or shredded in a food processor)
3 tablespoons chopped fresh mint
3 tablespoons coarsely chopped dry-roasted peanuts (optional)

1. After trimming away any fat or gristle, put the chicken breasts in a bowl.
2. Drop the ingredients of the Marinade, in descending order, through the feed tube of a food processor fitted with a metal blade, while the machine is running, and process to a fine paste. Add the marinade to the chicken breasts and mix with your hands, tossing to coat. Cover with plastic wrap and let the marinated chicken stand at room temperature for 2 hours.
3. To prepare the Vietnamese Dressing, soak the crushed red chiles or the chile flakes in the lime juice for several minutes. Add the garlic, sugar, and fish sauce, and stir to dissolve the sugar. Transfer the dressing to a serving dish.

4. Arrange the lettuce and carrots in separate concentric circles in a serving bowl.

5. Prepare a medium-hot fire for grilling or preheat the broiler. Arrange the chicken breasts 3 inches from the source of heat and grill or broil them about 8 to 10 minutes per side. Remove, let cool slightly, and cut them on the diagonal into thin slices. Arrange the chicken over the vegetables. Pour the dressing over the salad (or let everyone at the table dress their own salad). Garnish with the chopped mint and optional peanuts.

☯ Similar to lemon, lemon grass is believed to quench thirst and to drive summer heat from the body.

Chicken Saté

Saté is a traditional Indonesian dish that can be prepared with pork or beef, as well as chicken. The sauce, though delicious, can be slightly heavy, having peanut butter and coconut milk in it. I find that a good-quality "light" coconut milk, which is thinner and has less fat, works beautifully.

SIX SERVINGS

2 whole boned chicken breasts (about 1 pound each), trimmed of fat

Marinade
3 tablespoons fish sauce
3 tablespoons minced fresh lemon grass, ends trimmed and outer leaves removed
1 tablespoon minced garlic

14 10-inch bamboo skewers, softened in cold water to cover for 1 hour
2 1/2 cups grated carrots (about 4, peeled and ends trimmed)
3 cups Boston lettuce, rinsed, drained, and cut into thin julienne shreds

1 1/2 cups bean sprouts, rinsed and drained

Saté Sauce
1/2 cup smooth peanut butter
1 cup light coconut milk
3 tablespoons fish sauce
3 tablespoons minced fresh ginger
2 1/2 tablespoons light-brown sugar
1 tablespoon soy sauce
1 teaspoon crushed dried red chiles

2 tablespoons canola or corn oil
3 tablespoons minced fresh cilantro

☯ Peanuts are looked upon fondly by Chinese mothers since they regulate blood, stimulate the spleen, and improve the appetite. Mothers often give their children dishes cooked with peanuts, particularly to encourage growth and make their sons taller.

1. Place the chicken breasts flat on a cutting board. Holding the blade of your knife at a slant to the board, cut the chicken into thin diagonal slices and put them in a bowl. Add the Marinade ingredients and mix, tossing lightly, to coat the slices. Cover with plastic wrap, and let the chicken sit at least 2 hours in the refrigerator. Thread the chicken slices onto the skewers, reserving the marinade.
2. Arrange the carrots, lettuce, and bean sprouts in separate concentric circles on a serving platter, reserving room in the center for the chicken.
3. Process the ingredients of the Saté Sauce in descending order in a food processor fitted with a steel blade or in a blender until smooth. Pour into a serving bowl.

4. Heat a large, heavy skillet or a grill, brush the surface with the oil, and heat until near smoking. Sear or grill batches of the skewered chicken over high heat for about 3 to 4 minutes on each side, until golden brown and firm to the touch. Turn only once, and add more oil as needed. Arrange the cooked chicken over the vegetables, and sprinkle the cilantro on top. Serve with the Saté Sauce, spooning a little over each portion. Serve as an appetizer or an entrée.

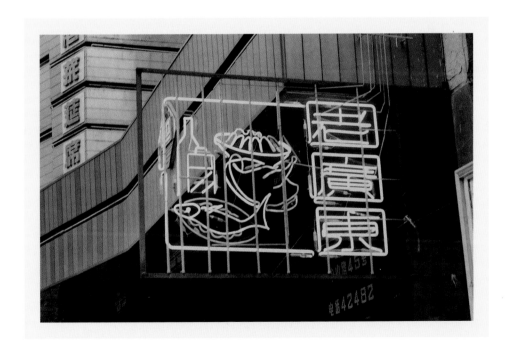

Smoky Chicken Salad with Fresh Herb Dressing

Tea-smoking is a process that may have originated as a preserving technique, but it is now used more often to give a flavor. Orange peel, cinnamon, fennel, and anise seed as well as star anise can all be used with the tea, and the flavor changes subtly with the different seasonings.

2 whole chicken breasts with bones (about 1¹/4 pounds each), trimmed of fat

Marinade

¹/4 cup rice wine or sake

2 tablespoons soy sauce

10 whole scallions, ends trimmed, and smashed lightly with the flat side of a knife

10 slices fresh ginger, about the size of a quarter, smashed lightly with the flat side of a knife

2 star anise, smashed lightly

Tea-Smoking Mixture (mixed together)

2 tablespoons loose black tea

¹/4 cup light-brown sugar

Rind of 1 orange, cut into ¹/2-inch lengths

2 teaspoons ground cinnamon

1 teaspoon toasted sesame oil (for brushing on smoked chicken)

1 teaspoon canola or corn oil

1 tablespoon minced garlic

1 pound snow peas, ends snapped off and veiny strings removed

2 tablespoons rice wine or sake

20 cherry tomatoes, rinsed and cut in half

Vinaigrette (mixed together)

¹/2 cup soy sauce

¹/3 cup clear rice vinegar

2 teaspoons toasted sesame oil

2 tablespoons sugar, or to taste

3 heaping tablespoons minced fresh cilantro

1. Rinse the chicken breasts, drain thoroughly, and put them in a large bowl. Add the Marinade ingredients, toss lightly with your hands to coat, cover with plastic wrap, and let the breasts marinate in the refrigerator for at least 1 hour.

2. Fill a wok or a pot with several inches of water and bring to a boil. Arrange the chicken breasts, skin side up, on a tray or a rack suspended over the boiling water. Cover and steam about 20 to 25 minutes, or until just cooked. Remove and let cool slightly.

3. Line a wok or a large, heavy pot and its cover with heavy-duty aluminum foil. Spread

the Tea-Smoking Mixture in the bottom of the pan. Arrange 6 crisscrossed chopsticks or a rack over the smoking mixture to hold the chicken. Arrange the chicken, breast side up, over the smoking mixture and put on the cover, crimping the edges of the aluminum foil so that no smoke can escape. Place over high heat and cook for about 15 minutes from the time the smoky smell is first apparent. Remove from the heat and let stand covered for 10 minutes. Remove the chicken breasts and let them cool slightly, then brush them with a little toasted sesame oil.

4. With the heel of your hand, press down on the central cartilage of each breastbone. Now turn the breast skin side down and remove the breastbone. Using a sharp knife, cut each breast lengthwise in half, then each half crosswise into $1/2$-inch-thick slices. By hand or with a knife, shred the chicken into julienne strips.

5. Heat a wok or a heavy skillet, add the canola or corn oil, and heat until very hot. Add the garlic and snow peas, and toss lightly over high heat for 20 seconds, then add the rice wine. Continue cooking for 1 minute, until crisp-tender. Add the cherry tomatoes, toss lightly about 15 seconds, then scoop the vegetables onto a serving platter. Arrange the smoked chicken shreds on top. Before serving, pour the Vinaigrette over the chicken and vegetables. Serve warm, at room temperature, or cold.

☯ Star anise is a warming spice, which will disperse inner cold in the body and aid digestion: It is often brewed in hot water, the resulting tea drunk as a simple digestive.

Chicken Salad with Fresh Mint

SIX SERVINGS

2 pounds chicken legs or thighs, rinsed
  and drained
3 cups water
1/4 cup rice wine or sake
2 stalks fresh lemon grass, ends trimmed,
  tough outer husks removed, and cut
  into 2-inch lengths (if unavailable, substitute dried lemon grass, soaked 1 hour
  in hot water)
1 1/2 red onions, cut into thin julienne
  slices (about 2 1/2 cups)
1 cup clear rice vinegar

Vietnamese Dressing
2 small fresh red chiles, ends trimmed, seeds
  removed, and cut into fine julienne shreds
3 tablespoons minced garlic
1/2 cup fish sauce
5 1/2 tablespoons sugar, or more to taste

5 cups julienned leafy or Boston lettuce
1/3 to 1/2 cup coarsely shredded mint
  leaves

1. Put the chicken parts, water, rice wine or sake, and lemon grass in a pot and bring to a boil. Reduce the heat to low, and cook for 25 minutes, or until the chicken is cooked. (Pierce the thigh with a knife; clear liquid should come out.) Remove the chicken and let it cool. (Save the broth for another use.) Remove and discard the skin and bones and cut the meat into thin julienne shreds.

2. Place the red onion slices in a bowl and pour the rice vinegar on top. Let the onion sit 15 to 20 minutes. Mix together the Vietnamese Dressing ingredients in a bowl and set aside.

3. Arrange the lettuce on a serving platter, and sprinkle the chicken evenly over it. Drain and sprinkle on the onions, adding the vinegar to the dressing. Sprinkle the fresh mint on top. Before serving, pour the dressing over the salad.

☯ Field mint or corn mint, a species with smaller leaves, is the Asian cousin to peppermint. In Europe, peppermint has been used medicinally for thousands of years. It is often prescribed for nausea, travel sickness, indigestion, and migraines. Penelope Ody, author of *The Complete Medicinal Herbal* (Dorling Kindersley, 1993), suggests putting a few fresh leaves in boiling water and inhaling the fumes to ease nasal congestion.

Chicken Yakitori

Anyone who has had the opportunity to visit the intricate network of yakitori stalls in Tokyo will always savor the experience. Customers stand informally around counters drinking beer and eating continuously from the charcoal braziers lined with skewered meats and vegetables; chicken is the most popular. This is my slightly simplified version of this classic dish.

Yakitori Marinade
1 cup soy sauce
1/2 cup sweetened rice wine (*mirin*)
1/2 cup sake
3 tablespoons minced fresh ginger
3/4 teaspoon dried chile flakes

1 1/2 pounds boned chicken thighs or
    breasts, skin removed
10 scallions, ends trimmed and cut into
    1-inch lengths
3 medium green peppers, cored, seeded,
    and cut into 1-inch squares
14 6-inch bamboo skewers, softened
    about 1 hour in cold water to cover
1 tablespoon canola or corn oil

SIX SERVINGS

1. Mix the Yakitori Marinade ingredients in a saucepan and bring to a boil. Reduce the heat to low and cook for 5 minutes. Cool slightly.

2. Trim the chicken of any fat or gristle. Cut into 1/2-inch cubes. Thread the chicken, scallions, and green peppers alternately onto the skewers, starting and ending with the green peppers. Place the skewered chicken in a flat pan. Pour the warm marinade on top, cover with plastic wrap, and let the chicken and vegetables marinate for 1 hour in the refrigerator.

3. Heat a heavy skillet or a grill, brush the surface with the oil and heat until very hot. Cook batches of the skewered chicken and vegetables over high heat about 3 1/2 to 4 minutes, until golden brown and firm to the touch on both sides, turning once. Baste the chicken and vegetables several times with the marinade as it cooks. Brush the pan or grill with more oil as needed. Remove the cooked meat and arrange on a serving platter. Serve as an appetizer, or as an entrée with steamed rice.

❂ The spicy seasonings and roasting technique make this dish very warming. Serve it with ice-cold drinks, like beer, as they do in Japan.

Saucy Ground Turkey Wrapped in Lettuce Leaves

I love to serve this unusual turkey dish as an appetizer or even an entrée. It can be made with almost any type of ground meat, such as pork or beef, if ground turkey is unavailable.

SIX SERVINGS

1 1/2 pounds ground turkey

Seasonings
3 1/2 tablespoons minced scallions, white part only
1 1/2 tablespoons minced fresh ginger
1 tablespoon minced garlic
1/2 tablespoon toasted sesame oil

2 bunches Boston lettuce, rinsed, drained, and stems trimmed
1 tablespoon canola or corn oil
2 cups canned water chestnuts, blanched

in boiling water for 10 seconds, refreshed in cold water, and drained (see page 21)
3 cups scallion greens cut into 1-inch sections

Spicy Sauce (mixed together)
5 tablespoons Chinese sweet bean paste or ground bean paste
2 tablespoons sugar
1 tablespoon toasted sesame oil
1 1/2 teaspoons hot chile paste

☯ Although turkey is not widely available in China, like chicken it has warming properties.

1. Put the ground turkey in a bowl, add the Seasonings, and mix together with your hands.
2. Lightly flatten the lettuce leaves with the flat side of a cleaver or knife and arrange in a basket or a bowl for serving.
3. Heat a wok or a heavy skillet, add half the oil, and when hot, about 30 seconds, add the turkey and stir-fry over medium-high heat, mashing and breaking it up. Cook until it changes color and separates. Drain in a colander and wipe out the pan.
4. Reheat the pan, add the remaining 1/2 tablespoon oil, and when very hot add the water chestnuts and scallion greens, tossing them over high heat about 1 minute. Add the premixed Spicy Sauce and stir, letting it thicken. Return the cooked turkey to the pan and toss to coat with the sauce. Scoop the mixture onto a serving platter. To serve, pass the platter and basket of lettuce leaves; each diner spoons some of the cooked meat onto a lettuce leaf, rolls it up, and eats it.

Braised Duck with Tangerine Peel and Sweet Potatoes

This sumptuous stew with its pungent seasonings is hearty and warming—perfect for a cold winter day.

1 duck, about 5 to 6 pounds, trimmed of
   fat and excess skin
2 tablespoons soy sauce
1 1/2 teaspoons canola or corn oil

Seasonings
4 6-inch strips dried tangerine or orange peel*
8 cloves garlic, smashed lightly with the flat
   side of a knife and sliced thinly
8 whole scallions, ends trimmed, cut into 1-
   inch sections, smashed lightly
8 slices fresh ginger, about the size of a
   quarter, smashed lightly with the flat side
   of a knife

Broth (mixed together)
3 1/2 cups water
1/2 cup soy sauce
1/2 cup rice wine or sake
1 tablespoon sugar

4 sweet potatoes or yams, about 2 pounds,
   peeled and cut into 1 1/2-inch cubes
1 1/2 teaspoons cornstarch mixed with 1
   tablespoon water

1. Preheat the oven to 475°F. Rub the soy sauce all over the duck, inside and out. Using a sharp knife or a cleaver, cut the duck, through the bones, into 3-inch sections. Arrange the duck pieces, skin side up, on a rack in a shallow roasting pan. Pour 1/2 cup water into the pan to prevent the duck fat from smoking. Roast the duck parts for 20 minutes, or until golden brown. Remove and set aside.

2. Meanwhile, boil the dried tangerine or orange peel for 1 1/2 minutes in water to cover. Let it sit for 20 minutes, then scrape away the pith to remove any bitterness.

3. Heat a casserole or Dutch oven with a lid, add the oil, and heat until hot. Add the citrus peel and the rest of the Seasonings and stir-fry until fragrant, about 15 seconds. Add the Broth ingredients and bring to a boil. Add the roasted duck pieces and bring to a

*Dried tangerine peel is a seasoning often used in "red-cooked" or soy-braised dishes. It is available at Asian specialty markets. If unavailable, substitute fresh orange or clementine peel and blanch as directed but do not soak.

boil again. Reduce the heat to low, partially cover, and simmer for 1^1/$_4$ hours, or until the duck is tender. Remove the duck pieces to a plate and strain the broth, discarding the seasonings and skimming the surface to remove all fat.

4. Return the broth to the casserole, add the sweet potatoes, partially cover, and cook for 12 to 14 minutes, or until just tender. Add the cornstarch and water, and heat the sauce until it begins to boil, stirring to prevent lumps. Put the duck back in and carefully turn the pieces in the sauce. Heat briefly, and either serve the duck from the pot, with steamed rice, or transfer to a serving bowl.

☯ Duck, though neutral in nature, increases the yin energy in the body, thereby strengthening it. Cooked with asparagus, duck is eaten for fevers due to a yin deficiency, and duck dishes are often prescribed to alleviate dizziness from hypertension.

☯ Tangerine and orange peel are reputed to warm the body, clear any congested energy channels, and help regulate energy flow. According to Dr. Henry Lu, the red, outer layer disperses energy and the white, inner layer (which I scrape away in cooked dishes because it is bitter) can eliminate oil from the body and harmonize the stomach.

Roasted Malaysian Cornish Game Hens

I usually reserve Rock Cornish game hens for a festive occasion, but this simple recipe is easy enough to prepare at any time. The pungent seasonings and high heat blend together to flavor the birds to a succulent tenderness.

SIX SERVINGS

3 Rock Cornish game hens, about 1 1/2 pounds each

Seasonings
2 slices peeled fresh ginger, about the size of a quarter
6 small shallots, ends trimmed, and peeled
5 cloves peeled garlic
1 stalk fresh lemon grass, ends trimmed, tough outer husks removed, and cut into 1-inch lengths

1 1/2 teaspoons ground cumin
3/4 teaspoon salt
1/2 teaspoon ground turmeric
1/4 teaspoon freshly ground black pepper
1 tablespoon fish sauce

3 tablespoons coarsely chopped fresh cilantro (optional)

1. Preheat the oven to 400°F. Remove any excess fat from around the cavity of the Rock Cornish game hens. Rinse and drain.
2. Drop the Seasonings in descending order into the feed tube of a food processor fitted with a steel blade while the machine is running, or into a blender. Blend to a paste.
3. Working carefully with your fingers, make a small pocket under the skin at the breast of each game hen. Slip some of the seasonings mixture inside and use your fingers to spread it out evenly over the breast. Rub the rest inside the cavity and all over the skin.
4. Place the game hens on a rack in a shallow roasting pan, breast side up, and roast 1 hour, or until the juices run clear when the leg is pierced with a knife. Remove from the oven and cool slightly; then cut each game hen in half. Sprinkle the cilantro on top and spoon some of the roasting juices over the breasts. Serve with a vegetable and rice or crusty bread.

To round out the meal, serve with Flash-Cooked Bean Sprouts (page 161) or Grilled Leeks in a Garlic-Soy Dressing (page 174).

Pork, Beef, and Lamb

Meat and Madame Siong Mui

The class at Madame Ng Siong Mui's Chinese Harvest Home Cooking School in Singapore began with the brewing of tea. Madame Ng, who is a well-known authority on holistic Chinese cooking, slowly poured hot water into a pot containing her own personal tea blend.

The tea was delectably sweet and soothing, and Madame Ng explained the different ingredients: "This tea is a tonic for the body," she said. "There's a little *pu erh,* a type of fermented black tea for flavor, and lotus seeds for the brain and stomach, dried longan to bolster mental energy, wolfberries or boxthorn fruit to improve eyesight, and a little rock sugar for sweetness."

Madame Ng's curriculum ranges from an "Introduction to a Traditional Chinese Health Diet" to specialized topics like "Diet for Mothers-to-Be" and "Rejuvenate Through Chinese Cooking." The menu the day I was in class included a demonstration of several meat dishes, including Red-Cooked Lamb and Flash-Cooked Ginger Beef.

Madame Ng, like many traditionalists, believes that herbs and medicine do not keep one healthy. Her approach, which was originally developed by ancient Chinese physicians, is more preventative in nature, relying on the daily consumption of ingredients like vegetables, fruits, nuts, berries, poultry, fish, and occasionally meat.

"Besides eating meat for nutrients," she says, "the Chinese eat a part of an animal to benefit that organ. For instance, eating liver will help the liver, just as eating kidneys will strengthen the kidneys."

Furthermore, Madame Ng subscribes to the "five-element" theory of Traditional Chinese Medicine: Specific human organs correspond to and can be affected by different animals. For instance, poultry is beneficial to the liver; sheep or lamb are good for the heart; cattle or beef should be eaten for the spleen/pancreas; horse or fish is a tonic for the lungs; and pig is beneficial to the kidneys. Some even believe that petting the live animal benefits a weakened organ.

Madame Ng was born into a family of food lovers. Her grandparents, who had fled to Singapore from China, sold homemade noodles and congee (rice porridge). Her father took over the business and opened a restaurant, so Madame Ng grew up working in the kitchen. Her interest in healthful foods developed when she married her husband, who is an herbalist, and she has accompanied him on numerous trips to China, meeting herbalists and Chinese nutritionists. She began teaching in 1987.

After the tea, Madame Ng showed me the clay pot in which she was to braise the mutton. "Traditionally, clay pots are used to braise and simmer, but a saucepan or a wok with a lid will do," she said. "The clay pot should be used over a small fire and will keep the food warm and moist." Madame Ng put all of the braising ingredients, including ginger, garlic, tangerine peel, star anise, cinnamon stick, and water, in the pot. After blanching the mutton, she added it to the braising mixture. She then left it to cook.

According to Madame Ng, a lamb or mutton stew should be consumed only by people with very weak or cooling body conditions, and it is best eaten during the winter. "The Cantonese say that no blanket is needed after eating mutton, because of its warming qualities."

As far as an overall diet is concerned, the Chinese actually favor eggs, fish, and poultry because they are more easily digested than pork, beef, and lamb. But beef and lamb are warming foods, usually reserved for the cold weather or for yin conditions. Pork is neutral, but it is believed to moisten dryness and is prescribed for those with thin, nervous, or weak constitutions.

When eating meat, Asians consume it in small quantities with plenty of vegetables and a staple such as rice, noodles, or bread. Vegetables such as leafy greens or cabbage and broccoli are often paired with meat since they help in the digestion of the protein. Marinades made with rice wine, garlic, lemon juice, tamarind juice, and vinegar are also added to break down the fats and proteins. And the use of ginger is common because it is believed to cleanse the body of toxins from meat dishes.

After cutting up and organizing the ingredients for the flash-cooked beef, Madame Ng deftly cooked the dish, tossing the sliced meat in hot oil and then further stir-frying it with ginger, garlic, scallions, and bean sprouts.

Next she scooped the stir-fry onto a platter and tested the red-cooked lamb for doneness. It was tender, so she directed everyone over to the table, where bowls and chopsticks were neatly laid out. We tasted the lamb: It was butter-tender, redolent with the seasonings of cinnamon, star anise, and tangerine peel. I ate another biteful, and the tips of my earlobes started to feel warm.

"Your body is on a curvy S line," Madame Ng explained as we devoured the stir-fried beef. "It changes every day depending on the weather, your activities, your natural constitution, and age. If you eat the correct food, your body will go in the direction you want."

Five-Spice Pork Roll-Ups

This homemade five-spice rub, made with a blending of fresh and dried ingredients—such as fresh ginger and garlic, ground allspice and coriander, crushed dried chiles—gives the tender pork a unique and spicy flavor. Once seared, the meat is then wrapped in a steamed spring roll skin, stuffed with additional fresh vegetables, and dipped in a tart cilantro dressing. The overall flavor is truly unforgettable.

SIX SERVINGS

1 1/2 pounds center-cut boneless pork loin, trimmed of fat or gristle

Seasonings (mixed together)
2 tablespoons minced garlic
1 1/2 tablespoons minced fresh ginger
1/4 cup soy sauce
1/4 cup rice wine or sake
3 tablespoons toasted sesame oil
1 1/2 tablespoons sugar
1 1/2 teaspoons ground allspice
1 1/2 teaspoons ground coriander
1 teaspoon crushed dried chiles or dried chile flakes

1 1/2 cups leafy lettuce, rinsed, drained, leaves separated, and cut into julienne strips about 1/2 inch wide

2 cups finely shredded or grated carrot
1 1/2 cups bean sprouts, rinsed and drained

Fresh Cilantro Vinaigrette (mixed together)
1/3 cup soy sauce
1/4 cup clear rice vinegar
3 tablespoons toasted sesame oil
1 1/2 tablespoons sugar
1 1/2 tablespoons rice wine or sake
1/3 cup chopped fresh cilantro leaves

24 spring roll skins (or substitute Filipino lumpia wrappers, or flour tortillas), separated and folded in quarters
5 tablespoons canola or corn oil

1. Cut the pork loin across the grain into very thin slices about 1/8 inch thick, then cut into 1 1/2-inch squares. Put the slices in a bowl, add the premixed Seasonings, and toss lightly to coat the slices. Cover with plastic wrap, and let the pork marinate for 1 hour, or longer if possible.

2. Arrange the shredded vegetables and bean sprouts on a deep platter or in a shallow bowl in separate concentric circles, leaving a space in the middle for the pork.

3. Whisk together the ingredients for the Cilantro Vinaigrette, except for the cilantro, stirring to dissolve the sugar. Pour into a serving bowl, sprinkle in the cilantro, and stir.

4. Steam the spring roll skins for 10 minutes. Set aside, covered.

5. Heat a wok or a large skillet, add $2^{1}/_{2}$ tablespoons of the oil, and heat until very hot. Add half the pork slices and stir-fry over high heat until the pork changes color and is cooked, about $2^{1}/_{2}$ minutes. Remove with a slotted spoon and drain. Reheat the pan, add $2^{1}/_{2}$ tablespoons of oil and the remaining pork, and stir-fry as directed. Remove and drain. Arrange the pork slices in the center of the vegetables. Serve with the steamed wrappers or flour tortillas and Fresh Cilantro Vinaigrette. Each diner takes a wrapper, arranges some pork on top, spoons a little vinaigrette over, and rolls it up like a spring roll, folding in the sides to form a compact package.

☯ According to Madame Ng Siong Mui, not only does the spice blend with allspice enhance the flavor of meat, but also the seasonings warm the stomach and intestines while aiding digestion.

Healthy Mu Shu Pork

While mu shu pork is one of the most bastardized dishes in Chinese cooking, it is also one of the most popular. Here is my rendition of this classic, chock-full of smoky black mushrooms, leeks, cabbage, and crunchy wood ears. These days, I substitute good-quality flour tortillas for Mandarin pancakes, brush them lightly with toasted sesame oil, and steam them briefly. Stuffed with the stir-fried meat and vegetable mixture, they are quite delicious and filling—a meal-in-one main course.

SIX SERVINGS

🌀 Wood ears have been used in Chinese medicine for thousands of years, often to treat hemorrhoids and as a stomach tonic. A simple remedy of 15 grams of the dried wood ear powder in 1 cup of boiling water twice a day is prescribed as an anticoagulant and to help build energy.

1 pound center-cut boneless pork loin, trimmed of fat or gristle

Marinade
2 tablespoons soy sauce
1 1/2 tablespoons rice wine or sake
1/2 teaspoon toasted sesame oil
2 teaspoons cornstarch

4 1/2 tablespoons canola or corn oil
24 spring roll skins or flour tortillas, separated and folded into quarters
1 large egg, lightly beaten

Seasonings
2 tablespoons minced garlic
3 tablespoons minced fresh ginger
10 dried Chinese black mushrooms, softened in hot water to cover for 20 minutes, stems removed, and caps shredded

2 leeks, ends trimmed, cleaned, and cut into thin julienne shreds (about 3 cups)

1/2 small Napa cabbage, cut into thin julienne strips, stem sections and leafy sections separated (about 4 cups)
1/4 cup dried wood ears, softened in hot water to cover for 20 minutes, drained, hard ends removed, and cut into thin julienne strips
2 tablespoons rice wine or sake

Sauce (mixed together)
1/4 cup soy sauce
1/4 cup rice wine or sake
1 teaspoon sugar
1/3 teaspoon freshly ground black pepper
1 teaspoon cornstarch

3/4 cup hoisin sauce, mixed with 1 tablespoon soy sauce and 2 1/2 tablespoons water

1. Cut the pork loin across the grain into thin slices about $1/4$ inch thick, then cut into thin, matchstick-size shreds about 1 inch long. Put the shreds in a bowl, add the Marinade, and toss lightly to coat them. Cover with plastic wrap, and let the pork marinate for 1 hour, or longer if possible.

2. Heat a wok or a heavy skillet, add $2^1/_2$ tablespoons of the oil, and heat until very hot. Add the pork and stir-fry over high heat about $2^1/_2$ to 3 minutes, until the meat changes color and is cooked. Scoop it into a colander and drain. Rinse out the pan and dry it.

3. Steam the spring roll skins or tortillas for 5 minutes. Set aside, covered.

4. Reheat the pan, add 1 tablespoon of the oil, and heat until hot. Add the egg, and stir-fry over high heat to scramble, then move to the side of the pan.

5. Add another tablespoon of oil, heat until very hot, and add the Seasonings. Stir-fry for 10 seconds until fragrant, then add the leeks and toss lightly over high heat for $1^1/_2$ minutes. Add the cabbage stems and wood ears, and continue to stir-fry over high heat for 30 seconds. Add the rice wine and leafy cabbage sections, and cook until the vegetables are crisp-tender, about 1 minute. Add the premixed Sauce and the meat, and toss lightly to thicken. Scoop onto a serving platter. Put the hoisin into a small serving bowl and the steamed spring roll skins on a plate. Each diner takes a wrapper, smears a tablespoon of the hoisin mixture on it, and spoons some of the stir-fried mixture on top. It is then rolled up and eaten immediately.

Spicy Pork Tenderloin with Leeks and Fennel

I like to stir-fry leeks and strips of fresh fennel with garlicky roasted pork slices, as in the recipe below or when there's leftover roasted pork. This dish is delicious either hot, cold, or at room temperature. On a brisk winter day, the meat and chile paste will ward off any chill.

SIX SERVINGS

1¹/2 pounds pork tenderloin, trimmed of any fat or gristle

Marinade
2 tablespoons soy sauce
2 tablespoons rice wine or sake
1¹/2 tablespoons minced garlic
2 teaspoons honey
1/2 teaspoon toasted sesame oil

1¹/2 pounds fennel bulbs with stalks, rinsed and trimmed
1 teaspoon canola or corn oil

2 leeks, ends trimmed, cleaned, and cut into thin julienne slices (about 2 cups)
2 tablespoons finely minced fresh ginger
1¹/4 teaspoons hot chile paste or crushed dried chiles
2 tablespoons rice wine or sake

Dressing (mixed together)
1/4 cup soy sauce
2¹/2 tablespoons Chinese black vinegar or Worcestershire sauce
1¹/2 tablespoons sugar

2 tablespoons minced scallion greens

1. Place the pork tenderloin in a shallow heatproof dish. Add the ingredients of the Marinade and turn to coat the pork. Cover with plastic wrap and let the meat sit 1 hour at room temperature or 3 hours or longer in the refrigerator. Preheat the oven to 400°F.
2. Cut each fennel bulb lengthwise in half, then cut the fennel into thin julienne slices about 2 inches long. Heat a large pot of water until boiling, add the fennel slices, and cook about 2 minutes, or until crisp-tender. Drain in a colander, refresh in cold water, and drain thoroughly.

☯ Chinese herbalists have found that garlic, leeks, and fennel seem effective in expelling internal cold and dampness from the body.

3. Roast the pork, with its marinade, for 50 to 55 minutes, or until the internal temperature reads 155°F. Baste occasionally with the marinade. Cool the pork, then cut it into
very thin slices, and cut those slices into $1^1/_2$-inch squares.

4. Heat a wok or heavy skillet, add the oil, heat until hot, and add the leeks, ginger, and
chile paste, and toss lightly over high heat about 1 minute. Add the rice wine and stir-fry
about $1^1/_2$ minutes, then add the fennel. Toss lightly and add the pork slices. Cook until
heated through, then add the premixed Dressing. Toss again to coat the meat and vegetables, scoop out onto a serving platter, and sprinkle the minced scallion greens on
top. Serve with steamed rice.

Spicy Spareribs in Squash or Pumpkin

Few dishes are as festive or sumptuous as this, with the spicy barbecued spareribs served on top of baked squash or pumpkin. Squashes are believed to have been introduced to Asia by the Spanish or Portuguese. You may use a Japanese pumpkin, which can be purchased at an Asian market, or the more accessible Western squashes specified in the recipe.

SIX SERVINGS

3 1/2 pounds country-style spareribs	1/2 teaspoon hot chile paste or crushed dried chiles
Sparerib Marinade	1 teaspoon toasted sesame oil
1/2 cup hoisin sauce	1/2 tablespoon sugar
3 1/2 tablespoons soy sauce	
2 tablespoons rice wine or sake	2 acorn or 1 butternut squash, about 4
1 1/2 tablespoons minced garlic	pounds
1 1/2 tablespoons minced fresh ginger	2 tablespoons minced scallion greens

☯ Squash or pumpkin tones and energizes the body, especially the middle region, and is believed to relieve pain.

1. Direct the butcher to separate the spareribs and cut them into shorter pieces, so that they measure about 2 to 2 1/2 inches in length. Trim away the excess fat.

2. Bring a large pot of water to a boil. Add the spareribs and return to a boil. Reduce the heat to medium and cook about 20 minutes. Remove the ribs, drain, and cool slightly.

3. Put the ribs in a bowl with the Sparerib Marinade. Toss lightly to coat the ribs, and cover with plastic wrap. Let the spareribs marinate in the refrigerator for 3 hours, or overnight.

4. Preheat the oven to 375°F. Cut the squash in half and scoop out the seeds with a spoon, slightly enlarging the cavity. Arrange the squash halves, cut surface up, on a cookie sheet lined with aluminum foil. Bake the squash for 30 minutes before the spareribs go in.

5. Put the spareribs, and the marinade, on another cookie sheet lined with aluminum foil and place in the oven with the squash. Bake for 30 minutes, then turn the ribs over with tongs and bake them, and the squash, another 15 minutes. Test the squash for doneness by piercing the flesh with the tip of a knife. If it needs more time, continue baking.

6. Remove and cut each squash half into about 6 sections. Arrange the squash on a serving platter. Spoon the ribs and some of their sauce on top. Sprinkle the minced scallions over the spareribs. Serve with steamed or boiled rice.

Black Bean Spareribs in Squash: Prepare step 1 and 2 as directed in Spicy Spareribs in Squash or Pumpkin (above) and prepare the following Seasonings and Sauce:

Seasonings	Sauce (mixed together)
2 tablespoons fermented or salted black beans, rinsed, drained, and minced	3 cups chicken broth (preferably Classic Chicken Broth, page 27) or water
2 tablespoons minced garlic	5 1/2 tablespoons soy sauce
1 1/2 tablespoons minced fresh ginger	1/4 cup rice wine or sake
1/2 teaspoon dried chile flakes	1 1/2 tablespoons sugar
	2 tablespoons cornstarch

Heat a wok or large skillet, add 1 1/2 tablespoons canola or corn oil, and heat until very hot. Add the Seasonings, and stir-fry over medium-high heat about 15 seconds, until fragrant. Add the premixed Sauce and heat until boiling, stirring until thickened. Let it cool slightly, then add two thirds of the sauce to the spareribs when they have been laid out on the lined cookie sheet, without the marinade. Coat them thoroughly. Pour the remaining third of the sauce over the cut squash. Bake the spareribs and squash as directed.

Braised Home-Style Pork

Cool weather is the perfect time to prepare this hearty, slow-cooked dish. Beef or lamb is also excellent prepared in the same way.

2 pounds boneless pork loin or butt for braising, trimmed of fat and gristle

1 1/2 pounds bok choy, collard greens, or spinach, cleaned and trimmed (stem and leaf parts of bok choy separated; collard greens or spinach cut into large pieces)

2 teaspoons canola or corn oil

8 slices fresh ginger, about the size of a quarter, smashed lightly with the flat side of a knife

12 whole scallions, ends trimmed, smashed lightly with the flat side of a knife, cut into quarters

8 cloves garlic, peeled and smashed with the flat side of a knife

Cooking Liquid (mixed together)

2 1/2 cups water

3/4 cup rice wine or sake

1/2 cup soy sauce

2 tablespoons sugar

1. Cut the pork into 1¹/₂-inch cubes. Cut the bok choy on the diagonal into 1¹/₂-inch lengths. Separate the leafy sections from the harder stem sections.

2. In a casserole or Dutch oven, heat 1 teaspoon of the oil until hot, for about 30 seconds. Add half the pork cubes and sear the outside surface until golden brown over high heat, turning once. Remove with a slotted spoon. Add the remaining 1 teaspoon oil, sear the rest of the meat, and remove.

3. Reheat the pan, add the ginger, scallions, and garlic, and stir-fry briefly, about 15 seconds. Add the premixed Cooking Liquid and the meat, and bring to a boil. Reduce the heat to low, and simmer uncovered for 1 hour, until the pork is very tender.

4. Skim off any fat and impurities, discarding the ginger slices.

5. Bring about 4 cups water to a boil in a large pot. Add the stem sections of the bok choy, cover, and cook about 1¹/₂ to 2 minutes, until just tender. Add the leafier sections or the collard greens or spinach, if using, and cook about 30 seconds. Remove, refresh under cold water, and drain thoroughly. Add the vegetable to the braised meat, and heat briefly. Serve the braised pork with the vegetable and some sauce over steamed rice or noodles.

☯ Garlic, scallions, and ginger all add heat to the meat, making this a perfect cold-weather dish.

Garlic Beef with Broccoli

This venerable classic remains one of my favorite dishes. I often vary the recipe, however, by substituting turkey cutlets or chicken for the beef and using snow or snap peas instead of the broccoli.

1 1/2 pounds flank steak, London broil, or boneless sirloin, trimmed of fat and gristle

Marinade
3 1/2 tablespoons soy sauce
2 tablespoons rice wine or sake
2 tablespoons minced garlic
1 tablespoon cornstarch

1 1/2 pounds broccoli, broccoli rabe, or Chinese broccoli, ends trimmed
5 1/2 tablespoons canola or corn oil
2 tablespoons minced garlic
1 1/2 tablespoons minced fresh ginger

1/4 cup rice wine or sake, mixed with 3 tablespoons water

Sauce (mixed together)
1/2 cup chicken broth (preferably Classic Chicken Broth, page 27) or water
6 tablespoons oyster sauce
1 1/2 tablespoons rice wine or sake
1 1/2 tablespoons sugar
1 teaspoon soy sauce
1/2 teaspoon toasted sesame oil
1 1/2 teaspoons cornstarch

2 tablespoons minced scallion greens

1. Cut the beef across the grain into thin slices about 1/8 inch thick, then cut the slices into 1-inch squares. Put the beef in a bowl, add the premixed Marinade, and toss lightly to coat. Cover with plastic wrap, and let marinate for 1 hour at room temperature, or longer if possible in the refrigerator.

2. Peel the broccoli stem with a sharp knife. Separate the broccoli florets into bite-size pieces and cut the stem on the diagonal into 1-inch lengths.

3. Bring 6 cups water to a boil in a pot. Add the broccoli and cook for about 3 1/2 to 4 minutes, or until just tender. Drain in a colander and refresh under cold water. Drain again.

4. Heat a wok or large skillet, add 3 1/2 tablespoons of the oil, and heat until near smok-

ing. Add the beef, and stir-fry over high heat until it loses its raw color and the pieces separate. Remove with a slotted spoon and drain. Clean out the pan.

5. Reheat the pan, add the remaining 2 tablespoons oil, heat about 20 seconds, and add the garlic and fresh ginger. Stir-fry over high heat for 15 seconds, until fragrant, then add the cooked broccoli and rice wine–water mixture and toss lightly to heat through. Add the Sauce and cook until it thickens, tossing constantly to prevent lumps. Add the cooked beef and toss until the meat is heated through and everything is coated evenly with the sauce. Scoop the beef and broccoli onto a serving platter, sprinkle with scallion greens, and serve with rice.

☯ Broccoli with its cooling nature and beef with its warming nature make a compatible and balanced pair for a stir-fry. Beef also increases *qi,* or energy in the body, and is prescribed for general weakness.

Grilled Beef with Thai Spices

Tender beef takes on a whole new dimension when marinated in lemon grass, garlic, shallots, and soy sauce, then grilled over charcoal and quickly stir-fried with red onions and basil.

Marinade

4 cloves garlic, peeled

3 shallots, trimmed and peeled

2 tablespoons rice wine or sake

1 stalk lemon grass, tough outer husks peeled away, ends trimmed, and inner stalk cut into 1-inch sections

1 1/2 tablespoons sugar

1/4 cup soy sauce

1 1/2 pounds top round roast, trimmed of fat and gristle

2 tablespoons canola or corn oil

Seasonings

1 1/2 tablespoons chopped fresh red chiles, ends trimmed and seeds removed (or substitute 1 teaspoon crushed dried chiles)

2 tablespoons chopped garlic

3 medium red onions, peeled, and cut into thin julienne slices

Sauce (mixed together)

3 tablespoons fish sauce

1 1/2 tablespoons soy sauce

1 tablespoon sugar

1 1/2 tablespoons water

1 1/2 cups fresh whole Thai holy basil or sweet basil leaves, stems removed, leaves rinsed, drained, and coarsely shredded

1. Blend the Marinade ingredients to a paste, adding them in descending order through the feed tube of a food processor or in a blender with the machine running.

2. Put the beef in a bowl and spread the marinade all over its surface. Cover with plastic wrap and let the beef marinate an hour or longer in the refrigerator.

3. Prepare a medium-hot fire for grilling or preheat the broiler. Place the meat 3 inches from the source of heat and grill or broil about 5 to 7 minutes per side for rare. (Grill longer if you want the meat well done.) Remove the beef, let it cool slightly, then cut it on the diagonal into very thin slices, about 1/4 inch thick.

4. Heat a wok or large skillet, add the oil, and heat until very hot, about 30 seconds. Add

the Seasonings, and stir-fry over high heat about $1^1/_2$ to 2 minutes, or until the onions are tender, tossing over high heat. Add the premixed Sauce and bring to a boil. Add the sliced meat and basil, and toss lightly a few seconds. Scoop the beef and vegetables onto a serving platter and serve with rice and another vegetable, if desired.

To round out the meal, serve with Grilled Leeks in a Garlic-Soy Dressing (page 174) or Flash-Cooked Bean Sprouts (page 161).

☯ Holy basil and sweet basil are both considered tonics. Ayurvedic doctors use the juice as a general remedy for chills, coughs, and earaches. The leaves of basil (about $^1/_2$ cup) can be brewed in 2 cups hot water and taken as a warming and uplifting tea for exhaustion.

Flash-Cooked Ginger Beef

This dish was one of the first I learned when I began my studies of Chinese cooking in Taiwan. Don't be put off by the generous amount of fresh ginger and scallions; it gives the dish a remarkable flavor. This stir-fry is superb over rice or rolled in a steamed pancake or flour tortilla.

SIX SERVINGS

1^1/2 pounds flank steak, London broil, or boneless sirloin, trimmed of fat and gristle

Marinade
3^1/2 tablespoons soy sauce
2 tablespoons rice wine or sake
2 tablespoons minced garlic
1 tablespoon cornstarch

5^1/2 tablespoons canola or corn oil
2 tablespoons minced garlic

3/4 cup very finely shredded fresh ginger
4 whole scallions, ends trimmed, cut into very fine shreds
5 cups bean sprouts, rinsed lightly and drained

2^1/2 tablespoons rice wine or sake

Sauce (mixed together)
6 tablespoons soy sauce
1^1/2 tablespoons sugar
1 teaspoon toasted sesame oil

☯ Ginger is a seasoning commonly paired with beef since it is believed to rid the body of toxins and remove impurities from meat.

1. Cut the beef across the grain into thin slices about ^{1}/8 inch thick; cut those slices into 1-inch squares. Put the beef in a bowl, add the Marinade, and toss lightly to coat. Cover with plastic wrap, and let the beef marinate for 1 hour at room temperature, or longer if possible in the refrigerator.

2. Heat a wok or large skillet, add 3^1/2 tablespoons of the oil, and heat until near smoking. Add the beef and stir-fry over high heat until it loses its raw color and the slices separate. Remove with a slotted spoon and drain. Clean out the pan.

3. Reheat the pan, add the remaining 2 tablespoons oil, heat about 20 seconds, and add the garlic, ginger, and scallions. Cook for 20 seconds, until fragrant, then add the bean sprouts and toss lightly over high heat. Add the rice wine, and stir-fry for 1^1/2 minutes, then add the premixed Sauce and the cooked meat. Cook until the meat is heated through and everything is coated evenly with the sauce. Scoop the beef onto a serving platter and serve with rice and a vegetable, if desired.

Curried Malay Beef Stew

In Asia, every cook has his or her own individual curried spice mixture. I like to use a blend of fresh ginger, dried chiles, coriander, cumin, cinnamon, and turmeric. In addition to the usual vegetables—carrots and potatoes—I add parsnips, which sweeten the dish further.

SIX SERVINGS

1 1/2 pounds stewing beef, fat and gristle trimmed

Seasonings
8 small shallots, peeled
1 thick slice fresh ginger, about double the size of a quarter, peeled
1/2 teaspoon crushed red chiles or dried chile flakes, or more to taste
1 tablespoon ground coriander
1 1/2 teaspoons ground cumin
3/4 teaspoon ground cinnamon
1/2 teaspoon ground turmeric
1/2 teaspoon freshly ground black pepper

1 1/2 tablespoons canola or corn oil
2 1/2 cups water
5 carrots, peeled and cut into 1/2-inch slices
3 medium red potatoes, peeled and quartered
3 parsnips, peeled and cut into 1 1/2-inch slices
1 teaspoon salt, or to taste

1. Cut the meat into rough 1-inch cubes.
2. Drop the Seasonings in descending order through the feed tube of a food processor or into a blender with the machine running. Blend or process to a finely minced consistency.
3. Heat a casserole or a Dutch oven, add the oil, and heat until medium hot. Add the seasonings paste and cook over medium heat, stirring frequently, for 3 to 5 minutes, until very fragrant. Add the beef cubes, and toss them in the paste. Cook 3 minutes more, tossing constantly. Add the water and bring to a boil. Reduce the heat slightly and cook, covered, for 45 minutes. Add the carrots and potatoes, and cook for 20 minutes; then add the parsnips and cook 10 more minutes, or until the vegetables and meat are tender.
4. Skim any fat or oil from the surface and add the salt. Stir, and serve over steamed rice.

Parsnips are believed to benefit the spleen, pancreas, and stomach. They lubricate the intestines and are a mild diuretic. They are used in simple remedies for coughs, colds, rheumatism, and arthritis.

Korean Barbecued Beef

Barbecued beef, though expensive, is a popular Korean specialty. Traditionally, the beef, once marinated, was grilled over wood, but today in Korean restaurants and households tableside gas grills are more common.

1 1/2 pounds boneless sirloin steak, trimmed of fat and gristle	1 1/2 teaspoons toasted sesame oil
	1/4 teaspoon freshly ground black pepper
	1 teaspoon hot chile paste (optional)
Marinade/Sauce	
1/2 cup soy sauce	8 whole scallions, ends trimmed, cut into 1-inch lengths
1/3 cup rice wine or sake	
2 tablespoons sugar	1 head Boston lettuce, rinsed and drained
2 tablespoons minced garlic	

☯ Beef is considered one of the most warming foods, but its effect here is somewhat neutralized by the cool lettuce leaves, making the dish an excellent one to serve at any time of the year.

1. Cut the beef, with the grain, into long strips about 1 1/2 inches wide, and place them in a bowl.

2. Mix the ingredients of the Marinade, add one third of it to the beef, and toss lightly with your hands to coat the strips. Cover with plastic wrap and let the beef marinate for at least 1 hour at room temperature, or longer in the refrigerator. Mix the remaining two thirds of the marinade with the scallions and place in a saucepan.

3. Separate the lettuce leaves, trim the stems, and lightly flatten the leaves with a knife or a cleaver. Arrange the lettuce in a serving bowl. Bring the marinade to a boil and cook about 1 minute, stirring often, then pour it into a serving bowl.

4. Prepare a medium-hot fire for grilling, and place the grill about 3 inches above the coals. Arrange the meat on the grill and cook about 3 to 3 1/2 minutes on each side, or until medium-rare, basting occasionally with the marinade. Alternatively, you may sear the meat over high heat in a heavy skillet that has been lightly brushed with oil. Cook about 2 minutes on each side. Remove the meat and cut across the grain into thin slices.

5. To eat, each diner arranges several meat slices on a lettuce leaf, spoons some of the sauce with scallions on top, folds the leaf over, and eats the bundle with the fingers. Serve with a vegetable and rice.

To round out the meal, serve with Wilted Greens with a Spicy Garlic Dressing (page 160).

Red-Cooked Lamb with Sweet Potatoes

Once it is simmered in the fragrant soy sauce braising mixture, the meat in this recipe becomes tender and redolent of cinnamon, ginger, and anise seed. Sweet potatoes or yams are the ultimate complement to this savory stew. You may substitute beef or chicken for the lamb and adjust the cooking time accordingly.

SIX SERVINGS

1 teaspoon canola or corn oil

Seasonings
8 cloves garlic, smashed lightly with the flat
    side of a knife and sliced thinly
8 whole scallions, ends trimmed, cut into 1-
    inch sections, smashed lightly
8 slices fresh ginger, about the size of a
    quarter, smashed lightly
1 teaspoon hot chile paste, or more to taste
2 sticks cinnamon
1 teaspoon anise seed

Broth (mixed together)
5 cups water
1/2 cup low-sodium soy sauce
3 tablespoons rice wine or sake
1 tablespoon sugar

3 pounds lamb shoulder for stewing,
    trimmed of any fat or gristle, and cut
    into 1 1/2-inch cubes
4 sweet potatoes or yams, about 2
    pounds, peeled and cut into 1 1/2-inch
    squares
1/2 pound fresh spinach, stems trimmed,
    leaves rinsed and drained

❂ According to the Chinese, lamb is one of the most "warming" of meats for the body and is relished in all types of wintertime dishes. The meat increases *qi,* or body energy, and is used to treat general weakness, anemia, or impotence.

1. Heat a Dutch oven or heavy casserole, add the oil, and heat until hot. Add the Seasonings and stir-fry until fragrant, about 15 seconds. Add the Broth and bring to a boil. Add the lamb and boil again. Reduce the heat to low, partially cover, and simmer for 1 hour, until the lamb is just tender, skimming the surface to remove any fat or gristle.
2. Add the sweet potatoes and continue cooking, partially covered, for 20 minutes, or until tender. Skim the surface to remove any fat or impurities. Remove the ginger slices and cinnamon sticks, and discard. Add the spinach leaves, carefully mixing them in but leaving some on top. Cover and cook until wilted, about 30 seconds to a minute. Remove from the heat, and serve the lamb and sweet potatoes with steamed rice.

Katy Luis's Vindaloo Lamb

Katy Luis, an extraordinarily talented Malaysian home cook, prepared this dish for me during a visit to Penang. She explained that the recipe was from her mother-in-law, who was Portuguese. Katy, who is Chinese, adapted it slightly, but such is the rich ethnic mix of Malaysian cooking. The dish is spicy, but full-bodied because of its eclectic seasonings.

Seasonings (mixed together)

15 fresh small red chiles or 4 3-inch fresh red chiles, stems trimmed and seeds removed (when minced, about 3 tablespoons)

2 fresh jalapeño chiles, ends and seeds removed

1 1-inch piece fresh ginger, peeled

20 small shallots, peeled and cut lengthwise in half (about 3/4 pound)

12 cloves garlic

1 1/2 teaspoons cumin seeds

1 1/2 teaspoons black mustard seeds

1/4 cup canola or corn oil

2 pounds lamb for stewing, trimmed of fat or gristle and cut into pieces 1 1/2 inches square

1 1/2 cups water

3 tablespoons distilled white vinegar, or to taste

1 teaspoon salt

3 teaspoons sugar

2 tablespoons chopped fresh cilantro

SIX SERVINGS

❂ Ayurvedic doctors credit cumin seeds with removing impurities from the blood and increasing milk while nursing. For a skin rash, add to bathwater 1 cup of water that has been boiled with 3 tablespoons of cumin seeds. Repeat several times.

To round out the meal, serve with Flash-Cooked Greens with Garlic (page 159) or Flash-Cooked Bean Sprouts (page 161).

1. In descending order, put the Seasonings into a blender or a food processor with the blade running, and process to a paste.

2. Heat a heavy casserole or Dutch oven, add the oil, and heat until hot. Add the paste and cook it, stirring frequently, for about 10 to 15 minutes, until dry and very fragrant.

3. Add the lamb and mix in with the seasonings over medium heat, cooking for about 10 minutes. Add the water and simmer over low heat, partially covered, about 45 minutes, stirring periodically, until the lamb is pretty tender. Add the vinegar, salt, and sugar and cook partially covered until the sauce has reduced and thickened, about 5 minutes. Remove from the heat and sprinkle the top with the chopped cilantro. Serve with rice and a vegetable or chutney.

Vegetables: Stir-Fries, Pickles, and Salads

Vegetables and Dr. Kok Kheng Tan

I was standing in the fragrantly earthy bowels of the Everbloom Mushroom Company in Singapore. The air was humid and slightly musty, and I was surrounded by rectangular logs of sawdust covered with endless rows of tiny sprouting mushrooms. They seemed as precious as newborn babies in a nursery.

"Shiitake mushrooms and other types of fungi have always been relished by the Chinese for their flavor, but, most important, they are valued for their curative properties," explained Dr. Kok Kheng Tan, a scholarly-looking Singaporean bio-technologist who started the company in 1980. Dr. Tan's business was fueled by his belief in the shiitake's medicinal qualities. "The ancient Chinese considered the shiitake as an 'elixir of life' and used it in soups, teas, and extracts." As he talked, he looked at the small mushrooms tenderly, like a new father.

I had come to visit Dr. Tan's mushroom factory and to learn more about the medicinal value of mushrooms.

It is believed that mushrooms were used as early as A.D. 100 by the Chinese to maintain health. In the Ming dynasty (1368–1644), a famous physician, Wu Rui, prescribed shiitake mushrooms for a number of ailments, ranging from heart disease to impotence.

According to Dr. Tan, recent scientific and medical studies in Asia have shown that mushrooms contain certain toniclike components, such as lentinan, a polysaccharide, which has proven to be effective in bolstering the immune system and to have antitumor effects. A synthesized version of lentinan is now given routinely to a number of cancer patients in Japan before chemotherapy and radiation. Shiitakes also contain eritadenine, which lowers blood lipids, and LEM (lentinus edodes mycelium), which has been shown to inhibit the HIV virus.

In addition to shiitakes, Dr. Tan's company grows maitake and enokitake mushrooms. Originally, he sold the mushrooms fresh to restaurants and markets, but now increasingly large amounts are bought by Chinese medicinal companies. Tan incorporates the mushrooms into prepared herbal soups, which are available in cans, and he also sells mushroom pills (made up of dried shiitake and reishi mushrooms) and essence of shiitake in bottles.

Shiitake mushrooms are not the only mushrooms credited with having therapeutic effects. According to Dr. Tan, almost half of the ten thousand mushroom species known to man may have medicinal value, including black fungus, enokitake, maitake, and the oyster mushroom. (See the mushroom glossary on page 164.)

Medicinal mushrooms have become increasingly popular today. All Chinese herbal shops boast a selection of dried mushrooms and fungi. Health food stores now offer pills containing dried reishi, shiitake, and maitake powder. And in the fresh mushroom season in the fall, particularly in Japan, the countryside is dotted with foragers scouting out different wild varieties such as maitake, enokitake, and shiitake.

Mushrooms are but one element of the broad category of vegetables essential to the Asian holistic kitchen. From the very beginning of Traditional Chinese Medicine, vegetables, plants, and herbs have played a crucial role in diet and health. In *The Yellow Emperor's Classic of Internal Medicine,* China's earliest theoretical medical text, which was believed to have been compiled between the fourth and first centuries B.C., it was written, "One should have grains or cereals for growth, fruits for assistance, meat for nutrition, and vegetables for supplement."

Taoists, who were influential in defining the balanced approach to life that many Chinese have adopted, went even further. They abstained from eating meat and grains in order to achieve immortality, and chose instead to subsist on a diet of vegetables, herbs, plants, nuts, and seeds. Most Asians choose a less severe regimen, but vegetables play a prominent role in the contemporary diet.

From early times, vegetables, like any food, were credited with having specific properties and corresponding effects on the body, such as warming, cooling, and neutral. In general, raw vegetables have a cooling or cold nature, but many (apart from being eaten in a daily diet) are used for simple remedies: Cucumber soup is recommended for preventing laryngitis or a sore throat; cabbage cooked with honey is often administered for easing ulcer pain; and pumpkin steamed with glutinous rice is suggested for malnutrition.

In general, **cooling** vegetables include asparagus, celery, Chinese cabbage, cucumber, lettuce, mushrooms, water chestnuts, and spinach. These vegetables are best for children, as well as active and robust adults (those who are yang in nature). To balance their cooling effect, they are often cooked with warming ingredients or eaten in warmer weather.

Neutral vegetables, such as green cabbage, carrots, cauliflower, long beans, green beans, beets, pumpkin, pea shoots, snow peas, squash, corn, sweet potatoes, and yams, are not necessarily curatives on their own, but they are influenced by the seasonings they are cooked with. Cooking neutral vegetables by stir-frying, steaming, roasting, or boiling makes them become more warming.

Hot or warming vegetables, such as leeks, onions, garlic, fennel, garlic chives, scallions, shallots, hot peppers, cilantro, dill, and other spicy seasonings, are often paired with cooling vegetables in dishes to create a balance. They should not be eaten excessively by those with a yang, or warming, nature. You can neutralize warming vegetables by boiling them or by pairing them with cooling vegetables and other ingredients.

The ancient Taoist sages agreed with many of the opinions now held by health-minded, contemporary cooks: They preached that fresh vegetables should be eaten in harmony with the seasons and that they should be locally grown whenever possible. Ideally, they should also be **organic.**

Vegetable Chart

Cooling

asparagus, broccoli, bamboo shoots, celery, Chinese cabbage, cucumber, lettuce, mushrooms, water chestnuts, spinach, summer squash, zucchini

Neutral

green cabbage, carrots, cauliflower, long beans, beets, pea shoots, snow peas, corn, sweet potatoes, yams

Hot or warming

leeks, onions, garlic, pumpkin, fennel, garlic chives, scallions, shallots, hot peppers, cilantro, dill, winter squash

Flash-Cooked Greens with Garlic

Simple but delicious, this basic stir-fry is excellent prepared with almost any leafy green, including spinach, watercress, or cabbage.

1 1/4 pounds (or 2 10-ounce packages) fresh spinach, water spinach, or *convolvulus* (available in Asian markets), watercress, snow pea shoots, or other greens	1 teaspoon canola or corn oil 8 to 10 cloves garlic, cut into paper-thin slices 2 1/2 tablespoons rice wine or sake 1/2 to 3/4 teaspoon salt

1. Tear the stems from the spinach. If using other greens, cut away the tough ends. Toss the greens in a colander, and rinse thoroughly under cold running water. Drain and place in a bowl near the stove.
2. Heat a wok or a skillet, add the oil, and heat until near smoking. Add the greens and garlic and toss lightly with a spatula for about 20 seconds, then add the rice wine and salt and toss lightly over high heat about 1 minute or less, until the greens are slightly wilted but still bright green. Scoop out the greens and garlic, leaving most of the liquid, and arrange on a serving platter. Serve hot, at room temperature, or cold.

☯ Watercress is a relative newcomer to the Chinese holistic kitchen, but it has become very popular. Similar to spinach, it is coolish and is believed to dissipate heat and detoxify the body. It is rarely eaten cold. To treat canker sores, boil 1/2 pound watercress and 4 sliced carrots in water for 1 hour and drink the soup.

Wilted Greens with a Spicy Garlic Dressing

I often prepare this dish in advance and serve it at room temperature—as a delicious garnish for any meat, poultry, or seafood dish.

SIX SERVINGS

1¼ pounds (or 2 10-ounce packages) fresh spinach, watercress, or other leafy green vegetables	Garlic Dressing (mixed together)
	3 tablespoons soy sauce
	2 tablespoons rice wine or sake
1 teaspoon canola or corn oil	1 tablespoon minced garlic
1 teaspoon toasted sesame oil	1 teaspoon sugar
	1 teaspoon hot chile paste (optional)

1. Tear the stems from the spinach and toss the leaves into a colander. Rinse thoroughly under cold, running water, drain, and set by the stove.

2. Heat a wok or large pot, add the oils, and heat until near smoking. Add the spinach and toss lightly with a slotted spoon over high heat about 1 minute. Add the Garlic Dressing and continue stir-frying about 30 seconds more, until the leaves are slightly wilted but still bright green. Scoop the greens and sauce into a serving bowl. Serve hot, at room temperature, or cold.

Spinach is considered sweet and coolish in nature. It mainly affects the stomach and large intestines, while also nourishing the blood and replenishing wetness in the body. A simple porridge of spinach and rice is often prescribed for hemorrhoidal bleeding. Similarly, a soup made of spinach with its roots is drunk as a tea for hangovers. According to recent Western studies, the strong folic acid in spinach may alleviate or prevent depression.

Flash-Cooked Bean Sprouts

Stir-fried, or flash-cooked, vegetables should be just tender, and ideally you should taste the fire in the food. The secret is to use the highest level of heat and to heat the pan and oil as much as possible before adding the vegetables and seasonings.

1 teaspoon canola or corn oil

2 cups Chinese garlic chives, ends trimmed, cut into 1 1/2-inch lengths (or substitute whole scallions, cut in half lengthwise, then cut into 1-inch sections and combined with 1 tablespoon minced garlic)

2 tablespoons rice wine or sake

5 1/2 cups bean sprouts, rinsed and drained

Dressing (mixed together)

3 tablespoons soy sauce

1 1/2 tablespoons rice wine or sake

1/2 teaspoon sugar

1/2 teaspoon toasted sesame oil

SIX SERVINGS

1. Heat a wok or large skillet until very hot. Add the oil and heat until almost smoking. Add the garlic chives (or scallions and garlic) and cook over high heat, tossing about with a slotted spoon, then add the rice wine and continue to stir-fry about 1 minute.

2. Add the bean sprouts and cook, tossing, about 30 seconds, then add the Dressing and cook, tossing constantly to coat the vegetables with the sauce. Scoop onto a serving platter and serve.

☯ Mung beans and their sprouts are often eaten during the hot summer months since they keep the body cool. They are said to detoxify the body and dissipate heat from it. As a result, they are often prescribed for boils and canker sores. According to Dr. Albert Leung, recent scientific studies in China have shown that mung beans also lower lipid and fat levels in the blood, indicating that they may be useful in treating heart disease.

Spicy Garlic Broccoli with Pine Nuts

For me, garlic and broccoli seem to go hand in hand, one flavor beautifully complementing the other. A light soy dressing and toasted pine nuts round out this wonderful dish.

SIX SERVINGS

1 1/2 pounds broccoli or broccoli rabe
1/4 cup pine nuts
1 1/2 teaspoons canola or corn oil
1 1/2 teaspoons toasted sesame oil
1 teaspoon hot chile paste or 3/4 teaspoon crushed dried chiles
2 tablespoons minced garlic

2 1/2 tablespoons rice wine or sake, mixed with 2 tablespoons water

Sauce (mixed together in a bowl until the sugar is dissolved)
1 1/2 tablespoons soy sauce
1 teaspoon sugar

☯ Opinions vary as to whether broccoli is neutral or cooling. It is often prescribed by Chinese doctors for eye inflammations and nearsightedness.

1. Trim the ends of the broccoli, separate the florets, peel the outer skin of the stem and cut it on the diagonal into 1-inch lengths.

2. Toast the pine nuts until golden in a 300°F. oven, turning them occasionally so that they cook evenly for about 20 minutes.

3. Heat a wok or large skillet, add the oils, and heat until hot, about 20 seconds. Add the chile paste or crushed chiles and garlic, and stir-fry, tossing with a slotted spoon over medium heat until fragrant, about 15 seconds. Turn the heat to high.

4. Add the stem sections of the broccoli and stir-fry. Pour in the rice wine and water and cook, tossing, about 30 seconds, then cover and cook about 1 1/2 to 2 minutes, until the stems are just tender. Add the florets or leafy sections and toss over high heat, cooking for about 1 1/2 minutes or until just tender.

5. Add the premixed Sauce and toss lightly for 15 seconds. Add the toasted pine nuts and stir-fry a few seconds to combine the ingredients. Scoop the ingredients into a serving bowl and serve immediately.

Curried Coconut Green Beans

Neutral vegetables, such as green beans, become enlivened with pungent flavorings like cumin, coriander, and chiles, as in the dish below.

2 pounds green beans

Curry Seasonings
3 dried red chiles or 1 1/2 teaspoons dried chile flakes
2 1/2-inch slices fresh ginger, peeled
1 1/2 teaspoons ground cumin
1 1/2 teaspoons ground coriander
1/2 teaspoon freshly ground black pepper
1 teaspoon salt

2 tablespoons canola or corn oil
3 medium red onions, peeled and cut into thin julienne slices
2 tablespoons rice wine or sake

Sauce (mixed together)
1 cup light coconut milk (if not available, substitute regular coconut milk)
2 1/2 tablespoons fish sauce
1 tablespoon sugar

1/2 cup fresh basil leaves, cut into thin strips

SIX SERVINGS

🌓 According to Chinese pharmacologists, green beans strengthen the spleen and tone the kidneys. A soup of boiled green beans and water is excellent to relieve recurring thirst.

🌓 Because it is so easily digested and effective in dispelling gas, cumin is routinely prescribed by Ayurvedic doctors for diarrhea. Ground coriander with cold water is applied to the eyes to cure conjunctivitis.

1. Cutting on the diagonal with a sharp knife, trim the ends of the green beans and slice the longer beans in two. Toss the beans into a colander, rinse lightly, and drain.
2. Drop the Curry Seasonings into the feed tube of a food processor fitted with a metal blade while the machine is running. Turn the machine on and off to chop the seasonings evenly, mincing them to a coarse powder. Pour it into a bowl.
3. Heat a wok or large skillet, add the oil, and heat until hot, about 20 seconds. Add the Curry Seasonings and red onions, stirring over medium-low heat with a wooden spoon for 3 to 4 minutes, until the onion is tender and the mixture is fragrant. Turn the heat to high, add the green beans and rice wine or sake, and stir-fry about 1 minute, until the beans are a vivid green. Add the premixed Sauce and heat until boiling. Reduce the heat to medium-low and cook, partially covered, for about 8 to 9 minutes, or until the beans are just tender. Sprinkle in the fresh basil and toss lightly for a few seconds. Scoop the beans and sauce into a serving bowl and serve immediately.

Wild Asian Mushroom Glossary

The produce bins of any well-stocked supermarket now hold a treasure trove of fresh wild mushrooms. In addition to the more familiar porcini and portobello mushrooms are a number of new varieties. The following glossary gives some general information and cooking tips for these new and old Asian varieties. When purchasing any fresh mushrooms, choose firm, fresh-looking caps with a woodsy odor or no odor at all. Avoid mushy or slimy caps.

• **Enoki** (or enokitake) mushrooms, with their long, slender stalks and miniature golden caps, have a delicate, sweet flavor and a lovely crispness. They are usually sold in clumps. Traditionally, they are a winter mushroom, but they are now grown and available year-round. They are often called for in soups and stews, where they retain their crisp texture. The enoki mushroom is believed to possess antitumor properties.

• Japanese, Korean, and French cooks relish **maitake** mushrooms, or "hen-of-the-woods," which are also called "dancing" mushrooms—because, supposedly, hunters were known to dance with joy after discovering them. They are also reputed to have medicinal properties that fight cancer. Maitake mushrooms have fan-shaped caps with stalks that may be fused together in massive clumps. They are superb in soups, stir-fries, or sautés, and are used as a garnish in savory dishes. Maitake mushrooms have been shown to reduce blood pressure. They also are believed to aid the prevention of cancer.

• For the Japanese, there's no mushroom finer than the **matsutake** (Japanese truffle), with its dark-brown cap, spicy fragrance, and thick, meaty stem. The flavor has been likened to a mixture of pine boughs and cinnamon. They are gathered from red pines in mid-autumn. Because they are under limited cultivation, they are extremely expensive. Matsutake should be cooked simply—lightly stir-fried, grilled, or used to garnish soups.

• The **oyster** mushroom, with its subtle taste of the sea and gray-beige cap, is also known as an abalone mushroom. Like other mushrooms, oyster mushrooms grow on decayed tree stumps. According to Marge Leibenstein in *The Edible Mushroom* (Fawcett, 1986), "they grow in large overlapping rows like tiles on a roof and their meat is thick and fleshy." They are ideal for stir-frying and in soups. Oyster mushrooms are credited with having antitumor qualities and are used for joint and muscle relaxation in China.

• **Shiitake** mushrooms, nicknamed "the monarch of mushrooms," are closely related to the black mushrooms of China and they can be used interchangeably. They are used extensively, fresh and dried. Fresh shiitakes have a delicate, woodsy flavor and are excellent in stir-fried dishes and soups. The stem of the fresh shiitake usually needs to be trimmed, since it tends to be tough. (The stems of the dried, reconstituted shiitake are always removed and discarded or saved for stock.)

Once dried, shiitake mushrooms develop a pleasantly smoky flavor. They should be reconstituted in hot water, and then the stems should be removed. The caps are usually served in soups, stews, and stir-fries. Recent research has credited shiitake mushrooms, like the reishi mushroom, with components that bolster the immune system, prolong life in cancer patients, and are useful in the treatment of chronic fatigue syndrome and AIDS. Dried shiitakes are best stored in the freezer, where they will keep almost indefinitely.

• **Wood ears,** tree ears, black fungus, or Jew's ears, as they are frequently called, are an edible form of fungus or mushroom. They have been used for thousands of years to treat hemorrhoids and as a stomach tonic. They also increase physical and mental energy as well as act as an anticoagulant. The Chinese relish them for their crunchy texture. Wood ears are available dried and must be reconstituted in hot water. Choose the smaller variety, if possible, and discard any tough stem ends. They will keep indefinitely stored in a cool, dry place.

Stir-Fried Wild Mushrooms with Snap Peas in Oyster Sauce

I love the flavor and textural contrast of meaty mushrooms and crisp snap peas, particularly when drenched in a sumptuous oyster sauce. If snap peas are unavailable, use snow peas and decrease the cooking time briefly.

SIX SERVINGS

☯ Snap peas, snow peas, and snow pea greens have similar tonic qualities: Chinese doctors feel not only that they are rich in iron and vitamins, but also that they promote urination and counteract the effects of ulcers.

Shiitake mushrooms are especially effective in bolstering the immune system, while oyster mushrooms are credited with inhibiting tumors. (See mushroom glossary, page 164.)

1/2 pound shiitake mushrooms, stems trimmed and lightly rinsed

1/2 pound oyster mushrooms, stems trimmed and lightly rinsed (if unavailable, substitute shiitake mushrooms)

1/2 pound cremini mushrooms, stems trimmed and lightly rinsed

Seasonings
1 tablespoon minced garlic
1 tablespoon minced fresh ginger

2 1/2 teaspoons canola or corn oil

1 pound snap peas, ends snapped and veiny strings removed, rinsed and drained
1 tablespoon minced garlic
2 tablespoons rice wine or sake
1/2 teaspoon salt, or to taste

Oyster Sauce (mixed together)
3 1/2 tablespoons good-quality oyster sauce
1 1/2 tablespoons rice wine or sake
1 1/4 teaspoons sugar
1/2 teaspoon toasted sesame oil
1/2 cup chicken broth or water
1 teaspoon cornstarch

1. With a sharp knife, cut all the mushrooms into quarters, depending on the size.
2. Prepare the Seasonings and set by the stove.
3. Heat a wok or heavy skillet until very hot, add 1 teaspoon of the oil and heat until hot. Add the snap peas, minced garlic, rice wine or sake, and salt, and toss lightly over high heat about 1 1/2 minutes, until the peas are just tender (snow peas will take slightly less time). Remove from the pan and arrange the peas around the outside of a serving plate.
4. Reheat the pan and the remaining 1 1/2 teaspoons oil until very hot. Add the Seasonings and stir-fry about 10 seconds, until fragrant. Add the mushrooms and toss lightly with a spatula over high heat about 1 minute. Add the premixed Oyster Sauce and toss lightly to thicken it, stirring constantly to prevent lumps. Scoop the mushrooms and sauce onto the circle inside the snow peas. Serve immediately.

Spicy Stir-Fried Sweet Potatoes

I vividly remember the call of the sweet potato man in Taiwan who used to cruise the alleys of the city in the winter, selling hot baked potatoes. The delectable flavor of those potatoes inspired this dish. Serve it with grilled or roasted meats or poultry.

SIX SERVINGS

1¹/2 pounds sweet potatoes (about 4 medium-size)

Zest of 1 navel orange, removed with a vegetable peeler and cut into fine julienne strips

Seasonings

1¹/2 tablespoons minced garlic

1 tablespoon minced fresh ginger

1/2 teaspoon hot chile paste, or to taste

Sweet and Sour Sauce (mixed together)

3/4 cup chicken broth or water

3¹/2 tablespoons soy sauce

3 tablespoons rice wine or sake

1¹/2 tablespoons clear rice vinegar

2 teaspoons sugar

2 teaspoon toasted sesame oil

1/4 teaspoon freshly ground black pepper

2 teaspoons canola or corn oil

1¹/2 teaspoons cornstarch mixed with 2 tablespoons water

1 tablespoon minced scallion greens

🌀 Sweet potatoes are sweet and neutral in nature. A simple home remedy to relieve frostbite is to apply mashed sweet potato to the affected area.

1. Peel the sweet potatoes and cut them lengthwise into 3 slices. Cut the slices lengthwise into 1/2-inch-wide sticks, then cut the sticks diagonally into 1/2-inch-long pieces.

2. Blanch the orange zest for 1¹/2 minutes in a small saucepan with water to cover. Drain on paper towels.

3. Prepare the Seasonings and mix the Sweet and Sour ingredients. Set near the stove.

4. Heat a wok or large skillet, add the oil, and heat until very hot. Add the seasonings and orange peel, and stir-fry until fragrant, about 10 seconds. Add the sweet potatoes and stir-fry about 30 seconds.

5. Give the Sweet and Sour Sauce another stir and add it to the sweet potatoes. Heat until boiling, cover, and cook over medium heat for 10 to 12 minutes, or until the potatoes are tender but not too soft. Stir the cornstarch and add while stirring the sauce continuously, to prevent lumps. Transfer potatoes and sauce to a serving platter and sprinkle the scallion greens on top.

Saucy Braised Eggplant

Braised eggplant was a specialty of one of my Sichuanese chef-teachers. He first deep-fried it and then stir-fried it with meat in a spicy sauce. I've adapted and lightened the flavor by braising the eggplant and leaving out the meat. Despite the changes, I think the flavor of my dish is certainly comparable to his.

1¹/₂ pounds eggplant, rinsed, ends trimmed, and cut lengthwise into ¹/₂-inch-thick slices

1 teaspoon salt

Seasonings

1¹/₂ teaspoons hot chile paste

1¹/₂ tablespoons minced garlic

1¹/₂ tablespoons minced fresh ginger

Braising Liquid

1¹/₂ cups chicken broth

2¹/₂ tablespoons soy sauce

1¹/₂ tablespoons rice wine or sake

1 tablespoon Chinese black vinegar or Worcestershire sauce

1 tablespoon sugar

1 teaspoon cornstarch

1 tablespoon canola or corn oil

2 cups red onion cut into ¹/₂-inch dice

1 medium red pepper, cored, seeded, and cut into ¹/₂-inch dice

2 tablespoons minced scallion greens

1. Arrange eggplant slices on a cookie sheet lined with paper towels and sprinkle both sides with salt. Let them sit 1 hour, then pat them dry and cut into 1¹/₂-inch-long pieces.

2. Prepare the Seasonings and mix the Braising Liquid ingredients in a bowl. Set by the stove.

3. Heat a large flameproof casserole or Dutch oven. Add the oil and heat until hot. Add the chile paste and stir-fry for 5 seconds over high heat, then add the other seasonings and stir-fry until fragrant. Add the red onions and sauté about 1¹/₂ minutes, then add the red pepper and sauté another minute. Add the eggplant cubes and stir-fry for 2 to 3 minutes.

4. Add the Braising Liquid, cover, and heat until boiling. Reduce the heat to medium, cover, and cook about 12 to 14 minutes, or until the eggplant is tender. Uncover, increase the heat to high, and cook until the sauce is reduced to a glaze. Transfer to a serving platter and sprinkle with the scallion greens.

☯ Eggplant has a sweet flavor and a cool nature. Chinese physicians prescribe it for easing bowel movements with hemorrhoids. A simple remedy of roasted eggplants steeped in rice wine is often recommended for a chronic cough.

Mu Shu Vegetable Rolls

I first was introduced to mu shu pork at Joyce Chen's Cambridge restaurant years ago. Since then I have tasted many a mu shu, and it still remains one of my favorites, but these days I prefer a vegetarian version, such as the dish below.

SIX SERVINGS

Seasonings

3 tablespoons minced garlic

3 tablespoons minced fresh ginger

3 1/2 cups Chinese garlic chives, cut into 1-inch lengths (or substitute leeks, cleaned, ends trimmed, and cut into thin julienne shreds)

1/4 cup dried wood ears, softened in hot water to cover for 20 minutes, drained, hard ends removed, and cut into thin julienne strips

3/4 pound fresh shiitake mushrooms, stems removed, rinsed, drained, and cut into thin slices

5 cups julienned Napa cabbage (stem and leafy shreds separated)

2 tablespoons canola or corn oil

1 large egg, lightly beaten

2 tablespoons rice wine or sake

Sauce (mixed together)

1/4 cup soy sauce

1/4 cup rice wine or sake

1 teaspoon sugar

1/3 teaspoon freshly ground black pepper

1 teaspoon cornstarch

Accompaniments

24 spring roll skins, lumpia wrappers, Mandarin pancakes, or flour tortillas, separated, folded into quarters, and steamed for 10 minutes

3/4 cup hoisin sauce, mixed with 1 tablespoon soy sauce and 2 1/2 tablespoons water in a serving dish

1. Prepare the Seasonings and vegetables, and set by the stove.

2. Heat a pan, add 1 tablespoon of the oil, and heat until hot. Add the beaten egg and stir-fry over high heat to scramble, then remove to a plate.

3. Add the other tablespoon of oil, heat until very hot, and add the Seasonings. Stir-fry for 10 seconds, until fragrant, then add the chives or leeks, wood ears, and mushrooms. Toss lightly over high heat for 1 1/2 minutes, then add the cabbage stem shreds, and continue to stir-fry over high heat for 30 seconds. Add the rice wine and leafy cabbage shreds, and cook until the vegetables are crisp-tender, about 1 minute. Return the

cooked egg to the pan, stir, then add the Sauce. Toss lightly to thicken it, stirring constantly to prevent lumps. Scoop the food onto a serving platter.

4. To eat, each diner arranges a wrapper on a plate, smears a tablespoon of the hoisin mixture over a wrapper, and spoons some of the stir-fried mixture on top. Roll it up, tucking the ends in, and eat immediately.

☯ Chinese physicians consider wood ears, a type of fungus, to be mild and sweet. Wood ears are reputed to activate blood and to increase physical and mental energy. Because they are also used to stop bleeding, a common postpartum tonic is made of wood ears soaked in vinegar. Although tests have been done only with animals, wood ears have been shown to lower total cholesterol and lipid levels.

Steamed Hot and Sour Hearts of Bok Choy

Steaming vegetables preserves their infinite goodness. I prefer the beautiful hearts of baby bok choy for this recipe, but, if unavailable, substitute adult bok choy, cutting the stalks to 2-inch lengths.

SIX SERVINGS

2 1/2 pounds hearts of baby bok choy or large bok choy, stem end and leaf tips trimmed

2 1/2 tablespoons minced fresh ginger

2 1/2 tablespoons minced scallions, white part only

Dressing (mixed together)

1/4 cup soy sauce

1 1/2 tablespoons Chinese black vinegar or Worcestershire sauce

1/2 tablespoon sugar

1 tablespoon minced garlic

3/4 teaspoon hot chile paste or dried chile flakes

1. Trim the tough, outer leaves from the bok choy. Rinse and drain. Cut the leaves along the length in half. Cut the halves and stems into 2-inch sections. Using your hands, toss the fresh ginger and scallions with the bok choy in a bowl.

2. Arrange the bok choy on a heatproof plate or on a piece of parchment or waxed paper in a steamer basket.

3. Fill a pot or wok with several inches of water and heat until boiling. Place the cabbage in the steamer (if using a plate, set it on a tunafish can with ends removed) and steam 5 to 6 minutes, or until the cabbage is tender.

4. Arrange the steamed bok choy on a serving platter, spoon some of the Dressing on top, and serve.

☯ Chinese cabbage has a sweet flavor and is cooling to the system when cooked by itself or neutral when cooked with spicy seasonings, such as ginger and scallions. A simple remedy of Chinese cabbage soup with honey is prescribed for coughs and sore throats.

Broccoli or Cauliflower with a Soy-Lemon Dressing

Tossed in a light, lemony dressing, broccoli or cauliflower takes on new life as a delicious side dish to meat, poultry, or seafood.

| 2 pounds broccoli or cauliflower (about 2 bunches) | Soy-Lemon Dressing (mixed together)
3 tablespoons to 1/4 cup soy sauce
2 tablespoons fresh lemon juice
11/2 tablespoons minced garlic
11/2 tablespoons sugar | SIX SERVINGS |

1. Using a sharp paring knife, peel the tough skin from the broccoli stems and cut away the stem ends. Cut off the florets and cut the peeled stems on the diagonal into 1¹/₂-inch-thick sections. Separate the larger florets, so all are approximately the same size. If cooking cauliflower, remove any leaves and break or cut into florets, about 1¹/₂ inches wide.

2. Arrange the broccoli or cauliflower in a steamer tray or on a plate set on a rack. Fill a wok or pot with several inches of water and heat until boiling. Place the vegetable over the boiling water and steam 8 to 10 minutes, or until tender.

3. Drain any water from the broccoli or cauliflower. Put the vegetable in a serving bowl, add the Dressing, toss lightly, and serve.

❸ Broccoli is especially popular for combating summer heat. Chinese doctors feel it is very beneficial for the eyes, and it is often prescribed for eye inflammations and nearsightedness. Some cooks suggest that if it is cooked until just tender, it will not cause gas.

Grilled Leeks in a Garlic-Soy Dressing

Grilling leeks brings out their inherent sweetness, a delectable counterpoint to the garlic-soy dressing in the dish below.

SIX SERVINGS

10 leeks
1 1/2 to 2 tablespoons virgin olive oil

Garlic-Soy Dressing
6 tablespoons soy sauce
1/4 cup rice wine or sake
1 tablespoon minced garlic
1 1/2 tablespoons minced fresh ginger
1 tablespoon sugar, or to taste
1 teaspoon toasted sesame oil

1. Using a sharp knife, trim away some of the root end of the leeks, but save enough so that the stalks will stay together. Slit each stalk in half lengthwise, cutting away the green leaves an inch from the white stalk. Fan out the leaves and rinse under cold running water to clean out the grit. Drain thoroughly. Use a toothpick to thread the green leaves together at the end so they will remain whole. Place the leek halves on a cookie sheet and brush lightly with the olive oil.

2. Prepare a medium-low fire for grilling, and place the grill 3 to 4 inches from the heat. Arrange the skewered leeks on the grill and cook about 6 to 7 minutes on each side, or until the centers are tender and the edges are golden brown and crisp. Arrange the leeks on a serving platter. Remove the toothpicks.

3. Put the ingredients for the Garlic-Soy Dressing in a saucepan, mix well, and heat until boiling, stirring to dissolve the sugar. Pour it over the grilled leeks and serve them warm, at room temperature, or cold.

☯ Like scallions and onions, leeks are warm and pungent. They are also considered to be astringent, and are believed to counteract bleeding and diarrhea.

Roasted Asparagus with a Sesame Vinaigrette

I was first introduced to roasted asparagus in Italy, and while the preparation is unknown in China, I feel confident that my master chef mentors would heartily approve of this dish.

2 pounds fresh asparagus, tough woody stems snapped off	Sesame Vinaigrette	SIX SERVINGS
2 teaspoons toasted sesame oil	1/3 cup soy sauce	
2 teaspoons virgin olive oil	3 tablespoons clear rice vinegar	
1/4 teaspoon salt	1/2 tablespoon toasted sesame oil	
	1 tablespoon sugar	
	2 tablespoons minced fresh parsley (optional)	

1. Preheat the oven to 475°F. Rinse the asparagus stalks and drain on paper towels. Spread the stalks out on a cookie sheet. Combine the sesame and olive oils and brush the asparagus with the oil, then sprinkle the salt over the stalks.
2. Roast the asparagus 10 to 12 minutes, or until they are tender when pierced with the tip of a knife. Alternatively, you may steam the asparagus for 4 to 5 minutes until tender. Arrange the asparagus on a serving plate.
3. Mix together the ingredients for the Sesame Vinaigrette and drizzle the dressing over the asparagus. Sprinkle the minced parsley on top. Serve hot or at room temperature.

Asparagus contains a diuretic, which explains why it is often prescribed for kidney problems; it is believed to have the capacity to draw water out of the kidneys. Since it is cooling in nature, it is also used to treat lung congestion. For constipation, eat some lightly steamed asparagus or Chinese cabbage.

A Mushroom Tale

When Anne Chang fell ill with hepatitis B more than eleven years ago, the best her doctors could offer her was treatment with Interferon, an immune system booster that had proven to be successful in only about 6 percent of cases and caused debilitating side effects of its own. When her excruciating aches and fatigue became almost unbearable, she pleaded with her husband to find an alternative. Dr. Raymond Chang, a doctor trained at Yale and New York Hospital and at the time an attending physician at Manhattan's Memorial Sloan Kettering, was stumped.

Then Chang, who was born in Hong Kong, recalled tales he had heard in childhood of Asian folk remedies. He had given them little heed. Now, he began investigating them intensively. Finally, after six months, he discovered a Japanese treatment that was being hailed as a wonder drug: reishi mushrooms.

Anne began taking an extraction of reishi, and within days she started to improve. She has been taking reishi ever since, and today there is no sign of hepatitis B virus in her blood.

As a result of the successful treatment and his subsequent research on the reishi mushroom, Chang has become very involved in alternative therapies. He is now the secretary general of the International Research Institute for Ganoderma or Reishi, a research organization, and he has become a recognized authority on the reishi mushroom.

In the spring of 1997, Dr. Chang founded the Institute of East-West Medicine in Manhattan, which is affiliated with New York Hospital and Cornell Medical College. At his clinic, patients receive an integrated combination of Western medical, Asian, and Ayurvedic (an age-old Indian philosophy regarding health and illness that parallels Traditional Chinese Medicine) treatments.

"I think modern medicine has come a long way," he says, "especially in the last few years, toward realizing that certain foods and alternative treatments may play a pivotal role in the areas of cancer prevention, heart disease modification, and the lessening of cholesterol and hormonal problems."

Dr. Chang also feels that until further research is done, herbs and foods should be used as disease preventatives by integrating them, as he does in his clinic, with conventional therapies.

Grilled Wild Mushrooms with a Teriyaki Dressing

I adore grilled mushrooms. When they are first drenched in a simple soy dressing such as this one, then seared over a hot fire, their smoky, juicy flavor, for me, is almost better than that of grilled meat.

SIX SERVINGS

1/2 pound (about 12) medium to large
    fresh shiitake mushrooms
1/2 pound (about 12) fresh oyster, cèpe,
    maitake, or other available wild mush-
    rooms
10 to 12 whole scallions, trimmed and cut
    into 1 1/2-inch lengths
About 16 to 20 bamboo skewers, soaked
    in cold water for 1 hour

Teriyaki Dressing
1/2 cup soy sauce
1/3 cup rice wine or sake
3 tablespoons water
2 tablespoons sugar
1 tablespoon toasted sesame oil
1 1/2 tablespoons minced fresh ginger

☯ Shiitake, cèpes, and oyster mushrooms are all sweet and neutral in nature. They are believed to bolster the immune system, inhibit tumors, and decrease cholesterol in the blood. Chinese doctors also suggest that they will promote good health if eaten on a regular basis.

1. Trim the stem ends of the mushrooms, rinse lightly, and drain thoroughly. If the mushroom caps are large, cut in half. Thread 2 mushrooms and 3 scallion sections alternately onto each skewer, starting and ending with the scallions. Arrange the skewered vegetables on a cookie sheet.

2. Combine the Teriyaki Dressing ingredients in a saucepan. Heat until boiling, stirring to dissolve the sugar. Use one third to liberally brush the mushrooms and scallions with the sauce. Pour the remaining two thirds into a serving bowl.

3. Prepare a medium-low fire for grilling and place the grill 3 to 4 inches from the heat. Arrange the skewered mushrooms and scallions on the grill and cook, turning frequently, about 4 or 5 minutes, or until golden brown and slightly crisp at the edges. Arrange on a serving platter.

4. Serve with the warm Teriyaki Dressing for dipping.

Black Bean Acorn Squash

Black bean sauce is remarkably versatile; it goes well with all types of winter squash, eggplant, and sweet potatoes. This dish is so satisfying that it would make a lovely light lunch or dinner served with steamed rice.

2¹/2 to 3 pounds acorn, butternut, or other type of winter squash

Seasonings
2 tablespoons fermented black beans, rinsed, drained, and minced
2 tablespoons minced scallions, white part only
1¹/2 tablespoons minced garlic
1 tablespoon minced fresh ginger
¹/2 teaspoon dried chile flakes (optional)
2 teaspoons canola or corn oil

Sauce (mixed together)
¹/2 cup chicken broth or water
1¹/2 tablespoons soy sauce
1¹/2 tablespoons rice wine or sake
2 teaspoons sugar
1 teaspoon toasted sesame oil
1¹/2 teaspoons cornstarch

2 tablespoons minced scallion greens

SIX SERVINGS

1. Lightly rinse the squash. Using a sharp knife or a cleaver, cut each one vertically in half. Scoop out the seeds and, if necessary, cut a thin slice from the bottom so the halves will sit flat. Arrange the squash halves in a heatproof quiche or pie pan. Preheat the oven to 425°F. Alternatively, you may arrange the squash in a steamer tray.

2. To make the black bean sauce, heat a wok or large skillet until hot, add the oil, and heat until very hot. Add the Seasonings and stir-fry about 10 seconds with a spatula or slotted spoon until fragrant. Add the Sauce and heat until boiling. Cook, stirring constantly to prevent lumps from forming, until thickened. Spoon the thickened sauce over the squash halves. If baking, cover the squash with aluminum foil.

3. Bake about 40 to 45 minutes, or until the squash is tender when pierced with the tip of a knife. Or steam for about 30 minutes, or until tender. Remove and sprinkle with the minced scallion greens. Serve.

☯ Winter squash is slightly warming in nature (whereas summer squash and zucchini tend to be cooling in nature and are eaten to overcome summer heat). Fresh squash pulp is sometimes applied to burns to alleviate the pain.

Curried Pumpkin or Squash

There are many different types of curry blends: This one is rich with the flavor of mustard seeds, cumin, garlic, and coriander. I then add some sweetness, from brown sugar and coconut.

SIX SERVINGS

2 1/2 pounds pumpkin or acorn squash

1 1/2 tablespoons corn or canola oil

1 red onion, peeled and cut into 1/4-inch dice

1 teaspoon black mustard seeds

Seasonings

1 1/2 teaspoons minced garlic

1 1/2 teaspoons ground cumin

1 teaspoon black mustard seeds

1 teaspoon dried coriander

1/2 teaspoon ground turmeric

2 cups water

1 teaspoon salt

1 tablespoon light-brown sugar

3 tablespoons grated coconut

1. Peel the squash or pumpkin and remove the seeds. Cut into 1 1/2-inch squares. Prepare the Seasonings.

2. Heat a casserole or Dutch oven, add the oil, and heat until hot. Add the onion and cook, over medium-low heat, until just soft. Turn the heat up slightly and add the mustard seeds, frying until they pop. Add the Seasonings and stir-fry over medium heat for 30 seconds, until very fragrant. Add the water and salt, and heat until boiling. Add the squash pieces.

3. Reduce the heat to moderate and cook, partially covered, about 20 minutes. Add the brown sugar and coconut, and cook, uncovered, until the squash is tender and the liquid has reduced completely. Spoon the cooked squash and sauce into a serving bowl and serve.

☯ Pumpkin, though slightly different from the Western variety, is grown all over China. It has a faintly sweet flavor and a warm nature. It is believed to help the pancreas by regulating blood sugar. An old folk remedy suggests applying fresh pumpkin alone or with aloe vera gel for treating burns.

Celery Hearts in a Spicy Sesame Dressing

In Chinese restaurants, customers are never allowed to go hungry: Pickles and light dishes such as this one are placed on the table to munch on while glancing at the menu. Serve this light salad as a starter or a side dish for any main entrée.

1 1/2 pounds celery stalks	Tart Dressing (mixed together)	SIX SERVINGS
3 tablespoons toasted sesame oil	3 1/2 tablespoons clear rice vinegar	
1 tablespoon canola or corn oil	1 tablespoon sugar	
1/2 to 3/4 teaspoon crushed dried chiles	1 teaspoon salt	
3 tablespoons minced scallions, white part only		
1 tablespoon rice wine or sake		

1. Rinse the celery stalks, and peel away the tough outer skin, if necessary. Cut off the root ends and leafy tops. Cut the celery sections into 2-inch lengths. Cut each section lengthwise into thin slices about 1/4 inch thick. (You should have about 7 cups.)
2. Heat a wok or large skillet, add the toasted sesame oil and canola or corn oil, and heat until hot. Add the crushed chiles and scallions, and stir-fry over high heat until fragrant, about 10 seconds. Add the celery and rice wine or sake, and toss lightly with a spatula or slotted spoon over high heat about 30 seconds, then add the Tart Dressing. Continue cooking over high heat for another 30 seconds, until the celery is just tender; spoon into a serving dish. Eat hot, at room temperature, or cold.

☯ According to Chinese doctors, celery is sweet and coolish in nature. Chinese celery is slender and preferable to Western celery for medicinal purposes. It is believed to have a calming effect on the body, and 3 cups of heated celery juice per day is recommended for hypertension. Many Chinese women also believe that it will regulate the menstrual cycle.

Grilled Scallops and Rainbow Peppers over Wilted Greens in a Fresh Cilantro Dressing

This is one of my favorite summer lunches or light dinners, and it can be prepared easily in advance. I often substitute shrimp or squid for the scallops, depending on their availability.

SIX SERVINGS

1¹/2 pounds sea scallops, rinsed and
   drained

Ginger Marinade
2 tablespoons rice wine or sake
2 tablespoons soy sauce
1 tablespoon minced fresh ginger
1 teaspoon toasted sesame oil

1 red bell pepper, cored, seeded, and cut
   into 1¹/2-inch squares
1 yellow pepper, cored, seeded, and cut
   into 1¹/2-inch squares
1 orange pepper, cored, seeded, and cut
   into 1¹/2-inch squares

6 to 8 10-inch bamboo or metal skewers (if
   bamboo, soaked in cold water to cover
   for 1 hour)

Cilantro Dressing
1/3 cup soy sauce
1/4 cup clear rice vinegar
2 tablespoons toasted sesame oil
1¹/2 tablespoons sugar
1¹/2 tablespoons rice wine or sake
1/3 cup chopped fresh cilantro, leaves only

1 pound snow pea shoots, tender spinach,
   or other baby greens, rinsed and drained
2 teaspoons canola or corn oil
1¹/2 tablespoons minced garlic
2 tablespoons rice wine or sake
1 teaspoon salt

1. Put the scallops in a bowl. Mix the Ginger Marinade ingredients and pour them over the scallops, tossing lightly to coat. Cover with plastic wrap, and let the scallops sit at least 30 minutes. Alternately thread the peppers and the scallops onto the bamboo skewers, starting and ending with the peppers. Brush the scallops and peppers with the marinade.

2. Mix the Cilantro Dressing ingredients in a bowl. Trim the wilted or any hard stems

Grilled Scallops and Peppers (continued)

from the snow pea shoots or baby greens and place near the stove. Pour the Cilantro Dressing into a serving container.

3. Heat a wok or large skillet, add the oil, and heat until near smoking. Add the greens and garlic and toss lightly about 20 seconds, then add the rice wine and salt, and toss lightly over high heat about 1 minute or less, until the greens are slightly wilted but still bright green. Spoon the greens onto a serving platter and mound slightly so that the scallops can be arranged on top.

4. Prepare a fire for grilling and arrange the skewers of scallops and peppers about 3 inches from the source of heat. Broil or grill about 3 to 4 minutes on each side, turning once and brushing with the marinade. Arrange the cooked scallops and peppers over the wilted greens, leaving them on the skewers or removing them. Spoon the Cilantro Dressing on top or serve on the side. Serve warm.

☯ Snow pea shoots and snow peas are sweet and neutral in nature, so they naturally complement many foods. They are reputed to reinforce the spleen and *qi* and promote the production of bodily fluids, thereby reducing thirst.

Cilantro is pungent and warming. Chinese doctors feel that it promotes blood circulation, and it is often prescribed internally and externally. Cilantro paste is often applied for easing the discomfort of chicken pox and measles.

Sweet and Sour Cucumber Slices

Chinese cucumbers are small, with few seeds, and have a delightfully crisp texture. Kirby or pickling cucumbers are most similar to them, although the long "seedless" variety works well also.

1 1/2 pounds Chinese, Kirby, or pickling cucumbers, or 2 seedless English cucumbers, rinsed and drained	Sweet and Sour Dressing (mixed together) 1 cup clear rice vinegar 1 cup sugar 1 teaspoon salt 1 1/2 tablespoons minced fresh ginger	**SIX SERVINGS**

1. Trim the ends of the cucumbers. Slice them lengthwise in half, then run the tines of a fork several times down the length to create a slight decoration. Scoop out the seeds with a spoon, and cut the cucumber halves into 3-inch sections. Cut the sections, along the length, into almost paper-thin slices. Place in a bowl.

2. Add the Sweet and Sour Dressing to the cucumbers. Toss lightly to coat the cucumber slices. Cover with plastic wrap and refrigerate for 30 minutes. Serve cold.

☯ Because of their coolish nature, cucumbers are especially popular in the summer since they dissipate heat. They are also considered to have diuretic and laxative effects. To soothe a scratchy throat or laryngitis, drink some cucumber soup. According to Dr. Chun-Han Zhu, the bitter end of the cucumber contains cucurbitacin C and is helpful in treating cancer.

Hot and Sour Cabbage Slaw

I first tasted this slaw in Hangzhou on a brutally hot summer's day. The vegetables were crisp and cool, while the seasoning was spicy—almost electrifying. The flavors were so memorable that they inspired me to create the dish below.

SIX SERVINGS

1 small head Chinese (Napa) cabbage (about 1 1/2 pounds)	1 1/2 cups grated carrots
1 teaspoon canola or corn oil	**Hot and Sour Dressing (mixed together)**
1 teaspoon toasted sesame oil	3 tablespoons soy sauce
1 teaspoon crushed dried chiles	1/2 teaspoon salt
2 1/2 tablespoons minced fresh ginger	2 tablespoons sugar
1 red bell pepper, cored, seeded, and cut into 1/4-inch dice	2 1/2 tablespoons Chinese black vinegar or Worcestershire sauce
1 1/2 tablespoons rice wine or sake	

1. Cut the cabbage stalks from the root end. Trim the leafy tip ends and discard. Rinse the stalks thoroughly and drain. Cut them into julienne strips about 1/2 inch wide, separating the stem sections from the leafy sections. (The leafy sections take less time to cook.)
2. Heat a wok or large skillet, add the oils, and heat until hot. Add the crushed dried chiles and minced ginger, and stir-fry over high heat about 15 seconds. Add the red pepper dice and stir-fry about 30 seconds, then add the rice wine or sake and continue stir-frying 30 seconds more. Add the stem sections of the cabbage, and the carrots, toss lightly over high heat, and cook for a minute. Now add the leafy sections, toss lightly, and pour on the Dressing. Continue tossing lightly to coat. Cook about 30 seconds and transfer to a serving bowl. Serve warm, at room temperature, or cold.

☯ Because of its high vitamin C content, Chinese (Napa) cabbage is believed by Chinese doctors to moisten the intestines and beautify the skin. For constipation, cabbage cooked with beets is often recommended. Carrots are believed to ease whooping cough and coughs in general. Drink hot carrot tea mixed with a little brown sugar for heartburn.

Wilted Spinach and Mushroom Salad

I love warm salads where a light dressing complements and accentuates the fresh flavors of the vegetables. This is such a dish. For a more substantial salad add some cooked shrimp or smoked turkey slices.

1 tablespoon canola or corn oil

Seasonings
3 tablespoons minced scallion greens
1 1/2 tablespoons minced fresh ginger
1 1/2 tablespoons minced garlic

1 pound fresh shiitake mushrooms, ends trimmed, and cut into thin slices
2 tablespoons rice wine or sake

Tart Dressing (mixed together)
6 tablespoons soy sauce
1 1/2 tablespoons sugar
3 1/2 tablespoons clear rice vinegar

1 1/4 pounds or 2 10-ounce packages fresh spinach, stems removed, rinsed thoroughly, drained, and torn into large pieces

1. Heat a wok or large skillet, add the oil, and heat until very hot. Add the Seasonings, and stir-fry lightly over high heat until fragrant, about 15 seconds. Add the sliced mushrooms and toss with a spatula or slotted spoon a few seconds. Then lower the heat slightly and cook for several minutes, until tender. Add the rice wine or sake and toss lightly over high heat for about 1 minute.
2. Add the Tart Dressing to the pan, and heat until boiling. Add the spinach, toss lightly over high heat for 30 seconds, or until the spinach becomes slightly wilted. Using a slotted spoon, scoop the spinach into a bowl, pour in some of the dressing, and serve.

🌜 According to Chinese dietary theory, spinach has a slightly slippery nature, which lubricates the body and improves secretion of all wastes. It is good for constipation and aids digestion. For acute conjunctivitis, drink a tea made by simmering spinach leaves and dried chrysanthemum flowers in hot water for 3 to 4 minutes.

Fresh Ginger Fennel

Fennel is such a subtle but delicious vegetable. I love its crunchy texture and slightly licoricey flavor. For a delightful contrast, serve this wonderful salad with red-cooked or braised dishes.

SIX SERVINGS

2 pounds fennel bulbs with stalks, rinsed and trimmed, leaving 1/8 inch of the root base to hold the fennel together

Ginger Dressing (mixed together)
3 tablespoons soy sauce

11/2 tablespoons Chinese black vinegar or Worcestershire sauce
1 tablespoon sugar
1 tablespoon minced fresh ginger

21/2 tablespoons minced fresh cilantro

1. Cut each fennel bulb lengthwise in half, then cut the fennel into slices, about 1/2 inch thick and 2 inches long.
2. Fill a large pot with 8 cups water and heat until boiling. Add the fennel slices and cook about 6 to 7 minutes, or until crisp-tender. Drain in a colander, refresh under cold water, and drain thoroughly. Place the fennel slices in a bowl.
3. Add the Ginger Dressing to the fennel slices. Toss lightly to coat with a spoon, and sprinkle cilantro on top. Serve at room temperature or chilled.

☯ Fennel seed has been a favorite herb of Chinese doctors for centuries. The seed, root, and leaf of the vegetable are all used for treating various maladies — one of the primary targets being bloating. The root is particularly good for balancing the internal region and promoting energy circulation. Similarly, it soothes stomach pain and stimulates the appetite. A flavoring of crushed roasted fennel seeds and minced ginger, fried until golden brown, is added to rice porridge and taken 3 times a day for digestive difficulties.

Fresh Corn and Roasted Bell Pepper Salad

Though a relative newcomer to the Far East, corn has become a popular vegetable in China, Taiwan, and Hong Kong. Steamed corn on the cob, still encased in its husks, is a common street food. (The husks are removed before eating the snack.) Try this fresh-tasting salad, which is delicious with either freshly picked sweet corn or frozen corn on the cob.

8 ears sweet corn, husked
4 red bell peppers
1¹/2 teaspoons canola or corn oil

Seasonings
2 tablespoons minced scallions, white part
　only
1 tablespoon minced fresh ginger

Sauce (mixed together)
2 tablespoons rice wine or sake
1 teaspoon toasted sesame oil
1 teaspoon salt, or to taste
1/4 teaspoon freshly ground black pepper

1. Cook the corn in a large pot of boiling water, about 3 to 4 minutes, or steam over high heat for 5 minutes, until cooked. Drain the corn, if necessary, and cool it under cold water. Using a sharp knife, cut off the kernels. (There should be about 5 cups.)
2. To roast the peppers, prepare a fire for grilling or preheat a broiler. Arrange the peppers about 3 inches from the source of heat and roast on all sides, turning occasionally, until blackened. Place in a paper bag, close the bag securely, and let the peppers steam until cool, about 15 minutes.
3. Using a sharp knife, remove the skin from the peppers and cut them lengthwise in half. Remove and discard the seeds, and cut the halves lengthwise into julienne strips. Cut the strips into small dice about ¹/4 inch square. (There should be about 1¹/2 cups.)
4. Heat a wok or a skillet, add the oil, and heat until very hot. Add the Seasonings and stir-fry over high heat for 15 seconds, until fragrant. Add the corn, roasted peppers, and the premixed Sauce. Toss lightly with a slotted spoon for a few seconds to mix the ingredients and coat them with the sauce. Spoon the vegetables into a serving bowl, and serve hot or at room temperature.

❧ Corn is often prescribed for a weak stomach, since it improves the appetite. A common remedy for urinary problems is a broth made from boiling the husks of 6 ears of corn in 3 cups water for 20 minutes.

Shrimp and Vegetable Salad with a Fresh Herb Dressing

This wonderful salad was inspired by the filling of Vietnamese spring rolls, which often consists of cooked shrimp, shredded vegetables, and rice noodles. Chopped fresh cilantro and basil and the fresh lime dressing further accentuate the freshness and delicacy of the mixture.

SIX SERVINGS

1 pound medium shrimp, shelled and deveined

1/3 pound thin rice stick noodles, softened in hot water for 15 to 20 minutes and drained

3 carrots, peeled and grated (about 21/2 cups)

21/2 cups leafy lettuce, rinsed, drained, and cut into thin julienne shreds

21/2 cups bean sprouts, rinsed and drained

Sweet and Sour Dressing

11/4 teaspoons crushed dried chiles or dried chile flakes

Juice of 5 limes or 21/2 lemons (about 2/3 cup)

1/3 cup fish sauce, or more to taste

1/3 cup sugar

11/2 tablespoons minced garlic

1/3 cup coarsely chopped fresh cilantro

1/3 cup coarsely chopped fresh basil

11/2 cups finely chopped scallion greens

1. Using a sharp knife, slice the shrimp in half lengthwise along the back. Heat 4 cups water in a saucepan until boiling, add the shrimp, and cook about 1¹/₂ minutes, after the water has reached a boil. Drain in a colander and rinse under cold water. Drain again.

2. In a large stockpot, heat 2 quarts water until boiling. Add the softened rice stick noodles and swirl in the hot water. Cook for 10 seconds, or until just tender. Drain thoroughly in a colander and rinse under cold water. Arrange the noodles on a deep serving platter.

3. Arrange the shrimp in the center of the platter with the carrots, lettuce, and bean sprouts in concentric circles around the shrimp.

4. In a medium bowl, soak the crushed red chiles or dried chile flakes in the lime juice for 2 to 3 minutes. Add the remaining Sweet and Sour Dressing ingredients, and stir to dissolve the sugar. Pour the dressing into a serving bowl.

5. Sprinkle the chopped cilantro, basil, and scallions on top of the shrimp and vegetables. Spoon the dressing over the salad, or serve on the side at room temperature or chilled.

☯ Cilantro, also called Chinese parsley or fresh coriander, has been used in Chinese medicine since A.D. 600. The herb and its seeds are said to aid digestion. The Cantonese recommend cilantro soup for treating bad breath. Cilantro-and-ginger tea is also drunk to relieve the symptoms of the common cold.

Basil has been used by Chinese doctors for centuries. It is believed to invigorate the body, promote circulation, and aid digestion. According to Dr. Albert Leung, author of *Better Health with (Mostly) Chinese Herbs and Foods* (AYSL Corporation, 1995), an eighth-century recipe for treating a cough consisted of a basil-ginger bread, to be eaten on an empty stomach.

Soybeans and Tofu

Soybeans, Tofu, and Dr. Albert Leung

This wasn't Beijing or Hong Kong. It was Glen Rock, New Jersey, and I was sitting in the resource library of Dr. Albert Leung, author of *Better Health with (Mostly) Chinese Herbs and Foods* and coauthor of the *Encyclopedia of Common Natural Ingredients Used in Food, Drugs and Cosmetics*. All around me were books and magazines with titles like *The Edible Fungi of China,* as well as the *American Journal of Chinese Medicine*. Every publication in Dr. Leung's vast collection, which is the largest of its kind outside of Asia, was dedicated to herbs, food, and Chinese medicine.

Dr. Leung is also the creator of a computer database on Chinese herbal medicine for the National Cancer Institute. (He has been working with the Chinese Institute of Materia Medica at the Academy of Traditional Chinese Medicine in Beijing to update his database.) His company, AYSL, develops various herbal "formulas" or remedies for numerous conditions, including migraine pain, menstrual discomfort, and allergies.

Dr. Leung was first introduced to food tonics as a child growing up in Hong Kong. His grandmother and mother frequently used remedies such as honeysuckle flowers and lotus seed embryos for fevers. His fascination with the subject persisted during his college years at the National Taiwan University and later at the University of Michigan, where he received M.S. and Ph.D. degrees in pharmacognosy (the science of natural drugs).

Frying tempeh

Like a growing number of doctors, Dr. Leung feels strongly that an integrated approach should be taken in the treatment of many diseases, one that draws from the strengths of both conventional and alternative therapies. He also concurs with Henry Lu that fortifying the immune system is critical to good health.

"Our immune system is the key to health and longevity and there are many factors that throw off our yin/yang balance," Dr. Leung says. "When this happens, Traditional Chinese Medicine often uses herbal tonics and food to help restore the balance."

Tofu is such a food. Chinese doctors classify its nature as cool and sweet. It is credited with clearing heat from the body, detoxifying the system, and strengthening the spleen and stomach. Western doctors also believe that soy products help to counter heart disease by lowering blood cholesterol and regulating blood sugar levels. Furthermore, they relieve menopausal symptoms because they contain phytoestrogens—natural chemicals that are similar to human estrogen.

Soy is also showing great promise in the fight against cancer. Doctors have isolated a soy phytonutrient, genistein, which has been shown in some studies to reduce the growth of malignant tumors. The National Cancer Institute is initiating studies of genistein as an anticancer drug. The researchers believe that soy's phytoestrogens may prevent cancer and help to slow the onset of osteoporosis.

Soybeans and soyfoods have been an integral staple in the Chinese diet for centuries. It is believed that tofu, or bean curd, was first made during the Han Dynasty (206 B.C.–A.D. 220), and soyfoods have long served as a vital source of protein.

According to Dr. Leung, two varieties of soybean are used in Chinese medicine: black and yellow. The first recorded use of black soybean dates back to the middle of the eighth century. The skin was credited with nourishing the blood, clearing vision, and driving away disease. Fermented black (soy)beans were used to treat illnesses affecting the lungs and digestive system. The yellow and black soybean are similar in nature and can be used interchangeably.

These days Western cooks have also discovered the beneficial qualities of soybeans and tofu. A visit to a supermarket or an Asian market will attest that soybeans are now available in many guises: fresh soybeans, which are sold seasonally and generally boiled and eaten sprinkled with salt as a nutritious snack, *edamame;* soybean sprouts, to be cooked in soups and stews; and soybean milk, flavored or plain, now a staple item in the dairy section. And there are the many condiments, including bean pastes and fermented black soybeans.

The actual process of making tofu is quite simple. The beans are first soaked and ground to a paste, then mixed with water and strained to make soybean milk. The milk is heated and a type of coagulant is added. The resulting custard that forms is called *silken* or *soft* tofu and is generally used for cold dishes and delicate soups. The curd is then poured into a press and weights are added to form *firm* tofu, which is stir-fried, deep-fried, or cooked in soups and stews. *Extra-firm* tofu results when the tofu is pressed longer. It holds together better for lengthy braised dishes and some stir-fries. It's also frequently stuffed with meat and vegetarian fillings. Five-spice tofu, which is firm tofu that has been cooked in soy sauce and seasonings, is now widely available and is excellent in salads and stir-fries.

Tempeh, a fermented cake or patty made with soybeans and rice, wheat, or millet, is now sold in many supermarkets. It is highly nutritious and quite versatile: It can be steamed, stir-fried, grilled, baked, and braised.

As doctors continue to research and confirm their toniclike effects and as cooks discover their remarkable versatility, soybeans and tofu are sure to figure prominently in the Western diet of the future.

Soybeans and Soyfoods

Product	Use	Storage Time in Refrigerator
Fresh soybeans	Boiled and served cold, salted as an appetizer	1 week
Soybean sprouts	Cooked in soups and stews	4 to 5 days
Miso	Added to marinades, soups, dressings, sauces, and pickles	2 to 3 months (pasteurized)
Soybean milk	Drunk plain or sweetened for breakfast and as a snack in between meals. Used to make tofu, confections, and dried soybean milk products	1 week (unpasteurized) 3 weeks (pasteurized)
Silken tofu	Used in sweet and savory soups, as an appetizer, in dips, desserts, and dressings	1 week in water
Soft tofu	Used in savory soups, sauces, and dressings	1 week in water
Firm tofu	Used in soups, salads, stir-fries, stuffings, stews, and baked dishes	1 week in water*
Extra-firm tofu	Used in salads, stir-fries, fillings, stews, and grilled dishes	1 week in water*
5-spice pressed tofu	Used in salads, stir-fries, fillings, and grilled dishes	2 weeks in package
Tempeh	Stir-fries, baked and grilled dishes	2 weeks in package

*Firm tofu and extra-firm tofu can be frozen and will keep for a month in the freezer. Freezing will change the texture, making it less slippery. This step is useful for cooks who prefer a firmer texture.

Japanese-Style Silken Tofu

Soft, or silken, tofu is voluptuous and custardlike. I adore it served simply with a few tablespoons of smoky dashi broth or sprinkled with soy sauce and wispy minced scallions. Serve it as a snack or a starter.

Dashi
1 4-inch square giant kelp (*konbu*)
2 cups cold water
2/3 cup dried bonito flakes (*katsuo bushi*)

Dipping Sauce (mixed together)
2 cups dashi (preceding)
1/4 cup soy sauce
3 tablespoons sweetened rice wine (*mirin*)

1 1/2 pounds silken tofu
1/4 cup minced scallion greens

1. Using a damp cloth, clean the kelp if necessary, removing any dirt, and place in the cold water. Bring the mixture to a boil over high heat. Remove the kelp immediately and reserve for another use.
2. Bring the water to a boil again, add the bonito flakes, stir, and remove from the heat. Let the flakes settle to the bottom of the pan, about 1 minute; then strain the liquid through a fine strainer or pour through a strainer lined with cheesecloth. Discard the bonito flakes and reserve this dashi for the Dipping Sauce.
3. Put the ingredients of the dipping sauce in a saucepan and heat to just under a simmer; keep it warm.
4. Cut the silken tofu into $1/2$-inch dice, or if it is too fragile, put it into a serving bowl. Sprinkle the top with the heated sauce and the minced scallion greens. Each diner scoops some tofu out of the broth with the sauce and scallions, and eats it immediately as a light appetizer, a side dish, or a snack.

◐ Tofu clears heat from the body and strengthens the spleen and stomach. This dish is perfect in warm weather, when it cools the body.

Soybean Sprouts and Leeks in Hot Chile Sauce

Soybean sprouts may be confused with mung bean sprouts. The main difference is that soybean sprouts have a large yellow bean on the end and they require more cooking. They usually are used in soups, stir-fries, and stews.

SIX SERVINGS

1¹/2 tablespoons canola or corn oil
2¹/2 tablespoons toasted sesame oil

Seasonings
1 teaspoon crushed dried chiles or 4 to 6
   small dried hot chiles, cut into ¹/4-inch
   lengths, seeds removed
1 tablespoon minced fresh ginger
1¹/2 tablespoons minced garlic

2 leeks, ends trimmed, cleaned and cut
   into thin julienne shreds (about 4 to 5
   cups)
3 cups soybean sprouts, rinsed and drained

Sauce (mixed together)
7 tablespoons soy sauce
2 tablespoons rice wine or sake
1¹/2 tablespoons sugar
3 tablespoons Chinese black vinegar or
   Worcestershire sauce
3 tablespoons minced fresh cilantro (optional)

1. Heat a wok or large, deep skillet, add the oils, and heat until very hot. Add the Seasonings and stir-fry about 15 seconds until fragrant. Add the leeks and stir-fry over high heat about 1¹/₂ minutes, until near tender.

2. Add the soybean sprouts and continue cooking over high heat, tossing, about 2 minutes. Add the premixed Sauce and cover. Cook about 1¹/₂ minutes, then spoon onto a serving plate. Serve as a side dish or an appetizer.

☯ According to the *Chinese Medicated Diet,* published by the Shanghai College of Traditional Chinese Medicine, raw soybeans (as in soybean milk) soothe the liver and regulate the circulation of *qi,* or the body's energy, while cooked soybeans (as in tofu) invigorate the body.

Rainbow Salad with Spicy Peanut Dressing

I simply couldn't write a book without including some version of a salad with my spicy peanut dressing—it is one of my most requested recipes. Serve it with any combination of shredded vegetables. Cooked noodles add substance to the dish.

1 pound firm tofu, cut into 1/2-inch slabs

1/2 pound spinach or egg fettuccine

1 teaspoon toasted sesame oil

2 cups grated carrots

1 1/2 cups grated cucumbers, seeds and skin removed

1 1/2 cups bean sprouts, rinsed and drained

1 red bell pepper, cored, seeded, and sliced into thin julienne strips

1 yellow pepper, cored, seeded, and sliced into thin julienne strips

Spicy Peanut Dressing

2 tablespoons minced fresh ginger or 2 1/4-inch-square peeled knob

1/2 tablespoon minced garlic

1 teaspoon hot chile paste, or more to taste

1/2 cup smooth peanut butter

1/4 cup soy sauce

3 1/2 tablespoons sugar

3 1/2 tablespoons Chinese black vinegar or Worcestershire sauce

3 tablespoons toasted sesame oil

5 to 6 tablespoons chicken broth or water

1. Wrap the tofu slabs in paper towels or a cotton towel, and place a heavy weight, such as a cast-iron skillet, on top. Let stand for 30 minutes to press out the excess water, then cut the tofu into matchstick-size shreds about 2 inches long.

2. Bring 3 quarts water to a boil, add the fettuccine, and cook until just tender. Drain in a colander, toss with the sesame oil, and arrange on a platter.

3. Arrange the carrots, cucumbers, bean sprouts, red and yellow pepper strips, and tofu in mounds or separate concentric circles on the serving platter with the noodles.

4. To prepare the Spicy Peanut Dressing, in a food processor fitted with a steel blade or a blender, chop the ginger and garlic until fine. Add the remaining ingredients in descending order, ending with the chicken broth or water. Process until smooth. The sauce should have the consistency of heavy cream. If it is too thick, add more water or chicken broth; if too thin, add more peanut butter. Pour the sauce into a serving container, and offer the vegetables and sauce to each diner to mix as desired.

☯ Chinese physicians prescribe tofu for those with an overheated blood system since soybeans on their own have a coolish tendency. Once cooked with water (cooling) to make tofu, the food becomes even more cooling.

Spicy Garlic Bean Curd Noodles

When customers walk into a traditional Chinese restaurant in Asia, small dishes are always served to nibble on as you contemplate the menu. This is such a dish. Fresh bean curd noodles are usually sold at Asian markets. If they are unavailable, press very firm tofu to remove excess water and cut into matchstick-size shreds.

SIX SERVINGS

1 pound bean curd noodles
2 tablespoons sesame seeds
1 teaspoon canola or corn oil
1 teaspoon toasted sesame oil
1 teaspoon hot chile paste (optional)
1 1/2 leeks, cleaned, ends trimmed, and cut into thin shreds 2 inches long (about 3 to 4 cups)

2 tablespoons rice wine or sake
3 cups bean sprouts, rinsed and drained

Garlic Dressing (mixed together)
1/2 cup soy sauce
5 1/2 tablespoons rice wine or sake
2 1/2 tablespoons minced garlic
2 1/2 teaspoons sugar

1. Bring 2 quarts water to a boil, add the bean curd noodles, and blanch for 1 minute. Drain in a colander and set aside.

2. Toast the sesame seeds until golden in a dry frying pan over medium-low heat for 15 minutes, tossing occasionally. Set aside.

3. Heat a wok or heavy skillet until hot, add the oils, and heat until hot. Add the hot chile paste and stir about 10 seconds, then add the leeks and toss to coat them. Add the rice wine or sake and stir-fry over high heat about 1 1/2 minutes, until just tender. Add the bean sprouts and toss lightly for 30 seconds.

4. Add the premixed Garlic Dressing and the bean curd noodles. Toss lightly over high heat until heated through. Remove and spoon onto a platter. Sprinkle the sesame seeds over the top. Serve hot or at room temperature.

☯ Tofu is extraordinarily versatile, and in noodle form it provides a wonderful staple for different foods and dressings. Since tofu is coolish in nature, it is not unusual for it to be cooked with pungent seasonings such as garlic and hot chiles to provide balance.

Vegetarian Roll-Ups

Despite their lack of meat, these rolls will satisfy even the most hardened carnivores. They are chock-full of vibrant seasonings, such as smoky black mushrooms, leeks, garlic, and fresh ginger. I serve them wrapped in steamed Chinese spring roll skins or flour tortillas for a delicious starter dish or a light entrée.

1 pound very firm tofu, cut into 1/2-inch slabs (substitute 5-spice tofu, if available, for extra bite)

24 spring roll skins, lumpia wrappers, or flour tortillas brushed with a little toasted sesame oil

2 tablespoons safflower or corn oil

Seasonings

2 1/2 tablespoons minced garlic

2 tablespoons minced fresh ginger

10 dried Chinese black mushrooms, softened in hot water for 20 minutes, stems removed and discarded, and caps shredded

2 leeks, ends trimmed, cleaned and cut into matchstick-size shreds (about 4 to 5 cups)

4 cups finely shredded Chinese (Napa) cabbage

2 carrots, peeled and grated (about 2 cups)

1 1/2 tablespoons rice wine or sake

Sauce (mixed together)

3 tablespoons soy sauce

1 1/2 teaspoons toasted sesame oil

1/4 teaspoon freshly ground black pepper

1/2 teaspoon cornstarch

1/2 cup hoisin sauce heated with 3 tablespoons water

MAKES ABOUT 24 ROLLS

1. Wrap the tofu slabs in paper towels or a cotton towel, and place a heavy weight such as a cast-iron skillet on top. Let stand for 30 minutes to press out the excess water, then cut into matchstick-size shreds about 2 inches long.

2. Separate the spring roll skins (or lumpia wrappers or flour tortillas), fold in half, arrange in a steamer, and steam for 5 minutes. Cover and keep warm.

3. Heat a wok or large skillet, add the oil, and heat until hot. Add the Seasonings and stir-fry about 10 seconds. Add the leeks, and stir-fry about 1 minute, then add the cabbage, carrots, and rice wine and cook, tossing, until the vegetables are crisp-tender. Add the premixed Sauce and stir-fry until thickened. Scoop the vegetables onto a platter.

4. To serve, smear a spring roll skin, lumpia wrapper, or flour tortilla with a dollop of hoisin sauce, arrange some of the stir-fried vegetarian mixture on top, roll up, and eat.

☯ Tofu is a superb substitute for meat, especially when seasoned with vibrant flavorings and stir-fried with assorted vegetables. Chinese nutritionists advise marinating tofu in garlic and ginger, then baking it to reduce its cool nature.

Fragrant Steamed Pearl Balls

This dish was inspired by the wonderful balls of ground meat coated with sweet rice that are so popular in western China. I love this vegetarian version, which is fragrant with black mushrooms, fresh ginger, and toasted sesame oil. Serve the pearl balls as an appetizer or a snack. They can be made in advance, and they reheat beautifully.

MAKES 36 BALLS

1 cup sweet (glutinous) or Arborio rice

1 pound firm tofu, cut into 1/2-inch slabs

14 dried Chinese black mushrooms, softened in hot water for 20 minutes and stems removed

3/4 cup water chestnuts, blanched 15 seconds in boiling water, then refreshed under cold water (see page 21)

1 1/2 cups grated carrots (1/2 cup for garnish)

Seasonings

2 tablespoons minced fresh ginger

1 1/2 tablespoons minced scallions, white part only

1 1/2 tablespoons soy sauce

1 1/2 teaspoons salt, or to taste

1 1/2 teaspoons toasted sesame oil

1 egg, lightly beaten

1 egg white, lightly beaten

3 to 4 tablespoons cornstarch

1. Rinse the rice in a strainer under cold running water, raking it with your fingers, until the water runs clear. Drain the rice, and put it in cold water to cover. Let it sit for 1 hour, then drain it in a colander, pour it onto a tray or cookie sheet, and spread it out in an even layer.

2. Wrap the tofu slabs in paper towels or a cotton towel, and set a heavy weight, such as a cast-iron skillet, on top. Let the tofu stand for 30 minutes to press out excess water; then, using a fork, mash it until smooth in a large mixing bowl.

3. Shred the black mushroom caps by hand, or mince them in a food processor fitted with a steel blade. Blot the water chestnuts dry with paper towels and chop by hand or with a food processor fitted with a steel blade.

4. Add to the mashed tofu the black mushrooms, 1 cup of the carrots, the water chestnuts, and the Seasonings. Stir vigorously to combine the ingredients. Add the egg, egg white, and cornstarch, and mix until smooth and sticky. Add a little more cornstarch if the mixture is too loose.

○ In the East, tofu is believed to lubricate and detoxify the body, whereas in the West, now some studies are showing that soybean products contain phytoestrogens, which are helpful in relieving menopausal symptoms. They also may reduce the risk of breast cancer.

Fragrant Steamed Pearl Balls (continued)

5. Shape the tofu mixture into balls about 1 inch in diameter and roll each ball in the rice so that the outside is completely coated. Line a steamer tray with parchment paper or waxed paper and arrange the rice-coated balls in the tray. Alternatively, place the balls on an aluminum pie plate with holes on the bottom.

6. Fill a wok or large pot with several inches of water and heat until boiling. Arrange the steamer tray or pie plate on a rack over the boiling water, cover, and steam for 20 minutes. Arrange the pearl balls on a serving platter and sprinkle on top the remaining grated carrots. Serve with soy sauce for dipping. To reheat, steam for 5 minutes until piping hot.

Spicy Ma Po Tofu

According to legend, ma po bean curd, a classic Sichuan specialty, was first created in the late 1800s by a Mrs. Chen, who was reputed to have a pockmarked face, hence the Chinese name for the dish—*Chen ma po tofu* ("Chen's pockmarked bean curd").

1 pound firm tofu, cut into 1-inch slabs
1/2 pound lean ground pork

Marinade
1 tablespoon soy sauce
1 tablespoon rice wine or sake
1/2 teaspoon toasted sesame oil

2 teaspoons canola or corn oil

Seasonings
3 tablespoons minced scallions, white part
    only

1 1/2 tablespoons minced fresh ginger
1 1/2 tablespoons minced garlic
1 teaspoon hot chile paste, or to taste

Braising Mixture (mixed together)
1 1/2 cups chicken broth or water
3 tablespoons soy sauce
1 tablespoon rice wine or sake

1 tablespoon cornstarch mixed with 1 1/2
    tablespoons water
3 tablespoons minced scallion greens

1. Wrap the tofu slabs in paper towels or a cotton towel and set a heavy weight, such as a cast-iron skillet, on top. Let stand for 30 minutes to press out the excess water, then cut the tofu into 1/4-inch-thick slices.

2. Put the ground pork in a bowl, add the Marinade, and mix with your hands.

3. Heat a wok or large skillet, add 1/2 teaspoon of the oil, and heat until hot. Add the meat and cook, mashing and chopping the meat with a slotted spoon or spatula to separate it. Cook, tossing lightly, until it changes color; then remove it with the slotted spoon and drain it in a colander. Clean the pan.

4. Heat the remaining 1 1/2 teaspoons of oil until hot. Add the Seasonings and stir-fry for 15 seconds, until fragrant. Add the Braising Mixture and bring to a boil. Add the tofu and meat and reduce the heat to low. Partially cover and cook the tofu for 20 minutes. Uncover and slowly add the cornstarch, stirring while it thickens. Shovel into a serving bowl, sprinkle the top with the minced scallions, and serve with steamed rice.

☯ Traditionally, this dish is made with pork, but for treating irregular menstruation, Chinese doctors urge their patients to substitute lamb and add a generous portion of fresh ginger.

Cantonese-Style Tofu in Black Bean Sauce

Few dishes are as delicious or satisfying as those made with this garlicky black bean sauce. The tofu rendition here is superb as a rice-sending dish, and it makes a wonderful meal-in-one dinner.

SIX SERVINGS

1 1/2 pounds tofu, cut into 1/2-inch slabs

Garlic Marinade
3 tablespoons soy sauce
2 tablespoons minced garlic
1 teaspoon toasted sesame oil

3 1/2 tablespoons canola or corn oil

Minced Seasonings
3 tablespoons fermented black beans, rinsed, drained, and minced
2 tablespoons minced garlic
2 tablespoons minced fresh ginger
1 teaspoon hot chile paste

2 red onions, peeled and thinly sliced
1 red bell pepper, cored, seeded, and cut into thin julienne strips
1 yellow bell pepper, cored, seeded, and cut into thin julienne strips
1/2 pound snow peas, ends snapped and veiny strings removed

Sauce (mixed together)
1 1/2 cups Classic Chicken Broth (page 27)
3 tablespoons soy sauce
3 tablespoons rice wine or sake
1 tablespoon sugar
2 teaspoons cornstarch

☯ For many Cantonese, tofu cooked with ginger is a surefire way to "sweat out" a cold. According to Dr. Albert Leung, black beans have been used for centuries by the Chinese in treating illnesses that involve the lungs and the digestive system.

1. Wrap the tofu slabs in paper towels or a cotton towel, and set a heavy weight, such as a cast-iron skillet, on top. Let them stand for 30 minutes to press out excess water. Then cut them into slices about 1/2 inch thick and 2 1/2 inches long. Put them in a bowl.

2. Mix the Garlic Marinade and pour it over the tofu slices. Toss lightly to coat, cover with plastic wrap, and let the tofu sit at room temperature for 30 minutes.

3. Heat a heavy skillet, and add 2 1/2 tablespoons of the oil. When hot, arrange some of the tofu slices in the pan and sear over very high heat for 2 to 3 minutes on each side, or until golden brown. Remove with a slotted spoon and drain. Reheat the pan and continue frying the remaining slices. Remove and drain.

4. Heat the pan again, add the remaining 1 tablespoon oil and heat until hot, about 30 seconds; then add the Minced Seasonings. Stir-fry about 15 seconds, until fragrant, then add the onions and bell peppers. Toss lightly with a slotted spoon or spatula over high heat and cook about 2 minutes, until the onions and peppers are slightly tender. Add the snow peas and the Sauce, and toss lightly until the sauce has thickened. Add the fried tofu slices and stir the vegetables and sauce with a spatula to coat them. Scoop the tofu and vegetables onto a platter and serve with steamed rice.

Vegetarian Kung Pao with Broccoli and Peanuts

This hearty and delicious entrée incorporates the best of Sichuan cooking: The spicy sauce plays off the contrasting textures of tender tofu, crisp peanuts, and crunchy broccoli.

SIX SERVINGS

1 1/2 pounds firm tofu, cut into 1/2-inch slabs

1 pound broccoli, ends trimmed and stalks peeled

5 1/2 tablespoons canola or corn oil

Seasonings

3 tablespoons minced scallions, white part only

2 tablespoons minced garlic

2 tablespoons minced fresh ginger

1 teaspoon hot chile paste

1 cup 1-inch lengths scallion greens (about 3 scallions)

1 1/2 cups thinly sliced water chestnuts, blanched 10 seconds in boiling water, then refreshed in cold water and drained (see page 21)

Sauce (mixed together)

1 cup Classic Chicken Broth (page 27)

1 tablespoon soy sauce

3 1/2 tablespoons rice wine or sake

2 tablespoons sugar

1 teaspoon toasted sesame oil

1 tablespoon Chinese black vinegar or Worcestershire sauce

1 1/4 tablespoons cornstarch

1 1/4 cups dry-roasted peanuts

1. Wrap the tofu slabs in paper towels or a cotton towel, and place a heavy weight, such as a cast-iron skillet, on top. Let stand for 30 minutes to press out the excess water. Cut the tofu into slices about 1/2 inch thick and 2 1/2 inches long. Place them in a bowl.

2. Cut away the broccoli florets and separate into bite-size pieces. Cut the stalks on the diagonal into 1-inch pieces. Heat a large pot of water until boiling. Add the broccoli, and boil for 3 minutes. Drain, refresh under cold water, and drain again.

3. Heat a large, heavy skillet and add 2 1/2 tablespoons of the oil. Arrange some of the tofu slices in the pan and sear over high heat for 3 to 4 minutes on each side, or until golden brown. Remove with a spatula and drain in a colander. Reheat the pan and add 2 more tablespoons of oil. Continue frying the rest of the slices. Remove and drain.

4. Reheat the skillet or a wok, add the remaining tablespoon of oil, heat until hot, and add the Seasonings. Stir-fry briefly, about 15 seconds, then add the scallion greens and water chestnuts, and stir-fry over high heat about $1^1/_2$ minutes. Add the premixed Sauce, and cook, stirring continuously to prevent lumps, until it thickens. Add the broccoli, fried tofu, and peanuts. Toss lightly to coat and heat through. Scoop the dish onto a serving platter. Serve with steamed rice.

☯ Tofu stir-fried with vinegar is a traditional folk remedy for malaria and dysentery. Peanuts are believed to improve the appetite and lubricate the lungs. An age-old remedy for hypertension is ground peanut shells steeped in water to make a tea that is drunk 3 times a day for at least 20 days.

Curried Tofu

In Singapore and Malaysia, vibrant seasonings from India, China, Europe, and Thailand are blended to make superb-tasting spice mixtures. This dish, with its sumptuous sauce, would make an excellent, satisfying meal paired with rice.

SIX SERVINGS

1 pound firm tofu, cut into 1-inch slabs
1 1/2 teaspoons canola or corn oil

Seasonings
1 1/2 tablespoons minced garlic, about 5 to 6 cloves
1 1/2 tablespoons minced fresh ginger
1 teaspoon crushed dried chiles, or to taste
1 teaspoon ground turmeric
1 teaspoon fennel seeds
1 teaspoon dried oregano
1 teaspoon ground coriander
1 teaspoon ground cumin

2 medium onions, coarsely chopped (about 1 1/2 cups)
4 tomatoes, peeled, seeded, and diced, or 1 28-ounce can tomatoes, seeded and diced
1/4 cup light coconut milk (if unavailable, use regular coconut milk)
1 pound cauliflower or broccoli florets
2 cups fresh or frozen peas
1/4 cup plain nonfat yogurt
1 1/4 teaspoons salt, or to taste
1 tablespoon chopped fresh cilantro

☯ This nourishing stew, with its spicy seasonings, would be perfect on a cold winter's day, but it's equally appropriate for warm weather, when the tofu will drive the heat out of the body.

1. Wrap the tofu slabs in paper towels or a cotton towel, and place a heavy weight, such as a cast-iron skillet, on top. Let stand for 30 minutes to press out the excess water, then cut into 1/4-inch dice.
2. Heat a large casserole or Dutch oven, add the oil, and heat until hot. Add the Seasonings and stir-fry about 10 seconds, until fragrant. Reduce the heat to low and add the onions, cooking and stirring about 4 minutes, until soft and translucent.
3. Add the tomatoes and coconut milk, and cook at low heat, stirring, for 5 to 7 minutes. Add the tofu and cauliflower or broccoli and cook, covered, for 12 to 15 minutes, or until the vegetable is almost tender.
4. Add the peas, cover, and cook about 3 minutes, stirring once. Remove from the heat and stir in the yogurt and salt. Garnish with cilantro and ladle over rice.

Braised Cinnamon Tofu

Braised Cinnamon Beef used to be one of my favorite dishes, which would always soothe and nurture me as a student many years ago. I've revised the recipe slightly, substituting tofu for the beef, and the dish is equally delicious.

1 teaspoon safflower or corn oil

Seasonings
6 whole scallions, ends trimmed, smashed
   lightly with the flat side of a knife and cut
   into 1 1/2-inch sections
6 garlic cloves, smashed lightly with the flat
   side of a knife and sliced thinly
4 slices fresh ginger, about the size of a quarter, smashed lightly with the flat side of a
   knife

1 teaspoon hot chile paste
2 sticks cinnamon
1 teaspoon anise seed

1/2 cup soy sauce
6 cups water
2 pounds firm tofu, cut into 1-inch cubes
1 pound spinach, stems trimmed, rinsed,
   and drained
3 tablespoons minced scallion greens

1. Heat a large pot or casserole over medium-high heat, add the oil, heat until hot, about 30 seconds, and add the Seasonings. Stir-fry until fragrant, about 15 seconds, then add the soy sauce and water. Heat until boiling, add the tofu, and boil again. Reduce the heat to low, cover, and simmer, skimming the surface to remove impurities and fat. Cook for 1 hour, until the tofu is drenched with the flavors of the braising mixture. Remove the ginger slices and cinnamon sticks and discard.
2. Add the spinach clump by clump to the tofu and heat until boiling. Ladle the mixture into serving bowls, sprinkle scallion greens on top, and serve.

Although soybean milk has many nutritional benefits, it's difficult to digest. Tofu, which is cooked soybean milk that has become a curd, is far easier, and this dish, where the tofu is simmered in a soy sauce–based braising mixture enriched with anise seed and cinnamon sticks, is wonderfully soothing.

Simmered Tofu with Black Mushrooms

My surrogate Chinese grandfather adored this dish of tender tofu drenched in oyster sauce and garnished with smoky black mushrooms. I always make it at New Year's time in tribute to his memory.

1 pound firm tofu, cut into 1/2-inch slabs

10 dried Chinese black mushrooms, soaked in 1 1/2 cups hot water for 20 minutes (reserve 1 cup of the soaking liquid), stems removed

1 1/2 teaspoons canola or corn oil

1 1/2 tablespoons minced garlic

2 whole scallions, ends trimmed, and cut into 1-inch sections

Simmering Mixture (mixed together)

2 cups Classic Chicken Broth (page 27)

1 cup reserved mushroom liquid

2 1/2 tablespoons oyster sauce

1 1/2 tablespoons soy sauce

1 1/2 tablespoons rice wine or sake

1 teaspoon sugar

1 tablespoon cornstarch mixed with 2 tablespoons water

🌀 Since tofu is believed to lower cholesterol levels and influence hormonal levels, and black mushrooms bolster the immune system, I like to eat this dish or a variation once a week, especially during the cold and flu season.

1. Wrap the tofu slabs in paper towels or a cotton towel, and place a heavy weight, such as a cast-iron skillet, on top. Let stand for 30 minutes to press out the excess water, then cut into 1/2-inch thick slices about 1 1/2 inches long.

2. Cut the black mushroom caps into halves or thirds, depending on their size.

3. Heat a wok, casserole, or Dutch oven, add the oil, and heat until very hot. Add the garlic, scallions, and black mushrooms, and stir-fry about 10 seconds, until fragrant. Add the premixed Simmering Mixture and heat until boiling. Add the tofu slices and bring the liquid to a boil again. Reduce the heat to medium low, cover, and simmer for 20 minutes. Uncover, increase the heat to medium, and cook for 15 more minutes, until the sauce is reduced by half. Add the cornstarch mixture and cook, stirring continuously to prevent lumps, until the sauce has thickened. Ladle the tofu and sauce into a serving bowl and serve with steamed rice and a vegetable.

Fried Tempeh with Sweet and Sour Sauce

Tempeh, which is a fermented soybean cake, is extraordinarily versatile. I find that searing the cakes in a bit of oil really highlights its nutty flavor. Tempeh is a wonderful foil for a sweet and sour sauce.

6 tablespoons virgin olive oil

1 pound soy tempeh, cut into slices 1/2 inch thick and 2 inches long, then cut diagonally in half

1 tablespoon canola or corn oil

Seasonings

2 tablespoons minced scallions, white part only

11/2 tablespoons minced garlic

1 tablespoon minced fresh ginger

1 large red bell pepper, cored and seeded, and cut into 1/2-inch squares

Sweet and Sour Sauce (mixed together)

1 tablespoons ketchup

41/2 tablespoons clear rice vinegar

41/2 tablespoons sugar

11/2 tablespoons soy sauce

1 teaspoon toasted sesame oil

1 cup water

2 teaspoons cornstarch

11/2 cups canned cubed pineapple, drained

1/2 pound snow peas, ends snapped, veiny strings removed, blanched for 10 seconds in boiling water, refreshed under cold water, and drained

1. Heat a nonstick frying pan, add the olive oil, and heat until very hot, about 375°F. Fry the tempeh in batches until golden brown on both sides. Reheat the oil between each batch. Remove the tempeh with a slotted spoon and drain on paper towels. Discard the oil.

2. Reheat the pan, add the canola or corn oil, and heat until very hot. Add the Seasonings and stir-fry over high heat about 15 seconds, until fragrant. Add the red pepper and stir-fry for 11/2 minutes over high heat. Add the Sauce and cook, stirring continuously to prevent lumps. Add the pineapple and snow peas, and cook over high heat for about 2 to 3 minutes to heat, then add the tempeh slices. Toss lightly with your spatula to coat, and spoon onto a serving platter. Serve hot with steamed rice.

For many decades tempeh has been promoted as a healthy alternative to meat because of its high protein content. Since it's made of soybeans, it possesses many of the same admirable properties.

Spicy Stir-Fried Tempeh with Basil

I adore the taste of this sumptuous stir-fry, with its fresh flavorings of garlic, red onion, and Thai holy basil. Thai holy basil, with its small purple leaves, is slightly more intense than sweet basil. It's sold in Asian markets, but if it's unavailable, substitute sweet basil.

SIX SERVINGS

1 1/2 pounds soy tempeh, cut into slices 1/2 inch thick and 2 inches long, then cut diagonally in half

Marinade

3 tablespoons soy sauce

1 1/2 tablespoons rice wine or sake

1 1/2 tablespoons minced shallots

1 teaspoon toasted sesame oil

2 tablespoons canola or corn oil

Seasonings

2 tablespoons chopped fresh red chile, ends trimmed and seeds removed

2 tablespoons chopped garlic

2 medium red onions, peeled and cut into thin julienne slices

Sauce (mixed together)

2 tablespoons fish sauce

1 1/2 tablespoons soy sauce

1 tablespoon sugar

1 1/2 tablespoons water

1 1/2 cups fresh Thai holy basil or sweet basil leaves, stems removed, rinsed, drained, and coarsely shredded

☯ Tempeh is definitely the food of the future: It is extraordinarily nutritious and is often recommended in Asia for frail people. Also, along with other soy products, it is believed to be especially effective in preventing cancer and heart disease.

1. Put the tempeh in a bowl, add the Marinade, and mix to coat. Marinate 20 minutes.
2. Prepare a medium-hot fire for grilling or heat a heavy skillet for searing. Arrange the tempeh 3 inches from the source of heat and grill about 3 to 4 minutes per side. Alternatively, you may sear the tempeh on each side for 2 to 3 minutes in 1 teaspoon of hot oil. Remove, let cool slightly, and cut on the diagonal into thin slices.
3. Heat a wok or skillet, add the oil and heat until very hot, about 30 seconds. Add the Seasonings, and stir-fry about 1 1/2 to 2 minutes, or until the onions are tender, tossing over high heat. Give the premixed Sauce another stir and add to the pan. Bring to a boil. Add the cooked tempeh and fresh basil; baste the tempeh with the sauce. Transfer to a serving platter and serve with rice and a vegetable, if desired.

Ginger Teriyaki Tempeh

There are many variations of tempeh: Soybeans are usually the base, but they may be blended with rice, wheat, millet, or even peanuts. This wonderfully versatile food is especially delicious marinated first in this gingery teriyaki sauce and then grilled or broiled.

Ginger Teriyaki Marinade (mixed together)	1 1/2 pounds soy tempeh
1/3 cup soy sauce	2 red bell peppers, seeded, cored, and cut into 1-inch squares
1/3 cup rice wine or sake	16 small white boiling onions, peeled and blanched in boiling water for 10 minutes
4 1/2 tablespoons sugar	
1 1/2 tablespoons minced ginger	
1/2 teaspoon crushed dried chiles or dried chile flakes (optional)	12 10-inch bamboo or metal skewers (if bamboo, soak in cold water for 1 hour)
1 tablespoon cornstarch	

SIX SERVINGS

1. In a saucepan, combine the Ginger Teriyaki Marinade with 1/3 cup water and heat until thickened, stirring constantly to prevent lumps. Remove and let cool about 10 minutes.

2. Cut the tempeh into 1-inch squares. Thread the tempeh squares, red pepper, and onions alternately onto the skewers and arrange them in a deep dish. Pour the Ginger Teriyaki Marinade on top. Turn the skewers to thoroughly coat the tempeh and vegetables. Marinate for 1 hour.

3. Heat the broiler or prepare a fire for grilling and arrange the tempeh and vegetables about 3 inches from the source of heat. Broil or grill about 6 to 7 minutes on each side, turning once and brushing with the marinade. Remove, place on a serving platter, and serve.

☯ In Indonesia, where this soybean food originated, tempeh is often eaten to stop diarrhea. It's also believed to increase the body's resistance to infections.

The Neutralizers:
Rice, Breads, and Noodles

Rice, Breads, Noodles, and Dr. Yu

The banquet began like many others. There were eight appetizers: Paper-thin slices of fresh ginger were interlaced with crab. Crispy-fried beef was seasoned with chiles and orange peel. Steamed river shrimps were served with dodder, a vine in the morning glory family that is credited with quelling dizziness, and thin strips of succulent red-cooked eel, recommended for combating fatigue and alleviating hemorrhoids.

The main entrées were also sumptuous: There were sea cucumbers, which tone the kidney; red-cooked turtle, the ultimate yin delicacy; and luscious prawns with Chinese yam, which is a tonic for the lungs, spleen, and kidneys.

We were in Shanghai, but this meal was not at one of the city's many notable restaurants. We were eating in the private dining room of the Shanghai College of Traditional Medicine as guests of the college's president and Professor Xue Ru Yu, a practicing doctor and teacher there. Dr. Yu has also devoted the past sixteen years to the study of food as medicine.

Dr. Yu's research is exemplary of a new field in Chinese medicine called "dietotherapy." "Dietotherapy refers to the treatment of certain diseases by consuming common foods," Dr. Yu said as we feasted on tender quail served with cordyceps, an herb that enriches bone marrow and builds *qi* in the body.

Dr. Yu explained that her work has two stages: First she investigates the food's nature and ability to prevent and treat disease by researching ancient texts. Next, the clinical aspect comes into play as, in some cases, the food is combined with herbs, and then administered to patients for results.

Later that day, we were treated to another extraordinary meal. This time it was prepared at the Changhai Hospital in the outskirts of Shanghai. Here, master chefs under the direction of Yuan Zeng Xi, a nutritionist, prepared such extraordinary specialties as stir-fried shrimp with wolfberries, rolled fish with jade skin syrup, bean curd dumplings, and melon balls with the essence of rose petals. Ms. Xi explained that all of the dishes were developed by the Shanghai Medicated Diet and Dietotherapy experts, specially designed to nourish, preserve, and bolster good health, and to prevent disease.

The concept of dietotherapy is by no means new to China. But to consider it a science, which is now being taught in schools and used in selected hospitals, is quite recent. At the Academy of Traditional Chinese Medicine in Beijing, Dr. Jingfeng Cai, author of *Eating Your Way to Health—Dietotherapy in Traditional Chinese Medicine* (Foreign Language Press, 1988), is another pioneer.

"During the last few decades, cancer and cardiovascular diseases have replaced infectious diseases in China as a common threat to good health," Dr. Yu said. "These types of diseases, especially cardiovascular and some types of cancer, are closely tied to food habits."

As these doctors and others have noted, Chinese food habits (in China) have changed radically in the last few years. Previously the Chinese diet was based on staples, such as rice, noodles, breads, and other grains, with fresh and pickled vegetables, seafoods, and meats served as garnishes. But as the Chinese have prospered, they have revised their daily regimen, increasing the amount of meat and decreasing the amount of rice and other staples. As a result, their health has suffered, and they are now developing the "diseases of prosperity," such as diabetes, heart disease, hypertension, and cancer. (This fact has been proven conclusively by the Cornell, China, and Oxford Project on Nutrition, Health, and Environment, which began in 1983 and published its first results in 1990. The study is still ongoing.)

Eating rice or other grains as a staple can be traced back thousands of years. In the *Book of Songs,* written during the Chou period (1122 to 256 B.C.), it is stated, "The meat that he eats must at the very most not be enough to make his breath smell of meat rather than rice."

Rice, millet, sorghum, and wheat have long been highly regarded by the Chinese both for their nutritional value and their ability to flourish in different climates. While some grains are credited with different properties for various ailments, most are considered the neutralizers of the food chain. Rice tones the middle region, strengthens the spleen, harmonizes the stomach, and energizes. Wheat nourishes the heart, benefits the kidneys, and clears heat from the body. Most important, grains help to provide balance, the key to good health.

As Paul Pitchford writes in his masterful book, *Healing with Whole Foods: Oriental Traditions and Modern Nutrition* (North Atlantic Books, 1993), "If prepared in balance with individual needs, grains satisfy hunger and taste, provide energy and endurance, calm nerves, and encourage deep sleep."

Basic Cooked White Rice

Rice is the staff of life in much of Asia and, depending on the area, the rice may vary: The Japanese prefer short-grain sticky or sweet rice. The Chinese in Hong Kong and China like long-grain, while those in Taiwan like a slightly shorter grain. In much of the rest of Asia, particularly Thailand and Vietnam, long-grain jasmine rice is the rice of choice. Personally, I love the slightly nutty flavor of jasmine or basmati rice. Both of these varieties are available at well-stocked supermarkets.

SIX SERVINGS

2³/4 cups long-grain rice	4¹/4 cups water

☯ Chinese newborns who cannot tolerate their mothers' milk are often given an ancient remedy of a tea made from pan-roasted rice steeped in hot water. It is believed to soothe and strengthen the stomach.

1. Put the rice in a saucepan and, using your fingers as a rake, rinse it under cold running water to remove some of the talc. Drain it in a colander.
2. Place the rice and water in a heavy saucepan with a lid. Heat uncovered until the water boils. Reduce the heat to low, cover, and simmer about 17 to 18 minutes, or until the water has evaporated and craters appear on the surface. Remove from the heat and fluff lightly with a fork to separate the grains. Serve immediately or, if using it for fried rice, spread the rice out in a thin layer on a tray. Let it cool completely, cover with plastic wrap, and chill in the refrigerator overnight.

To steam rice: Fill a wok or a pot with water for steaming and heat until boiling. Spread the rice in a steamer tray lined with damp cheesecloth or parchment paper, or in a lined pie plate, with a tunafish can, both ends removed, for support. Place the steamer tray over boiling water, cover, and steam 35 to 40 minutes, or until tender. Fluff the rice with a fork and serve or spread out and chill on a tray as directed above.

Steamed Rice with Roasted Pine Nuts: Prepare the rice as directed in the recipe above, undercooking it by 10 minutes for each method. Toast ¹/4 cup pine nuts until golden in a 300°F. oven, about 20 minutes, turning the nuts occasionally so that they cook evenly. Sprinkle the pine nuts over the almost cooked rice and mix them in with 1 teaspoon salt. Cover and continue cooking for 10 minutes, or until tender. Serve.

Cinnamon Curry Rice

Cinnamon is considered one of the most warming herbs by the Chinese, since it is reputed to enhance circulation. Chinese cinnamon is from a type of laurel tree cultivated only in China. It marries particularly well with other seasonings, like the curry in this fried rice dish. Other vegetables and cubed meat may be added as garnishes.

4 sticks cinnamon

3 3/4 cups water

2 cups long-grain rice

2 1/2 teaspoons safflower or corn oil

1 1/2 cups thinly sliced leeks

1 1/2 tablespoons minced garlic

2 tablespoons good-quality curry powder

3 to 4 carrots, peeled and cut into 1/4-inch dice (about 1 1/2 cups)

3 to 4 turnips, peeled and cut into 1/4-inch dice (about 1 1/2 cups)

3 1/2 tablespoons rice wine or sake

1/2 cup water

1 1/2 cups cooked peas (if using frozen, thaw to room temperature)

Sauce (mixed together)

1 1/2 tablespoons soy sauce

1 tablespoon rice wine or sake

1 teaspoon salt

1/2 teaspoon freshly ground black pepper

SIX SERVINGS

Chinese cassia, or cinnamon, has been used by Asian doctors for thousands of years in treating colds, rheumatism, and diarrhea. Chinese scientists have discovered that it lowers high blood pressure and acts as a sedative. When consumed in large quantities, it will create a "hot" condition and should then be counteracted with coolish foods, such as mung beans and chrysanthemum tea. For coughs and sore throats, boil several strips in water, and inhale the vapors.

1. Put the cinnamon sticks and the water in a pot and bring to a boil. Cook about 5 minutes over medium heat. Under cold running water, rinse the rice in a saucepan until the water runs clear. Drain and add the rice to the cinnamon water. Bring the water to a boil again, reduce the heat to low, and cover. Simmer covered for 17 minutes, or until craters appear in the surface of the rice and the water has been absorbed. Remove from the heat and fluff the cooked grains with a fork. Cover and let sit for 15 minutes, then uncover and spread the rice out on a cookie sheet with a fork to cool completely. Discard the cinnamon sticks. (The rice should be cold or at least room temperature before stir-frying.)
2. Heat a wok or large skillet. Add the safflower or corn oil and heat until hot. Add the leeks and garlic, and stir-fry over medium heat until slightly softened and translucent. Add the curry powder and stir-fry for 10 seconds, until fragrant. Add the carrots, turnips, rice wine, and water, and partially cover. Cook about 5 to 8 minutes, until tender, then add the cooked rice, breaking it up with a spatula. Add the peas and the premixed Sauce. Toss lightly to coat the ingredients and spoon into a serving dish. Serve hot.

Seafood Rice Casserole

When I lived in Taipei, my surrogate Chinese mother would often make this as a meal-in-one dinner or Sunday lunch. The ingredients would vary depending on the seafood or vegetables in season or available.

SIX SERVINGS

1/2 pound firm-fleshed fish fillet, such as haddock, red snapper, or lake trout
1/2 pound medium shrimp, shelled

Marinade
3 tablespoons rice wine or sake
1 1/2 tablespoons minced fresh ginger
1 teaspoon sesame oil

1/2 pound fresh shiitake mushrooms, stems removed
1 teaspoon safflower or corn oil
4 cloves garlic, peeled and smashed lightly with the flat side of a knife
1 Chinese (Napa) cabbage, about 1 1/2 pounds, cut into 2-inch squares, stem and leafy sections separated
1/3 cup rice wine or sake
4 cups Classic Chicken Broth (page 27)
1 teaspoon salt
2 1/4 cups long-grain rice
1 bunch (1/2 pound) enoki mushrooms, stem ends trimmed, rinsed lightly, and drained
1/2 square firm tofu, about 1/2 pound, cut into 1/4-inch dice (optional)
2 whole scallions, ends trimmed, cut into thin diagonal slices

Mongolian Sauce (mixed together)
3/4 cup soy sauce
3 1/2 tablespoons rice wine or sake
3 1/2 tablespoons Chinese black vinegar or Worcestershire sauce
3 tablespoons minced scallions, white part only
2 tablespoons minced fresh ginger
2 tablespoons minced garlic
2 tablespoons sugar
1 teaspoon hot chile paste (optional)

This one-pot seafood rice dish is a wonderful meal-in-one lunch or dinner. The different components of fish (cold) balanced by the vegetables (cooling) and spicy sauce (hot), all complemented by the rice (neutral), make it a nicely balanced meal.

1. Cut the fish into 1-inch-square chunks and place them in a bowl. Cut the shrimp along the back almost all the way to butterfly them, and put them in the bowl with the fish. Add the Marinade, and stir to coat. Let the seafood marinate for 20 minutes. Cut the shiitake mushroom caps into thin slices.
2. Heat a 4-quart Dutch oven or a covered casserole, add the oil, and heat until hot, about 30 seconds. Add the garlic cloves and cabbage stems, and stir-fry for a minute

over medium-high heat. Add the rice wine, and toss lightly, then cover and cook for $1^1/_2$ minutes. Uncover, add the remaining cabbage, chicken broth, and salt. Partially cover and, once the broth reaches a boil, simmer for 5 minutes.

3. Meanwhile, put the rice in a bowl and, using your fingers as a rake, rinse it under cold water until the water runs clear. Drain it in a colander. Arrange the rice evenly over the bottom of a 4-quart casserole or a Dutch oven, and pour the cabbage with the broth on top. Cover, and cook on top of the stove for 15 minutes.

4. Preheat the oven to 450°F. Arrange the mushrooms and tofu in separate piles over the rice, leaving a space for the seafood. Cover and bake for 10 minutes. Uncover and arrange the seafood over the rice. Cover and bake another 8 minutes, or until the fish flakes when prodded with a fork.

5. Remove the casserole from the oven and sprinkle the scallions over the top. Let the food sit covered for a minute. Then spoon out individual portions of seafood, mushrooms, tofu, and rice into serving bowls, and sprinkle with the Mongolian Sauce. Serve immediately.

About Fried Rice

I've always loved fried rice, even as a child, when my family innocently (and incorrectly) ordered it as a side dish for our favorite Cantonese specialties like Lobster Cantonese and sweet and sour pork. It wasn't until I went to Taiwan, many years later, that I tasted *real* fried rice, which is far more delicate than the Americanized version, and learned that it is rarely ordered with entrées. I also discovered that it is extraordinarily versatile.

Throughout Asia, fried rice is traditionally served as a snack or as the main dish for a simple meal. In Taiwan, we would make soup and fried rice almost every Sunday for lunch. The recipe varied depending on what was available in the market and what was left over in the refrigerator. Occasionally, we even ate it for dinner, which is how I serve it now in my New England household. It's a light, easy, and totally satisfying meal.

Basically, fried rice is a dish principally made up of leftovers, starting with any leftover rice—even some ordered from a previous Chinese takeout meal. Myriad cooked meats, seafood, and vegetables can be diced and tossed with the cooked rice, creating a diverse repertoire. The kind of rice used can also vary: A friend in New York reports using leftover brown rice from several local Chinese restaurants. At first, I considered that variation a sacrilege, but inspired by her enthusiasm I experimented with brown rice, and the results were smashing.

The seasonings and ingredients usually vary depending on the cooks and their region. In eastern China, fried rice is loaded with shrimp, Chinese ham, black mushrooms, eggs, and peas. It is lightly seasoned with salt, black pepper, and chicken broth. Cantonese fried rice dishes are similar. Soy sauce is never added, since it darkens the dish. (Personally, I like to add a little for flavor.) Curry powder is another seasoning possibility. I often use vegetables and ingredients that correspond to the season: Sweet potatoes and squash make a sumptuous fried rice in the fall and winter, while corn, zucchini, fresh herbs, and grilled leftovers are delicious in warmer weather.

There are only a few set rules for fried rice. Long-grain rice, such as basmati, jasmine, or Carolina, is preferred, but brown rice is another option.

The following tips should help in the preparation of a perfect fried rice.

- Always begin with *cold,* or at least room-temperature, cooked rice. If the rice is still warm, it will clump together when it is fried. I suggest cooking the rice the day before and refrigerating it, fluffing and separating the grains before frying.

- Choose meat and vegetable garnishes that contrast in flavor, texture, and color. Cut them into uniform pieces so that the finished dish looks attractive.

- Aromatic seasonings like ginger, scallions, and curry powder can complement and enhance the taste of the garnishes. Use the stronger ones sparingly so that there is a full, even blending of flavors.

- While fried rice doesn't freeze well, it can be made in advance and reheated. To reheat fried rice, merely stir-fry or steam for several minutes before serving.

Wild Mushroom Fried Rice

Depending on the season and availability, I add whatever mushrooms happen to be on hand. Serve this as a side course–staple with barbecued or baked meat, seafood or chicken, or with soup as a light lunch or dinner.

SIX SERVINGS

2 tablespoons corn or safflower oil
8 cloves garlic, smashed lightly with the flat side of a knife, and sliced thinly
1/2 pound fresh shiitake mushrooms, rinsed, drained, stem ends trimmed, and caps thinly sliced
1/2 pound cremini mushrooms, rinsed, drained, stem ends trimmed, and caps thinly sliced

3 tablespoons rice wine or sake
2 cups minced scallion greens
5 cups cooked rice, chilled (see page 220)
31/2 tablespoons soy sauce
11/2 tablespoons chicken broth
1/2 teaspoon salt
1/2 teaspoon freshly ground black pepper
1/4 cup chopped fresh cilantro

1. Heat a wok or large, heavy skillet over high heat. Add the oil and heat until hot. Add the garlic and mushrooms and stir-fry for 1 to 2 minutes, until slightly softened. Lower the heat to medium high and add the rice wine. Partially cover and cook for $3^{1}/_{2}$ minutes, or until the mushrooms are tender. Uncover, add the scallions, and cook, tossing, to reduce the liquid by half.

2. Add the rice, breaking it up with a spatula. Cook 2 to 3 minutes, until heated through. Add the soy sauce, chicken broth, salt, and black pepper, and toss lightly to coat. Add the cilantro, toss to mix, and spoon the rice onto a platter and serve.

☯ During cold and flu season, I double the amount of shiitake mushrooms and add maitake for good measure, since both varieties bolster the immune system.

Scallion-Ginger Rice

Drawing inspiration from Cantonese cooks, who make a famous scallion-ginger noodle dish, I do the same with rice. This is delicious as an accompaniment to grilled, steamed, or stir-fried seafood. The rice is stir-fried until it's just heated through. Add a simple stir-fried or steamed green vegetable and you have a veritable feast.

2 tablespoons corn or canola oil	Sauce (mixed together)	SIX SERVINGS
2 1/2 cups minced whole scallions	3 tablespoons chicken broth	
3 tablespoons minced fresh ginger	1 tablespoon soy sauce	
1/3 cup rice wine or sake	1 1/2 teaspoons toasted sesame oil	
2 1/2 cups bean sprouts, rinsed and drained	1 1/2 teaspoons salt, or to taste	
5 cups cooked rice, chilled (see page 220), then separated with a fork	1/3 teaspoon freshly ground black pepper	

1. Heat a well-seasoned wok or a large nonstick skillet over high heat. Add the oil and heat until very hot. Add the scallions and ginger, and stir-fry over high heat until fragrant, about 20 seconds. Add the rice wine and bean sprouts, and toss lightly about 1 minute.

2. Add the rice and stir-fry about 2 to 3 minutes, until heated through. Add the premixed Sauce and toss lightly with a slotted spoon to coat the ingredients. Spoon onto a platter and serve.

☯ Rice is normally a neutral food, but with the addition of scallions and fresh ginger the overall effect is warming.

Shrimp Fried Rice

Shrimp Fried Rice is a Cantonese classic, and this is my adaptation. Unlike many of the versions prepared in Cantonese-American restaurants, authentic Shrimp Fried Rice is seasoned with salt, not soy sauce, which can darken the grains. I add a tiny bit of soy sauce, just for extra flavor.

2 tablespoons corn or safflower oil	Sauce (mixed together)
2 large eggs, lightly beaten	2 tablespoons chicken broth
2 cups minced whole scallions	2 tablespoons rice wine
1 tablespoon minced fresh ginger	1 tablespoon soy sauce
3/4 pound peeled, cooked shrimp, sliced in half along the back	1 teaspoon salt
	1 teaspoon toasted sesame oil
13/4 cups cooked fresh or defrosted frozen peas (10-ounce package)	1/4 teaspoon freshly ground black pepper
5 cups cooked rice, chilled (see page 220), and separated with a fork	

1. Heat a wok or large skillet, add the oil, and heat until hot. Add the eggs and stir-fry over high heat about 30 seconds to scramble them. Add the minced scallions and ginger and stir-fry about 1 minute.

2. Add the shrimp and peas and toss lightly to heat through, then add the rice. Stir-fry about 2 to 3 minutes, until heated through. Add the premixed Sauce and toss lightly to coat all the ingredients. Spoon the shrimp fried rice into a serving bowl and serve.

Basic Cooked Brown Rice

Brown rice used to be available only at health food stores. These days it is sold in most supermarkets, and different varieties, such as brown basmati rice, are even offered.

2 1/2 cups long-grain brown rice	4 1/4 cups water	SIX SERVINGS

1. Put the rice in a pot and, using your fingers as a rake, rinse it under cold running water. Drain it in a colander.
2. Place the water in a heavy saucepan with a lid. Heat uncovered until the water reaches a boil, add the rice, boil again, reduce the heat to low, cover, and simmer for 35 to 40 minutes, until the rice is just tender. Remove from the heat and fluff lightly with a fork to separate the grains. Serve hot with food, or cool before stir-frying: Drain the rice in a colander and let it cool, stirring from time to time, then spread it out on a tray. You may refrigerate before using. Use as directed in the following recipes.

☯ Brown rice is prescribed for nausea, diarrhea, and mental depression. It is believed to strengthen the spleen and pancreas and increase the body's *qi*.

Barbecued Pork Brown Rice

The brown rice in this dish adds just the right balance to the barbecued pork and leeks, and you can add soy sauce without worrying about muddying up the rice. This is a wonderful meal in itself.

SIX SERVINGS

1 pound center-cut pork loin (or purchase barbecued pork loin in Chinatown or use leftover roasted pork)

Barbecue Sauce
1/4 cup hoisin sauce
2 tablespoons soy sauce
1 tablespoon minced garlic
1 tablespoon ketchup
1/2 to 3/4 teaspoon five-spice powder (optional)

1 1/2 tablespoons corn or canola oil
1 1/2 tablespoons minced fresh ginger
2 1/2 cups minced leeks, cleaned thoroughly

1/2 pound fresh snow peas, ends snapped, veiny strings removed, and cut diagonally in half
2 1/2 tablespoons rice wine
5 cups cooked brown rice, chilled, then separated with a fork (see preceding recipe)

Sauce (mixed together)
3 1/2 tablespoons soy sauce
1 tablespoon chicken broth
1 teaspoon salt
1/4 teaspoon freshly ground black pepper

1. Preheat the oven to 350°F. To prepare the barbecued pork, trim any fat or gristle from the meat. Mix the Barbecue Sauce ingredients in a bowl, add the pork, and toss to coat. Place the pork in a baking pan lined with aluminum foil, and roast for 30 to 45 minutes, until cooked through. Let it cool, then cut it into thin slices about 1/4 inch thick, and then into small dice about 1/2 inch square. Skip this step if you are using already barbecued or roasted pork.

2. Heat a wok or large skillet, add the oil, and heat until hot. Add the ginger and leeks, and toss lightly over high heat about 1 1/2 minutes. Add the snow peas and cook briefly, then add the rice wine and stir-fry over high heat for a minute until crisp-tender. Add the brown rice, breaking it up with a spatula. Cook about 2 to 3 minutes, tossing, until heated through. Add the cooked pork and the premixed Sauce and toss lightly to coat. Spoon the rice into a serving dish and serve.

Chicken–Black Bean Brown Rice

Try this recipe with seafood, beef, turkey, or pork as well as with chicken. The black bean sauce has a vibrant flavor, and the snow peas and red onions add color and a pleasing crunchiness.

Garlic Marinade
3 tablespoons soy sauce
2 tablespoons minced garlic
1 teaspoon toasted sesame oil

1 whole boned chicken breast (about $3/4$ pound), split and skinned, or an already cooked chicken breast
$2^1/2$ tablespoons corn or safflower oil

Seasonings
3 tablespoons fermented black beans, rinsed, drained, and minced
2 tablespoons minced garlic
2 tablespoons minced fresh ginger

1 red onion, diced (about $1^1/2$ cups)
1 red bell pepper, cored, seeded, and diced (about 1 cup)
$1/2$ pound snow peas, ends snapped and strings removed, cut into $1/4$-inch crosswise strips
5 cups cooked brown rice, chilled, then separated with a fork (see page 229)

Sauce (mixed together)
1 tablespoon chicken broth
3 tablespoons soy sauce
$1^1/2$ tablespoons rice wine or sake
1 teaspoon sugar

1. Combine the Marinade and chicken breast halves in a bowl; toss to coat them. Prepare the remaining ingredients.

2. Heat a large, heavy skillet over medium heat. Add $1/2$ tablespoon of the oil and heat until hot. Add the chicken and cook for 6 to 7 minutes on each side, or until cooked thoroughly. Let it cool thoroughly, then cut it into $1/4$-inch dice.

3. Reheat the skillet or a wok over medium-high heat. Add the remaining 2 tablespoons oil and heat until hot. Add the Seasonings and stir-fry for 15 to 20 seconds, then add the diced onion and pepper and stir-fry for 2 minutes. Add the snow peas and rice. Cook, tossing, about $1^1/2$ to 2 minutes, until heated through. Add the premixed Sauce, and cooked chicken, and toss lightly to coat all the ingredients. Spoon the dish into a serving bowl, and serve immediately.

☯ According to Albert Leung, fermented black beans are prepared in a rather complicated process that involves first soaking the small black soybeans in water with mulberry leaves and a wormwood herb, then fermenting them in salt. They are sometimes used in the treatment of burns, which, once treated with this herb, are said to heal with no scars.

A Congee Tale

Professor Weng Weijian of the Beijing College of Traditional Chinese Medicine has the skin of a baby, remarkably sparkling eyes, and a lively manner. In his seventies, he claims that all are a testament to his diet and his beliefs in the rejuvenating and healthful powers of food and diet.

In addition to his professorial duties, he is a consultant to a number of companies developing functional foods, the inventor of Tang Long Beauty Slimming Wine, Anti-Snoring Drops, and Weng's Health and Beauty Tea. Professor Weijian is also the author of *Chinese Herbal Foods to Enhance Your Health*. And one of his favorite topics is congee.

"Healthy and therapeutic congees have a long and rich history in China," he says. "As early as the pre-Qin period [221–207 B.C.], there is a record of an illness-curing millet soup."

We know congee mainly as rice porridge, but in fact it may be made with any type of grain, including millet, sorghum, barley, and wheat. The amount of rice is often a fraction of that of the water, and it may be cooked for up to four hours. Some say the longer the congee cooks, the more therapeutic it becomes.

According to Dr. Weijian, optional nuts and dried fruits, such as dates, walnuts, or chestnuts, should be added at the beginning of the cooking period, with the uncooked grain and water. Vegetables can either be precooked and added at the end or cooked until tender with the rice.

For an herbal congee, the herbs should first be steeped in water; then the strained liquid is added to the cooked congee before serving. The following congees are suggested for treating certain conditions:

- **Asparagus Congee:** This will serve as a diuretic and will help to cleanse the arteries of cholesterol.
- **Carrot Congee:** A digestive aid that will ease flatulence.
- **Chicken or Lamb Congee:** This porridge will fortify weak constitutions, and invigorate and warm the body.
- **Ginger Congee:** This will heat the system, settle nausea, and cure diarrhea, vomiting, and indigestion.
- **Pear Congee:** This will cure coughing, ease throat irritation, alleviate dizziness and fever. A little honey is also recommended.
- **Black Sesame Seed Congee:** It will lubricate the intestines, prevent premature gray hair, and encourage lactation for nursing mothers.
- **Spinach Congee:** This will lubricate the lungs and act as a mild sedative.
- **Wild Mushroom Congee:** Shiitakes and maitakes bolster the immune system, making this dish one of the most therapeutic for fighting flu, colds, and life-threatening diseases.

Plain Congee with Garnishes

Congee, or rice porridge, is often one of the first solid foods that Chinese babies eat, so it is easy to understand why most Chinese develop a passion for it. Few things are as soothing or as comforting, especially for an upset stomach. In southern China, congee with assorted pickles, dried meat, or seafood—even the previous dinner's leftovers— are served universally for breakfast. Similarly, it is wonderful as a midday or evening snack. Many Chinese use long-grain rice, but, like the Japanese, I prefer the creamy consistency of congee made with short-grain rice.

SIX SERVINGS

1 cup short-grain or Arborio rice	Garnishes
8 cups water or chicken broth (preferably Classic Chicken Broth, page 27)	Cucumber pickle*
	Dried pickled turnip*
1 teaspoon salt	4 tablespoons minced scallion greens
	3 tablespoons minced fresh cilantro

1. Put the rice in a pot and, using your fingers as a rake, rinse it under cold running water to remove some of the talc, then drain it in a colander.

2. Put the rice and water in a heavy saucepan with a lid. Bring the water to a boil over high heat, uncovered. Reduce the heat to low, partially cover, and simmer for 1 hour, stirring occasionally. The resulting liquid will be a thick porridge with the consistency of heavy cream. Serve with any of the above garnishes, or reheated leftover meat, chicken, or seafood and vegetable dishes.

Asparagus Congee: Prepare the Plain Congee as directed above and mix the cooked congee with 1^1/$_2$ pounds cooked asparagus, cut into ^{1}/$_4$-inch rounds.

Wild Mushroom Congee: Prepare the Wild Mushroom mixture as described in Wild Mushroom Fried Rice (page 226) and mix with the cooked congee.

*May be purchased at any Asian market.

Rainbow Congee

Whenever my surrogate Chinese brothers and sister had the flu, my Chinese mother would make them a pot of this congee, which was generously garnished with diced pork, sweet potatoes, carrots, and peas—or other vegetables, depending on their availability at the market.

SIX SERVINGS

1/2 pound center-cut pork loin, trimmed of fat or gristle

Marinade
1 tablespoon minced garlic
1 tablespoon minced fresh ginger
2 tablespoons soy sauce
1 1/2 tablespoons rice wine or sake
1 teaspoon toasted sesame oil

2 sweet potatoes, peeled
2 carrots, ends trimmed and peeled
1 cup long-grain rice
1 tablespoon safflower or corn oil
12 cups low-salt chicken broth
1/4 teaspoon freshly ground black pepper
1 1/2 cups frozen peas, defrosted to room temperature
3 tablespoons minced scallion greens

1. Cut the pork loin across the grain into slices about 1/4 inch thick, then cut into 1/4-inch dice. Put the meat in a bowl, add the Marinade, and toss lightly to coat. Cover with plastic wrap, and let the pork marinate for 20 minutes.

2. Cut the sweet potatoes and carrots into 1/4-inch dice.

3. Clean the rice as directed in step 1 of Plain Congee (opposite page).

4. Heat a large casserole or Dutch oven, add the oil, and heat until very hot. Add the pork and stir-fry over high heat until cooked, about 2 minutes. Scoop out into a bowl and blot the pan with paper towels.

5. Add the rice and chicken broth to the casserole and bring the liquid to a boil. Reduce the heat to low, partially cover, and simmer for 40 minutes. Add the diced sweet potato and carrot, and continue cooking another 20 minutes. Add the pepper, the peas, the cooked pork, and salt to taste if necessary. Stir to blend the seasonings evenly. Ladle the congee into serving bowls and sprinkle a little of the minced scallion on top. Serve.

Turkey Congee with Barley

I have always been a fan of turkey soup. At Thanksgiving, I wait impatiently until the carcass is clean enough to start making soup. These days, with turkey parts widely available year round, you can make this dish anytime. It's a nourishing and soothing meal in itself.

SIX SERVINGS

1 1/2 pounds turkey bones or turkey parts
12 cups water
1/3 cup rice wine
3 slices fresh ginger, about the size of a quarter, smashed lightly with the side of a knife
3 whole scallions, ends trimmed, smashed lightly with the side of a knife
1 pound turkey meat, trimmed of fat or gristle

Marinade
2 tablespoons soy sauce
1 1/2 tablespoons rice wine
1 teaspoon toasted sesame oil

1 1/2 onions, peeled and cut into 1/4-inch dice
1 cup whole-grain barley or pearl barley, rinsed and drained
3 carrots, peeled and cut into 1/4-inch dice
3 stalks celery, ends trimmed and cut into 1/4-inch dice
1 teaspoon salt
1/4 teaspoon freshly ground black pepper

◑ Whole-grain barley, with its bran and germ intact, is preferable to pearl barley. This cooling grain is excellent for settling the stomach. It is believed to aid digestion and often recommended for diabetics, who tend to have over-heated blood systems.

1. Put the turkey parts, water, rice wine, ginger, and scallions in a large pot and bring to a boil. Reduce the heat to low and simmer for 1 hour. Remove the ginger and scallions.
2. While the stock is cooking, cut the turkey meat into 1/4-inch dice. Put the diced turkey in a bowl, add the Marinade, and toss lightly to coat.
3. Add the turkey, onions, and barley to the stock, and continue cooking over low heat for 45 minutes, then add the carrots and celery and cook another 30 minutes. Remove the turkey bones, skim the surface to remove any impurities, and add salt and pepper to taste. Ladle into soup bowls and serve.

Japanese Congee with Shiitake Mushrooms

This soothing congee has a silky consistency thanks to the short-grain rice. It's delicate yet filling with the shiitakes and eggs. You may add a blanched green vegetable for additional color and nourishment.

1 cup short-grain or sweet (glutinous) rice
8 cups water

Seasonings
3 tablespoons soy sauce
1 1/2 tablespoons sweetened rice wine or *mirin*
(if unavailable, substitute 1 1/2 tablespoons
rice wine and 1/2 tablespoon sugar)
1 teaspoon salt

1 1/2 cups scallion greens or Chinese garlic
chives, ends trimmed and cut into 1/4-
inch lengths
1/2 pound fresh shiitake mushrooms,
stems trimmed, and cut into thin slices
2 large eggs, lightly beaten

SIX SERVINGS

1. Put the rice in a pot and, using your fingers as a rake, rinse it under cold running water to remove some of the talc. Drain it in a colander.
2. Put the rice and water in a heavy saucepan with a lid. Heat uncovered until boiling. Reduce the heat to low, partially cover, and simmer for 1 hour, stirring occasionally.
3. Add the Seasonings, stir, and add the scallions and mushrooms. Cook over low heat for 5 minutes, then add the beaten eggs. Stir and cook the eggs, about 1 1/2 minutes. Remove from the heat and ladle into soup bowls. Serve.

Chinese Yeast Dough

This dough, once steamed, transforms into a light, airy bread thanks to the long rising period and the addition of baking powder in the final shaping. Make certain to thoroughly knead the powder into the dough so that the texture will be smooth and even. Once risen, the dough can be sculpted into myriad shapes.

2¹/2 tablespoons sugar	3 cups all-purpose flour
1 cup warm water	1¹/2 tablespoons corn oil
¹/2 tablespoon active dry yeast	

1. Mix the sugar and water in a small bowl with a wooden spoon, stirring to dissolve the sugar, then add the yeast and stir again to dissolve the yeast.
2. Put the flour in a large mixing bowl, add the yeast mixture and 1 tablespoon of the oil, and stir with the wooden spoon to form a rough dough. Turn the dough out onto a lightly floured surface, scraping the sides of the bowl. Knead lightly, until the dough is smooth and elastic, adding a little more flour if the dough is too sticky. (The consistency may vary slightly, depending on the weather: If the dough is too dry, add a little warm water.)
3. Brush the large mixing bowl with the remaining $^1/_2$ tablespoon oil and put the dough in the bowl. Cover with a damp cloth and place in a draft-free place (like an oven). Let the dough rise for 3 hours, until tripled in bulk. Use as directed in the recipes.

☯ Although wheat is slightly less nutritious than other grains, the Chinese credit it with nourishing the heart and mind, as well as improving insomnia and menopausal difficulties. And it is especially good for children and for frail individuals.

Steamed Flower Buns and Variations

Flower buns are one of the easiest and most attractive shapes to make with Chinese Yeast Dough. I serve these rolls as an unusual replacement for rice with meat, vegetable, or seafood dishes.

1 recipe Chinese Yeast Dough, prepared as directed in preceding recipe $1^{1}/4$ teaspoons baking powder	$2^{1}/2$ tablespoons toasted sesame oil $^{1}/4$ cup minced scallion greens or toasted sesame seeds	**MAKES 16 BUNS**

1. Turn the risen dough out onto a lightly floured working surface. Flatten into a circle with your hands and sprinkle the baking powder in the center. Sprinkle a tablespoon of water on top of the baking powder. Gather up the edges to enclose the baking powder and bring together and pinch in the center. Knead the dough thoroughly to incorporate the baking powder evenly.

2. Roll the dough out to a large rectangle measuring about 10 by 14 inches and $^{1}/8$ inch thick. Brush the surface with the toasted sesame oil. Starting with the long side, roll up the dough like a jelly roll. Pinch the ends to seal in the oil. Cut the roll crosswise into 16 sections with a sharp knife. Let the dough relax slightly, covered with a damp cloth, about 20 minutes.

3. Lightly stretch each portion of dough and wrap it maypole-style around your index finger, third finger, and thumb to form a ball, then tuck the ends underneath. Sprinkle the top with scallions or sesame seeds. Place the finished buns on a cookie sheet lined with waxed paper or parchment paper and let them rise for 20 minutes, covered with a cloth.

4. Fill a wok or a large pot with several inches of water and bring to a boil. Arrange the risen buns on a lightly oiled steaming tray or aluminum pie plate punched with holes. Perch the tray or plate over the boiling water (you can crisscross chopsticks or use a tunafish can with ends removed). Cover and steam for 15 minutes, or until the buns are light and springy. Remove with a spatula and serve hot or at room temperature. To reheat, steam for several minutes or microwave until hot, covered with a damp towel. Serve with any entrée instead of rice.

Flaky Scallion Pancakes

I will never forget my first taste of scallion pancakes as a student in Taipei. I bought them at a small stand next to the university where I was studying Mandarin. The aroma of fried scallions hit me first, causing my mouth to water. Freshly fried, the pancakes were crisp and slightly chewy. Serve these as a snack or a side dish with stir-fried meat, vegetables, or seafood.

MAKES 24 PANCAKES

3 cups cake flour	1/4 cup or more all-purpose flour, if necessary, for kneading
1/2 cup all-purpose flour	
1 teaspoon salt	1/4 cup toasted sesame oil
2 tablespoons corn oil	3/4 cup minced scallion greens
1 3/4 cups boiling water	3/4 cup canola or corn oil

☯ Scallion pancakes, with their fragrant scallion seasoning, are extremely warming, so they are ideal in the winter with meat dishes; they can be balanced, however, with coolish seafood entrées. I like to fry them in as little oil as possible.

1. Stir the flours and salt in a mixing bowl with a wooden spoon. Add the corn oil and the boiling water, and stir until a rough dough forms. If the dough is too soft, knead in about 1/4 cup more flour. Turn the dough out onto a lightly floured surface and knead for 5 minutes, or until smooth, kneading in more all-purpose flour as necessary. Cover with a cloth or wrap in plastic wrap and let rest for 30 minutes, or longer if possible.

2. On a very lightly floured work surface, roll the dough into a long snakelike roll about 1 inch in diameter. Cut the roll into 24 pieces. Keep the unused dough covered with a damp towel as you work.

3. With a rolling pin, roll out one piece of dough, cut side down on the work surface, into a 5-inch circle. Brush the top with a little sesame oil and sprinkle with some of the minced scallion greens. Roll up the circle like a jelly roll and pinch the ends to seal. Flatten the roll slightly with the rolling pin, and coil it into a snail shape, with the seam on the inside. Pinch the end to secure it and set aside on a lightly floured surface. Prepare the remaining pancakes, and let them rest for 30 minutes uncovered.

4. Reflour the work surface and roll each coiled pancake out to a 4-inch circle. Place them on a lightly floured tray. Let them rest for 30 minutes uncovered, or longer if possible. Preheat the oven to 200°F.

5. Heat a large, heavy skillet, add the oil, and heat to 350°F. Put a few of the pancakes in the pan, not touching, and fry over medium heat, turning once, until golden brown and

Flaky Scallion Pancakes (continued)

crisp on both sides, about 2 to 3 minutes. Remove with a spatula and drain briefly in a colander, then transfer to absorbent paper. Arrange the cooked pancakes on a cookie sheet and keep them warm in the oven while you fry the remaining pancakes, reheating the oil between batches. Serve immediately or keep them warm in the oven.

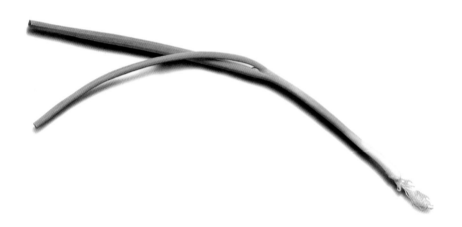

Japanese Wild Mushrooms with Soba

Soba noodles with their classic Japanese broth (dashi) have come to be one of my favorite dishes in the whole world. The nutty noodles make a lovely contrast to the smoky soup. And this dish is so easy to make! I like this vegetarian rendition with wild mushrooms, but you can add chicken or shrimp if you like.

Dashi
1 four-inch square giant kelp (*konbu*)
5 cups cold water
1 cup dried bonito flakes (*katsuo bushi*)

1/2 pound fresh shiitake mushrooms, stems trimmed

4 ounces oyster or maitake mushrooms, stems trimmed
1/2 pound soba noodles
2 1/2 tablespoons sweetened rice wine (*mirin*)
5 tablespoons soy sauce
4 whole scallions, ends trimmed and cut diagonally into 1/4-inch lengths

1. To make the Dashi, clean the kelp if necessary with a damp cloth, removing any dirt. Put into a large saucepan together with the water and bring to a boil over high heat. Remove the kelp immediately and reserve for another use.
2. Bring the water to a boil again, add the bonito flakes, stir, then remove from the heat. Let the flakes settle to the bottom of the pan, about 1 minute, and strain the liquid through a fine strainer or a strainer lined with cheesecloth, into a Dutch oven or a casserole. Discard the bonito flakes.
3. Cut the mushrooms into thin slices.
4. Bring 4 quarts water to a boil in a large pot. Drop the soba into the water, and stir to prevent them from sticking together. Bring to a boil again and cook 3 1/2 to 4 minutes, until just tender. Drain the noodles in a colander and rinse under warm water. Drain again and divide the noodles among six serving bowls.
5. Add the sweetened rice wine and soy sauce to the dashi, and heat to a gentle boil. Add the mushrooms and scallions, and cook for 4 to 5 minutes over medium-high heat. Skim any impurities from the surface.
6. Ladle the mushrooms, scallions, and hot broth over the noodles and serve.

☯ Soba noodles, which are made with buckwheat and wheat flour, were always considered a health food, and as early as 300 years ago were believed to relieve stress and cure ulcers. They cleanse and energize the body as well.

Udon with Shrimp

Udon are plump Japanese wheat-flour-and-water noodles that are usually served in soups and stews. I love them as much as I do soba. This dashi-based soup is soothing, filling, and satisfying.

Dashi
1 four-inch square giant kelp (*konbu*)
5 cups cold water
1 cup dried bonito flakes (*katsuo bushi*)

1/2 pound medium shrimp, shelled but tail intact
2 tablespoons rice wine or sake
1 teaspoon minced fresh ginger

1/2 pound udon or thick, round wheat-flour noodles, or spaghettini
2 1/2 tablespoons sweetened rice wine (*mirin*)
5 tablespoons soy sauce
1/2 pound snow peas, ends snapped off and veiny strings removed
4 tablespoons minced scallion greens

1. Prepare the Dashi as directed in the preceding recipe.
2. Clean and devein the shrimp, leaving the tail intact. Place them in a bowl, add the rice wine and ginger, and toss lightly to coat.
3. Bring 4 quarts water to a boil in a large pot. Drop the udon into the water, and stir to prevent them from sticking together. Heat until boiling and cook 10 to 12 minutes, until just tender. Drain the noodles in a colander and rinse under warm water. Drain again and divide the noodles among six serving bowls.
4. Pour the dashi, the sweetened rice wine, and the soy sauce into a casserole or a Dutch oven, and heat to a gentle boil. Add the shrimp, and cook for 1 1/2 to 2 minutes over medium heat, or until just cooked. Skim any impurities from the surface. Add the snow peas and cook about 30 seconds. Ladle some of the shrimp, snow peas, and broth over each bowl of udon and sprinkle minced scallion greens on top. Serve.

☯ This soup is the epitome of balance, making it an excellent meal by itself. The udon are deliciously filling and neutral, while the shrimp is nicely complemented by the rice wine and ginger.

Vegetarian *Pad Thai*

In this popular Thai dish, the flat, silken rice noodles soak up the sweet and sour sauce and provide a superb foil to the tender tofu and crunchy bean sprouts.

SIX SERVINGS

1 pound firm tofu

4 tablespoons safflower or corn oil

2 large eggs, lightly beaten

2 tablespoons minced garlic

Sauce (mixed together)

1/3 cup fish sauce

1/4 cup ketchup

1 1/2 tablespoons sugar

3 tablespoons water

1/2 pound Chinese rice stick noodles or vermicelli, softened in hot water for 15 to 20 minutes and drained

2 cups bean sprouts, rinsed lightly and drained

Topping

3 tablespoons minced scallion greens

1/2 teaspoon crushed red chiles

2 1/2 tablespoons coarsely chopped fresh cilantro

4 tablespoons finely chopped dry-roasted peanuts

2 limes, cut into six wedges each

1. Wrap the tofu in paper towels or a cotton towel and place a heavy weight, such as a cast-iron skillet, on top. Let drain for 20 minutes. Cut the tofu into 1/4-inch dice.

2. Heat a wok or heavy skillet, add 2 tablespoons of the oil, and heat until very hot, about 30 seconds. Add the tofu and stir-fry over high heat about 3 minutes. Remove with a handled strainer or slotted spoon and drain. Pour the oil out of the pan and wipe it clean.

3. Reheat the pan, add the remaining 2 tablespoons oil, and heat until hot, about 20 seconds. Add the eggs, stirring to scramble over medium-high heat. Add the garlic and stir-fry until fragrant, about 10 seconds. Add the premixed Sauce and the rice noodles, and toss over medium-high heat, cooking about 3 to 4 minutes, until the noodles are tender and the mixture is dry.

4. Add the bean sprouts and tofu, and toss to mix. Transfer to a serving platter. Sprinkle with the prepared Topping ingredients. Arrange the lime wedges on the side and serve. Each diner squeezes the lime onto an individual portion before eating.

Noodle dishes, such as *pad thai*, form a significant part of the Asian diet, and for good reason. They nurture and nourish. Like rice, noodles tone the body, energize the system, and strengthen the spleen.

Saucy Chicken Lo Mein

I was first introduced to a variation of this dish as a student in Taipei at one of my favorite noodle stands. It became a dish I craved during the winter, when the weather turned raw and damp. This noodle dish will fill the stomach and warm the soul.

1 pound boned chicken breast, skin removed

Garlic Marinade
2 tablespoons soy sauce
1 1/2 tablespoons rice wine or sake
1 tablespoon sugar
1 1/2 tablespoons minced garlic

8 dried Chinese black mushrooms, softened in hot water to cover for 20 minutes
2 leeks or 1/3 pound garlic chives, cleaned and ends trimmed
1/2 pound Chinese flour-and-water noodles or linguine
3 1/2 tablespoons safflower or corn oil

3 tablespoons minced fresh ginger
2 tablespoons minced garlic
2 1/2 tablespoons rice wine or sake

Sauce (mixed together)
2 1/4 cups Classic Chicken Broth (page 27) or water
7 1/2 tablespoons soy sauce
3 tablespoons rice wine or sake
1 1/2 teaspoons toasted sesame oil
1 1/2 teaspoons sugar
1/4 teaspoon freshly ground black pepper
2 1/2 tablespoons cornstarch

4 cups bean sprouts, rinsed lightly and drained

1. Lay the chicken breast meat flat on a cutting board. Holding the blade of your knife at a low slant to the board, cut the chicken into thin slices, then cut the slices into match-stick-size shreds; place them in a bowl. Add the Garlic Marinade and toss lightly with your hands to coat. Cover with plastic wrap and refrigerate for 30 minutes.

2. Remove and discard the stems from the black mushrooms and cut the caps into very thin shreds. Cut the leeks into thin julienne slices about 1 1/2 inches long. If using garlic chives, trim the ends and cut into 1-inch lengths.

3. Bring 3 quarts water to a boil, add the noodles, and cook about 10 to 12 minutes, until near tender; drain in a colander, rinse lightly to remove the starch, and drain again thoroughly in a colander.

4. Heat a wok or large skillet, add $2^1/_2$ tablespoons of the oil, and heat until very hot but not smoking. Add the chicken shreds and toss lightly over high heat until they change color and separate. Remove with a handled strainer or slotted spoon and drain. Clean out the pan.

5. Reheat the pan, add the remaining 1 tablespoon of oil, heat about 20 seconds, and add the ginger, garlic, and black mushrooms. Stir-fry over high heat about 15 seconds, then add the leeks or garlic chives. Stir-fry over high heat briefly, add the rice wine or sake, and cook about 1 minute, then add the premixed Sauce and cook, stirring continuously to prevent lumps, until it thickens. Add the cooked noodles and chicken, then the bean sprouts, and toss lightly to heat and combine the ingredients. Spoon the chicken lo mein onto a serving platter, and serve immediately.

The combination of chicken and leeks gives this dish its warming tendencies, but the addition of bean sprouts, which are cooling, offsets the heat. Bean sprouts also have been shown to lower lipid levels, making them useful in the prevention of heart disease.

Dan Dan Sesame Noodles

This quintessentially Sichuan dish illustrates the brilliance of western Chinese cooking: The silky noodles are superb drenched in the spicy sesame dressing. I make vats of the sauce in the summer and store it, covered, in my fridge for several weeks for an instant, satisfying meal. "*Dan dan*" is the Chinese equivalent for the distinctive noise made by the noodle vendor who sold this dish in the alleys of China.

SIX SERVINGS

1 pound boneless pork loin

Marinade
2 tablespoons soy sauce
1 1/2 tablespoons rice wine or sake
1 teaspoon toasted sesame oil
2 teaspoons cornstarch

1/2 teaspoon crushed Sichuan peppercorns (optional)

Spicy Sesame Dressing
8 cloves garlic
2 1-inch-square knobs fresh ginger, peeled
1 teaspoon crushed dried chiles or dried chile flakes

6 tablespoons Chinese toasted sesame paste (stirred well before adding)
4 tablespoons toasted sesame oil
5 tablespoons soy sauce
1/4 cup rice wine or sake
1 1/2 tablespoons Chinese black vinegar or Worcestershire sauce
1 1/2 tablespoons sugar
6 tablespoons chicken broth or water

1/2 pound thin egg noodles, such as angel hair or spaghettini
2 1/2 tablespoons canola or corn oil
2 cups minced scallion greens

1. Cut the pork loin into thin slices about 1/4 inch thick, then cut the slices into thin, matchstick-size shreds about 1 inch long. Put the shreds in a bowl, add the Marinade, and toss lightly to coat. Cover with plastic wrap, and let the pork marinate for 1 hour at room temperature, or longer if possible in the refrigerator.

2. Put the Sichuan peppercorns (if using) in a skillet, and toast over medium heat about 4 to 5 minutes, stirring occasionally until they are very fragrant. Let them cool slightly and then crush them into a powder with a rolling pin, mallet, or mortar and pestle.

3. Drop the seasonings of the Spicy Sesame Dressing in descending order into the feed tube of a food processor fitted with a steel blade while the machine is running. Mix together to a smooth sauce—it should have the consistency of heavy cream. Add the Sichuan peppercorn powder and mix. Pour into a serving bowl.

4. Bring 3 quarts water to a boil, add the noodles, and cook about 5 to 6 minutes, or until near tender. Drain in a colander, rinse lightly to remove the starch, and drain again thoroughly in a colander. Divide the noodles into six portions in soup bowls.

5. Heat a wok or large skillet, add the oil, and heat until very hot. Add the pork and stir-fry over high heat about $2^1/2$ to 3 minutes, until the meat changes color and is cooked. Scoop it into a colander to drain; then spoon it over the individual servings of noodles and sprinkle about $^1/_3$ cup minced scallion greens on top of each. Ladle some Spicy Sesame Dressing over all, and serve.

☯ Early records indicate that the sesame plant was introduced to China around the second century B.C.; its seeds have been used in Chinese medicine for over 2,000 years. Traditionally, they are believed to vitalize the internal organs and to moisten the body. According to Dr. Albert Leung, some Chinese studies have shown that they also lower the blood sugar level. In ancient China $^1/_2$ cup sesame seeds boiled in 1 cup water was drunk to relieve toothaches.

Garlic Beef with Golden Noodles

Tender beef with red onions and snap peas in oyster sauce is a delicious topping for crisp-fried noodles, but chicken, turkey, or pork may be substituted. For convenience, I often broil the noodles, as described below, instead of pan-frying them.

SIX SERVINGS

1 1/2 pounds flank steak, London broil, or boneless sirloin

Marinade
3 1/2 tablespoons soy sauce
2 tablespoons rice wine or sake
2 tablespoons minced garlic
1 tablespoon cornstarch

3/4 pound thin egg noodles, such as angel hair or vermicelli
1 1/2 teaspoons toasted sesame oil mixed with 1 teaspoon safflower or corn oil
5 1/2 tablespoons safflower or corn oil

2 tablespoons minced garlic
1 1/2 tablespoons minced fresh ginger
1 1/2 red onions, peeled and cut into thin julienne slices
3/4 pound fresh snap peas, ends trimmed and veiny strings removed
2 tablespoons rice wine or sake

Oyster Sauce (mixed together)
1 1/2 cups Classic Chicken Broth (page 27)
6 tablespoons oyster sauce
1 1/2 tablespoons rice wine or sake
1 teaspoon soy sauce
1 teaspoon toasted sesame oil
1 1/2 tablespoons cornstarch

1. Trim the meat of fat and gristle, cut lengthwise along the grain into strips about 2 1/2 inches wide, then cut across the grain into very thin slices about 1/8 inch thick. Put the slices in a bowl, add the Marinade, and toss lightly to coat. Cover the beef slices with plastic wrap and let them marinate for 20 minutes.

2. Bring 3 quarts water to a boil, add the noodles, and cook about 5 to 6 minutes, or until near tender. Drain in a colander, rinse lightly to remove the starch, and drain again thoroughly in a colander. Pour the toasted sesame oil–safflower oil over the noodles and toss to coat. Spread the noodles out on a large baking sheet.

3. Heat a broiler until very hot. Place the noodles 3 inches under the broiler and cook about 10 minutes, until they are golden brown. Flip them over with a spatula and brown on the other side. Cook until golden. Turn off the broiler and keep the noodles warm in an oven on low.

4. Heat a well-seasoned wok or large skillet, add $3^1/_2$ tablespoons of the oil, and heat until near smoking. Add the beef slices, and stir-fry over high heat until they lose their raw color and separate. Remove with a handled strainer and drain in a colander. Clean the pan.

5. Reheat the pan, add the remaining 2 tablespoons oil, heat about 20 seconds, and add the garlic, ginger, and red onions. Stir-fry for 2 minutes, until the onion is soft. Add the snap peas and rice wine, and stir-fry another 2 minutes, or until the snap peas are almost tender. Pour in the premixed Oyster Sauce and stir-fry until it thickens, taking care to prevent lumps. Add the cooked beef, and toss lightly in the sauce. Place the browned noodles on a platter and scoop the beef and snap peas on top. Serve.

☯ Like chicken soup, noodle dishes are nurturing and soothing. Since the beef and onions in this recipe heat the body, this is one of my favorite wintertime dishes. I often substitute chicken or seafood and add lots of different vegetables for a more neutral dish in warmer weather.

Sweet Flavors

Sweet Flavors and the Sweet 'N' Tart Cafe

For some customers, the menu of the Sweet 'N' Tart Cafe on Mott Street in Manhattan's Chinatown or its sister cafe in Flushing, Queens, looks the same as in any other Cantonese eatery. Won ton soup is there, and various noodle dishes, and steamed dumplings.

But for anyone well versed in the powers of "food as medicine," the dishes tell another story: Double-boiled pear soup with almonds is believed to be beneficial for the lungs and a scratchy throat. Cold mung beans in syrup are eaten as a refreshing snack in warm weather to drive heat from the body. And lotus seeds in sweet herbal tea are good for the liver and kidneys.

Here, *tong shui,* or "sweet soups," are the specialties of the house. Besides being delicious dishes that are served at the end of meals, or as snacks, *tong shui,* as the menu explains, "nourish, moderate, and balance the yin and yang of the body." They have a history of over a thousand years, and are still very popular with the Chinese.

The list of *tong shui* is extensive, and there are three main types: hot, double-boiled, and cold. Among the hot dishes are the special almond tea, fresh walnut *tong shui,* sesame paste with rice dumpling, tapioca pearl with coconut milk, and Chinese herbal *tong shui.* The double-boiled *tong shui* include Oriental pears with almonds, papaya with snow fungi, or silver tree ears, and snow fungi with almonds or lotus seeds. Among the cold *tong shui* are almond tea, pearl tapioca with coconut milk, lotus seeds with herbal tea, and red beans *tong shui*.

Tong shui and fresh fruit are typically served at the end of a Chinese meal, since they aid digestion and soothe the palate. Pastries and cakes—the dishes we consider to be desserts—are more often served as snacks. This custom is slowly changing as Asians adopt Western ways and as chefs integrate Western techniques with Eastern ingredients. It's in this spirit that I have brought together this selection of sweet dishes, and I have divided the recipes into three sections: fruit desserts, tea pastries, and sweet puddings and sumptuous treats.

Fruit has a particularly prominent role in the Asian diet. The nutritional and therapeutic benefits of the numerous varieties found in Asia are considerable: In general, many fruits are cooling and refreshing, hence their prominence in dishes designed for warm weather. When paired with pungent, warm seasonings, such as cinnamon, nutmeg, and ginger, and then baked, steamed, or poached and sweetened with honey and brown sugar, they become neutralized, an appropriate dish for colder times. Fruits also often act to cleanse the body and can balance the effect of rich and fatty foods. Ideally, fruits are best eaten in season, and, whenever possible, organic varieties are preferable.

At first glance, the custards and tapioca and rice puddings presented in this chapter might not be considered therapeutic, but I believe puddings and custards to be some of the most nurturing foods one can eat. Comfort foods like these are especially beneficial and soothing to the spirit.

Sugar, in moderation, is not considered as villainous in Asia as it is in the United States. Rock sugar is used moderately in Traditional Chinese Medicine as a way of harmonizing the stomach. Most sugars—rock, white, and brown—are believed to have some beneficial effects on the body: They lubricate the lungs, and produce fluids and nourish them. Honey is said to relieve pain and to counteract toxic effects.

The last category of sweet recipes is tea pastries and cakes. Eating sweet and savory pastries with tea is a time-honored tradition in many parts of the world. Green and black tea, as recent research suggests, is now being hailed as a powerful tonic with anticarcinogenic and antitumor properties.

Enjoyment is a key factor to be considered in one's diet and lifestyle. At a certain time of the day, there's nothing more civilized or relaxing than to enjoy a hot cup of tea and a light cookie or piece of cake on the side.

Balance is the key point to consider when dealing with sweet dishes: Savor them languorously and eat them in moderation.

Fruit Chart

Cooling

apple, banana, cantaloupe, grapefruit, kiwi, lemon, lime, mango, orange, pear, persimmon, strawberry, tangerine, watermelon

Neutral

apricot, coconut, fig, grape, loquat, papaya, pineapple, plum, prune, raspberry

Warming

cherry, date, litchee, peach

Cinnamon-Honey Orange Slices

Sliced orange sections are often served as a typical "dessert" at the end of a Chinese meal. I like to add honey and cinnamon, which accentuate the sweet and refreshing juiciness of the fruit.

SIX SERVINGS

5 navel oranges, peeled and cut into 1/2-inch-thick slices

4 tablespoons honey
1 teaspoon ground cinnamon

Put the orange slices in a bowl. Mix the honey and cinnamon, and add to the orange slices. Stir gently to coat. Let the orange slices sit for 15 minutes at room temperature, and serve.

☯ While oranges are cool in nature, the warmth from the cinnamon counterbalances this tendency nicely. The fruit is excellent for digestion and regenerates body fluids. Chinese physicians sometimes use the pith to help dissolve eye cysts.

Strawberries and Melon in Plum Wine

This is one of the simplest desserts, yet it's unique and very refreshing. I often add other fresh fruits depending on what is in season, as well as canned litchees, loquats, or arbutus with some of their syrup.

2 pints ripe strawberries, rinsed and hulled	3 cups ripe cantaloupe or honeydew	SIX SERVINGS
2 tablespoons sugar, or to taste (optional)	melon cut into balls or 1-inch diamonds	
	1 cup plum wine	

1. If the strawberries are large, cut in half lengthwise. If they are not very sweet, add the sugar, toss lightly to coat, and let them sit for 1 hour at room temperature. If they are sweet, reduce the sugar by half.
2. Place the strawberries in a serving bowl and add the cut-up melon. Add the plum wine, and stir gently to mix. Cover with plastic wrap and refrigerate for at least 1 hour. Spoon the fruit and sauce into bowls and serve.

☯ Like oranges, strawberries are believed to improve the appetite and generate body fluids. They also can relieve urinary difficulties. According to Paul Pitchford, author of *Healing with Whole Foods,* since strawberries are one of the first fruits to appear in the spring, they are excellent for cleansing and purifying the body. Strawberries are often prescribed for sore throats and hoarseness.

Cantaloupe is cooling and sweet. It clears exterior and interior body heat and quenches thirst.

Poached Pears in a Cinnamon-Ginger Syrup

This versatile dessert is delightfully refreshing served cold in the summer and soothing served warm in cooler weather.

SIX SERVINGS

10 cups water
1 1/2 cups sugar
2 cinnamon sticks
8 slices fresh, unpeeled ginger, about the

size of a quarter, smashed lightly with
the flat edge of a knife
6 slightly underripe Bosc or Anjou pears
2 lemons

1. In a large pot, combine the water, sugar, cinnamon sticks, and fresh ginger. Heat until boiling, reduce the heat to low, and cook for 30 minutes so that the flavors marry.

2. Using a vegetable peeler or a paring knife, peel the pears, and rub the outside with cut lemons to prevent them from turning brown.

3. Squeeze the juice from the lemons and add along with the pears to the cinnamon liquid. Heat until boiling and reduce the heat to low, so that the water barely boils. Cook uncovered for about 25 to 30 minutes, or until the pears are just tender. You can poke them with the tip of a knife to test them. Remove and place in a bowl.

4. Transfer about 3 cups of the cooking liquid to a smaller saucepan. (Discard any ginger and cinnamon sticks.) Heat until boiling, reduce the heat to medium, and cook about 35 minutes, or until the liquid thickens slightly. It should be like a syrup.

5. Arrange the pears in serving bowls and pour the cinnamon-ginger syrup on top. Serve. To serve cold, pour the syrup over the pears in a large bowl, cover with plastic wrap, and refrigerate for several hours before serving.

☯ On their own, pears are cooling in nature, but once poached in the cinnamon-ginger syrup, they become neutral, if not warming. This dish will ease a hacking cough and help digest deep-fried or spicy foods. Chinese women eat pears for menstrual pain, and for anemia during pregnancy, but they are careful, believing that eating too many may cause miscarriages.

Steamed Asian Pears with Honey and Almonds

Asian pears, also called Chinese pears or apple pears, are firm, crunchy, and surprisingly juicy. When I had a sore throat or a cold, my surrogate Chinese mother would make me steamed Asian pears with rock sugar or honey. Sometimes, she also added dried red dates that had been softened in water and sprinkled among the pears before steaming. Once steamed, the pears become tender and the broth is soothing and not overly sweet.

SIX SERVINGS

6 nearly ripe Asian pears
2 lemons
6 tablespoons honey
4 tablespoons "southern" Chinese

almonds or apricot or olive kernels (often labeled "apricot kernels" or "olive kernels" in markets; available at Asian markets)*

1. Cut a thin slice off the bottom of each pear so that it will stand upright. Peel the pears and rub the surface with a cut lemon half to prevent them from turning brown. Cut the top squarely off each pear, slicing about 2 inches from the top, and with a melon baller or spoon, carefully remove the core and seeds. Do not cut through to the bottom of the pear. Reserve the tops.

2. Arrange the pears on a pie plate or some kind of a heatproof plate. Spoon a tablespoon of the honey into each pear and sprinkle some of the almonds on top. Place the reserved tops on the pears, if necessary securing them with toothpicks. Place the plate in a steamer tray if using.

3. Fill a wok or large pot with enough water to reach the bottom of the steamer tray and bring to a boil. Or create your own steamer by balancing the plate on a tunafish can, both ends removed, that has been placed in the center of the pot. Cover and steam 40 to 45 minutes, or until the fruit is tender when pierced with a knife. Serve the Asian pears warm, at room temperature, or cold.

*You may substitute chopped candied ginger or dates for the almonds to get a different flavor.

☯ According to the Chinese, pears are considered a cooling fruit and they are excellent for fevers, ulcers, or other stomach ailments.

For the Chinese, almonds come in two main varieties: there are "northern" (bitter) and "southern" (sweet) almonds. Both are used by the Chinese for food and medicine. The word "almond" in Chinese also refers to apricot kernels. Sweet almonds have a neutral nature, while the bitter are warming, but both lubricate the intestines and temper coughs. Almond tea made with almonds steeped in boiling water, then sweetened with rock sugar, is often drunk as a remedy for coughing.

Baked Apples
with Honey, Cinnamon, and Jujubes

Apples (especially the imported varieties) are considered a delicacy in China, and I remember the shiny gift boxes of Red Delicious apples flown in from Washington State that were sold at Christmas and Chinese New Year. In this recipe, I blend my love of the East and West with the combination of baked apples and jujubes, or dried Chinese dates. Jujubes are sold in Asian markets and herbal shops, but, if unavailable, raisins may be used.

SIX SERVINGS

1/2 cup jujubes (dried Chinese dates) or
   raisins
6 Rome or Braeburn apples
1 lemon, cut in half

3 tablespoons honey
1 1/2 teaspoons ground cinnamon
2/3 cup apple cider

1. Rinse the jujubes and soften in boiling hot water to cover for 1 hour, changing the water twice. Drain, and remove the pits with a paring knife. Cut the softened dates into rings.

2. Preheat the oven to 375°F. Cut a slice about 1/2 inch thick off the top of each apple and set aside. (These will serve as lids.) Trim the bottom of each apple so that it will sit upright. Using a melon baller or a spoon, core and seed the apples. Squeeze a little lemon juice inside each apple.

3. Arrange the apples upright in a baking dish.

4. Mix the honey, cinnamon, and sliced dates. Spoon some of the mixture into each apple. Cover the apples with their "lids." Pour the apple cider in the baking dish around the apples. Cover the top of the baking dish with aluminum foil, sealing the edges. Place on the middle shelf of the oven. Alternatively, you may steam the apples (see Poached Pears in a Cinnamon-Ginger Syrup, page 258, for the procedure).

5. Bake the apples in the preheated oven for 50 to 60 minutes, or until very tender when pierced with a knife. Uncover and serve warm.

☯ Apples, like many fruits, are believed to produce fluids in the body, improve the appetite, and clear summer heat. Some Chinese also believe they relieve depression and stress.

Jujubes, or Chinese dates, are widely revered by the Chinese, as they build strength and—so it is believed—extend life. They tone the stomach and remove obstructions from the flow of *qi* in the body. In some cases, they are prescribed as a sedative and a laxative.

Fresh Mangoes and Silver Tree Ears in Syrup

This unusual soup is refreshing and delicious. Silver tree ears have a slightly crisp and pleasing texture, a lovely contrast to the tender, ripe fruit. Although mango is my favorite in this recipe, I like to change the fruit depending on what is in season.

SIX TO EIGHT
SERVINGS

1 ounce silver tree ears (available in Asian markets)
5 cups water

6 ounces rock, or crystal, sugar
3 ripe mangoes

1. Soak the silver tree ears in hot water to cover for 30 minutes. Drain in a colander and remove by hand any yellow bits from the edges. Put the tree ears in a heatproof bowl with the water.
2. Using a hammer, lightly break up the rock sugar into smaller pieces. Sprinkle evenly over the tree ears. Place the bowl in a steamer tray and cover with a lid.
3. Fill a wok or a pot with enough water to reach the bottom of a steamer tray and heat until boiling. Place the steamer tray over the boiling water, cover, and steam 1 hour over high heat, replenishing the boiling water in the pot as necessary. Alternatively, you may steam the soup in the oven: Preheat the oven to 425°F. Place the ingredients in a Dutch oven or casserole with a lid and, before covering, wrap the top tightly with heavy-duty aluminum foil; then cover. Place the pot in a lasagna pan or a casserole and fill with $1^1/_2$ inches boiling water. Bake for 1 hour, replenishing the boiling water as necessary.
4. Cut away one half of each mango, scraping away the flesh from the pit. Repeat for the other side. Score the flesh of the mango lengthwise and crosswise, but do not cut through the skin. The resulting diamond-shaped pieces should be about $1^1/_2$ inches on each side. Using a spoon, dislodge the mango pieces from the skin and add them to the silver tree ears in syrup. Steam them 5 minutes. Ladle the soup and fruit into serving bowls and serve, or chill and serve cold.

☯ Silver tree ears, snow fungus, and white tree ears are all names for the same dried plant that has been used by the Chinese for centuries as a *qi* tonic and immune enhancer. It is considered a delicacy. Chinese women believe that it will improve their complexion, regulate menstruation, and relieve constipation. Chinese doctors believe that it supplements the body's vital energy, strengthens the heart, and invigorates the brain.

Mangoes regenerate body fluids, clear heat, quench thirst, and settle nausea. Mango juice is drunk to improve digestion, and Chinese men drink tea made by boiling the peel and the pit for an enlarged prostate.

Rock, or crystal, sugar is considered the best type of sugar in Traditional Chinese Medicine. It tones the middle region, energizes the body, and lubricates the lungs.

Almond Soy Jelly with Litchees and Melon

Almond jelly is a classic Chinese dessert that is light and refreshing, though one sees the Western influence in this dessert. I have adapted the recipe, substituting soy milk for most of the cow's milk that's usually used. In this recipe, I've added melon and litchees, but almost any ripe, seasonal fruit is also delicious.

SIX TO EIGHT SERVINGS

2 1/2 tablespoons unflavored gelatin
3 cups water
2 tablespoons sugar
1 1/2 cups soy milk
1/2 cup sweetened condensed milk

1 1/4 tablespoons almond extract
3 cups ripe honeydew or cantaloupe cut into balls or squares
1 15-ounce can litchees in syrup

1. Chill a 9-inch square or round cake pan. Soften the gelatin in 1/2 cup water in a saucepan. Heat the mixture slightly, stirring constantly to dissolve the gelatin. Place the remaining water, sugar, the soy and condensed milk, and the almond extract in a bowl and stir to dissolve the sugar. Add the dissolved gelatin and stir again. Pour the mixture into the chilled pan and refrigerate until set, about 4 hours. Using a sharp knife, cut the gelatin into 1/2-inch diamond shapes.

2. In a large bowl, combine the melon and litchees in syrup. Carefully add the diamond-shaped pieces of gelatin to the fruit. Spoon into serving bowls and serve chilled.

☯ Almonds, while warming in nature, relieve stagnant *qi* in the lungs, so they are often prescribed for lung ailments and asthma. Ayurvedic doctors consider almonds the most beneficial nut, since they are believed to heighten spirituality and intellect.

Litchees, or litchee nuts, are another wondrous fruit. They regulate energy and produce and nourish fluids.

Banana-Coconut Pudding

This luscious pudding is simple, yet sumptuous. The coconut-tapioca pudding is generously studded with bits of banana and candied ginger.

1 tablespoon small pearl tapioca

1 13½-ounce can light coconut milk

2 heaping tablespoons coarsely chopped
candied ginger

¼ cup sugar

3 bananas

1. Soften the tapioca in warm water to cover for 1 hour. Drain.

2. While the tapioca is soaking, heat the coconut milk, candied ginger, and sugar in a saucepan, stirring constantly. When hot, remove from the heat and let the mixture stand for 10 minutes to infuse the coconut milk with the flavor of the ginger.

3. Peel the bananas and cut along the length in half. Cut along the length again and then cut across into dice about ½ inch square. Place the banana and tapioca in the coconut milk and slowly cook over low heat, stirring lightly so as not to break up the bananas. Cook about 5 minutes, until the bananas are barely poached. Remove from the heat, let cool slightly, then ladle into a serving bowl. Chill, and serve sprinkled with additional shredded candied ginger, if desired.

☯ Although coconut is rich with saturated fat (it is prescribed in Asia for malnutrition), the milk is warming, it clears summer heat (hence its popularity in warm climates), and it quenches thirst.

Bananas also clear heat while lubricating the intestines. A whole steamed banana with skin eaten twice a day on an empty stomach is prescribed to alleviate hemorrhoids.

In Praise of Malaysian Pastries

The Shanghai Restaurant in the Katong district of Singapore is like no other Chinese bakery. Amidst the humble wooden tables and green plastic chairs, there is a treasure trove of freshly made confections. The selection is extraordinary. Like Singapore itself, the foods reflect an exotic and colorful blending of Chinese, Malaysian, Indian, Thai, and Indonesian cultures.

The pastries technically are Chinese, or, more aptly, Nonya, a local hybrid cuisine that originated when Chinese traders settling in Singapore, Penang, and Malacca took Malay wives. Instead of the cloying and heavy preparations many foreigners associate with Chinese confections, these are light and enticing delicacies. There is *kueh talam*, neon-green and white slices of steamed sweet rice cake laced with coconut milk. *Abomb*, another pastry made of rice flour, is covered with a sweet sauce made of mapley palm sugar and chunks of banana. *Kueh ubi goreng* is a tapioca pancake flavored with the vanilla-like pandan leaf. The bakery offers a selection of 30 to 40 sweet and savory delicacies daily.

In Singapore, cakes are made with rice or tapioca flour and coconut milk and puddings. Porridgelike sweets are made with beans and rice. Many of the confections are neon green, colored by the juices of the pandan leaf. These dishes are not necessarily served as desserts, but, instead, are nibbled as snacks with tea or gobbled up quickly for breakfast.

Two-Spice Vanilla Tapioca Pudding

This is one of those creamy, finger-licking-good desserts that nurture the spirit as well as the body. I like to make an old-fashioned milk-based tapioca pudding, substituting soy milk for regular milk.

1/2 cup small pearl tapioca (if unavailable, use large pearl tapioca)

4 cups soy milk

3/4 cup sugar

1/2 teaspoon salt

2 egg yolks

1 tablespoon vanilla extract

1 1/2 teaspoons ground cinnamon

3/4 teaspoon ground nutmeg

3 egg whites, at room temperature

1/4 teaspoon cream of tartar

SIX TO EIGHT SERVINGS

1. Soak the tapioca in warm water to cover for 1 hour. Drain and set aside.
2. Preheat the oven to 375°F. Lightly butter a 12-inch oval or gratin baking dish and place it on a cookie sheet.
3. Mix the tapioca, soy milk, sugar, and salt in a heavy nonaluminum saucepan. Bring the soy milk to a boil over medium heat while whisking. Lower the heat and let the mixture simmer 10 minutes, whisking occasionally. Remove from the heat and quickly whisk in the egg yolks, vanilla extract, cinnamon, and nutmeg.
4. In another bowl, beat the egg whites with the cream of tartar until just stiff. Whisk half a cupful into the tapioca, then fold the remaining egg whites in. Pour the tapioca mixture into the prepared baking dish.
5. Place the baking dish and cookie sheet on the middle shelf of the oven and pour several inches of boiling water around the outside. Bake about 35 minutes, until the top is puffed and golden. The inside will still be a little soft. Remove, cool slightly, and serve warm or at room temperature.

☯ Puddings made with pearl tapioca and pearl sago, a similar starchy vegetable, are quite popular in Asia. Their nurturing effects are far greater than their therapeutic properties.

Soy milk, which is the base of this pudding, lubricates the body and clears the lungs. It is often prescribed for urinary disorders and constipation.

Walnut-Jujube Cream

Nut soups, or "creams" as the Chinese call them, are often served as snacks, desserts, and "in-between" dishes at multicourse banquets to clear the palate. This lovely soup is both soothing and delicate.

**EIGHT TO TEN
SERVINGS**

2 cups jujubes, or dried Chinese dates
(available at Asian markets or Chinese
herbal stores)
4 cups water

3/4 cup shelled walnuts
2 tablespoons cream of rice or wheat*
5 tablespoons sugar
1 tablespoon vanilla extract

1. Soften the jujubes in boiling water to cover for 1 hour, changing the water twice. Drain and remove the pits. Put the pitted dates in a food processor fitted with a steel blade or a blender, add $^1/_2$ cup water, and puree to a paste.

2. Add the walnuts, cream of rice or wheat, and 1 cup water, and blend until smooth. Pour the mixture into a saucepan and add the remaining $2^1/_2$ cups water and the sugar, stirring to blend.

3. Heat the walnut-jujube cream over low heat, stirring as it thickens, until just under a boil. Add the vanilla. Remove from the heat and ladle into serving bowls. Serve hot.

*If unavailable, soak 3 tablespoons glutinous, or sweet, rice in hot water for 1 hour, changing the water twice. Drain and puree to a paste in a food processor fitted with a steel blade.

☯ Jujubes, or Chinese dates, are considered to be effective in combating fatigue and anemia. They energize the body. They also strengthen the spleen and stomach. Postpartum women use them frequently in dishes to rebuild their strength and blood supply after childbirth.

Walnuts tone the kidneys and warm the lungs. Chinese doctors prescribe them for relieving asthma. A traditional remedy for coughs and constipation is 2 tablespoons ground walnuts mixed with 1 tablespoon honey.

Pumpkin Caramel Custard

This custard was created one dreary winter day when I was developing recipes for holiday menus. It's deliciously rich, but light. Once again I've replaced cow's milk with soy milk, creating a healthier, yet satisfying, dessert.

1 cup sugar

2 cups soy milk

1/2 cup cooked pumpkin puree or canned pumpkin puree

4 eggs, lightly beaten

2 tablespoons vanilla extract

1 1/2 teaspoons ground cinnamon

1/2 teaspoon ground nutmeg

1/2 teaspoon ground ginger

SIX SERVINGS

1. To make the caramel, combine 1/2 cup of the sugar and 1/4 cup water in a heavy saucepan. Cook the mixture over medium heat without stirring, and wash down the sides with a brush dipped in water to prevent crystals from forming. Once the sugar has dissolved, gently swirl the pan from time to time, cooking over medium heat until the mixture turns a deep caramel color, about 10 to 12 minutes.

2. Once the caramel has become golden, you need to work quickly: Pour one sixth of the caramel into the bottom of a 3/4-cup ramekin. Swirl the ramekin so that the caramel coats the bottom and a little of the sides. Repeat with the remaining ramekins. Preheat the oven to 350°F.

3. Scald the soy milk in a heavy saucepan. Mix the pumpkin, the remaining 1/2 cup sugar, eggs, vanilla, cinnamon, nutmeg, and ginger in a bowl. Whisk the hot soy milk into the pumpkin puree and ladle the mixture evenly among the ramekins.

4. Place the ramekins in a lasagna pan or baking dish, pour several inches of boiling water around the ramekins, and cover with aluminum foil. Bake 45 to 50 minutes, or until the custards have set. Remove the ramekins from the baking dish and let the custards cool on a rack. Run a knife around the side of each ramekin, invert onto a plate, and serve warm or chilled.

☯ Pumpkin, like other winter squashes, dispels dampness from the body and reduces pain and fever. The Chinese believe that a slice of pumpkin a day will improve diabetes.

Coconut Rice Pudding with Berries

I adore rice puddings of all kinds with fruit. In this dish, the combination of a coconut rice congee, tart raspberries, and a cinnamon–brown sugar topping is superb.

EIGHT TO TEN
SERVINGS

1 cup short-grain or Arborio rice
6 cups soy milk
3 cups coconut milk, preferably light
1 teaspoon salt
1 tablespoon vanilla extract

1 pint fresh berries (raspberries, blueberries, or blackberries), rinsed and drained
3 tablespoons cinnamon sugar, made with 1 tablespoon light-brown sugar, 2 tablespoons granulated sugar, and 1 teaspoon ground cinnamon

1. Put the rice in a pot and, using your fingers as a rake, rinse it under cold water to remove some of the talc. Drain the rice in a colander, then put it in a bowl and soak it in cold water to cover for 1 hour. Drain again.

2. Put the rice, soy milk, and coconut milk in a heavy saucepan with a lid. Heat uncovered until boiling. Reduce the heat to low, partially cover the pan, and simmer for 1 hour, stirring occasionally. The resulting liquid will be a thick porridge.

3. Ladle the congee into serving bowls and divide the fruit among them, arranging the berries on top. Sprinkle with cinnamon sugar and serve warm.

☯ For me, few sweets are as nurturing or psychologically therapeutic as rice pudding. For the benefits of congee, see page 232.

Chinese doctors revere dried unripe raspberries, which they say tone the liver and kidneys, enrich and cleanse the blood, and regulate menstruation. Ripe raspberries, they believe, improve vision. A paste of cooked, reduced raspberries is sometimes applied to the skin to improve eczema.

Soothing Pear Congee

This is the dish I crave when my throat aches before the onset of a cold. It is deliciously soothing and warming. I often vary the fruit, using apples, peaches, and even berries.

1/2 cup short-grain or Arborio rice

5 cups water

1/4 teaspoon salt

1 recipe Poached Pears in a Cinnamon-Ginger Syrup (page 258)

EIGHT TO TEN SERVINGS

1. Put the rice in a pot and, using your fingers as a rake, rinse it under cold water to remove some of the talc, then drain it in a colander.
2. Put the rice and water in a heavy saucepan with a lid. Heat uncovered until boiling. Reduce the heat to low, partially cover the pan, and simmer for 45 minutes, stirring occasionally.
3. Prepare the recipe for Poached Pears in a Cinnamon-Ginger Syrup, but after poaching the pears, remove them with a slotted spoon and cut them into 1/2-inch dice. Add the diced pears to the syrup and then mix into the porridge. Cook another 10 minutes. Mix, ladle into soup bowls, and serve

☯ According to Professor Weng Weijian, author of *Chinese Herbal Foods to Enhance Your Health,* pear congee should be eaten to ease coughs and congestion in the lungs. It will also, he claims, dissipate poor appetite, dizziness, and fever.

An Ode to Tea

There is some dispute as to when tea first made its auspicious debut in China. A popular myth credits the Emperor Shen Nong, the founder of Chinese agriculture (2737–2697 B.C.), as the creator of the drink. The emperor, so it is said, was fond of brewing drinks with different varieties of wild grass and one day several tea leaves innocently fell into the pot, producing the first official cup of tea. It is known that the plant grew wild in Asia as early as A.D. 350 and tea as we know it was drunk during the period of the Three Kingdoms (A.D. 222–277).

There are four main types of Chinese tea, which are classified according to the way the leaves are treated after picking:

- Green teas are merely leaves that have been picked directly from the plants and dried. The flavor is somewhat astringent, and many find these teas refreshing after a heavy meal.
- Semi-fermented (oxidized), or oolong, teas are made with leaves that have been partially cured. While the flavor differs according to the particular brand, oolongs tend to be subtler and less sharp than their fermented cousins. Some contend that oolong teas are the most desirable of all, combining the appealing characteristics of both black and green tea.
- Black, or red, teas are made with leaves that have been cured, or toasted. They tend to have a hearty, robust flavor. Black teas should always be made with boiling water to bring out their fullest taste.
- Flower teas, which are made by infusing hot water with dried flower petals, have become increasingly popular in Asia. They are believed to have originated during the Sung dynasty (A.D. 960–1280), when dried flowers were blended with inferior tea leaves to improve their flavor. Chrysanthemum, rose, cassia, lotus, plum, and orchid petals are all used to make flower tea.

According to Dr. Albert Leung, author of *Better Health with (Mostly) Chinese Herbs and Foods,* the use of tea in Traditional Chinese Medicine was first recorded in an early sixth-century herbal journal, where it was written that tea is "good for people who sleep too much." Tea was credited with clearing the mind, voice, and vision, quenching thirst, aiding digestion, relieving flatulence, and ridding the body of toxins.

The early pharmacological benefits derived mainly from its caffeine and tannin content. (Tannins, says Dr. Leung, have astringent, germ-killing, and anticarcinogenic properties.) But tea was also praised for easing dysentery, cholera, and diphtheria.

Some of the most traditional remedies made with tea are:

- A cup of strong black tea for a hangover.
- A teaspoon of strong black or green tea for diarrhea or gastritis.
- A poultice, made with tea leaves soaked in hot water, to help dry up poison ivy or poison oak.

Recently, green tea has been hailed as a cancer preventative. Since 1983, doctors at the Saitama Cancer Research Institute in Japan have been studying its remarkable anticarcinogenic and antitumor effects. (Recent studies have shown that black tea may possess the same or similar tonic properties as green. Researchers now believe that tea has antioxidant power equal to that of some fruits and vegetables.) In addition, they and U.S. doctors have reported evidence that green tea may reduce the risk of heart disease and stroke.

To make a good pot of tea:

1. Rinse the teapot with boiling water to heat it and remove resins from the last brewing.
2. Put loose tea in the pot, adding 1 heaping teaspoon for every cup of water.
3. Pour a little boiling water into the pot, swish it around, then pour it out. This step removes some of the tannin in the tea.
4. Pour boiling water into the pot, cover, and let the tea steep for 3 to 5 minutes before serving.

Almond Crisps

Almond cookies might be considered the quintessential Chinese dessert. I make a light, crisp whisper of a wafer, chock-full of sliced almonds and delectable with tea.

MAKES THIRTY-TWO
COOKIES

3 tablespoons unsalted butter
1/2 cup sliced almonds, sliced Chinese almonds, or "apricot kernels" (see note about almonds, page 260)
3/4 cup sugar

3 large egg whites
1/2 cup all-purpose flour
1 teaspoon cinnamon
1/2 teaspoon salt
1 tablespoon vanilla extract

1. Preheat the oven to 300°F. Lightly spray baking sheets with a vegetable oil spray or brush with 2 tablespoons melted butter.

2. Melt the 3 tablespoons butter in a small saucepan and add the sliced almonds. Stir over low heat until the butter and almonds are golden. Pour them into a mixing bowl, whisk in the sugar, and add the egg whites, flour, cinnamon, salt, and vanilla. Whisk until smooth.

3. Drop the batter by teaspoon 2 inches apart on the prepared cookie sheets. Smooth the batter into circles about 3 inches in diameter with the back of a spoon. Bake 10 to 12 minutes, or until lightly golden. Loosen the cookies with a spatula while still hot and drape a number of them over a rolling pin to shape them. They will set in seconds. Remove the set cookies to a cooling rack. Repeat for the remaining batter and cookies. Serve with green tea.

☯ The Chinese credit almonds with removing stagnant *qi* from the lungs and alleviating coughs, constipation, and asthma. To treat coughs and asthma, Chinese physicians often recommend drinking a paste made with ground almonds and fructose, a sweetener.

Debby's Steamed Banana Cake

One of my dearest friends, Debby Richards, has been cooking and sampling food with me since sixth grade. She has become a talented and creative cook in her own right. This is her recipe for banana cake. The original recipe calls for baking; Debby and I adapted the recipe slightly for steaming.

TWELVE SERVINGS

2 tablespoons unsalted butter, softened	3 large eggs, at room temperature
2 1/2 cups all-purpose flour	1 cup sugar
1 tablespoon baking powder	3 ripe bananas, mashed (roughly 2 cups)
1 1/2 teaspoons ground cinnamon	1/2 cup nonfat yogurt
1 teaspoon baking soda	2 tablespoons unsalted butter, melted
1/4 teaspoon salt	1 tablespoon vanilla extract

1. Generously grease a 10-inch tube pan with the softened butter, thoroughly coating it. Sift together the flour, baking powder, cinnamon, baking soda, and salt.

2. Break the eggs into a large bowl. Beat vigorously with an electric mixer at high speed about 5 minutes, until the eggs are light and lemon-colored and have tripled in volume. Add the sugar and beat for 3 minutes. Separately add the mashed bananas, yogurt, melted butter, and vanilla extract, beating well after each addition. Fold in the flour mixture. Pour the batter into the greased pan.

3. Fill a wok or large pot with enough water for steaming and heat until boiling. Place the cake pan in a steamer tray over the boiling water or balance it on a trivet or a tunafish can with ends removed in the center of the pan. Cover and steam over high heat for 50 minutes, or until the cake is springy to the touch; check the water level after 30 minutes and add more boiling water if necessary. Remove the cake from the steamer and let it cool slightly. Unmold it onto a platter, cut it into slices, and serve warm with tea. To reheat, steam for 10 minutes.

☯ Bananas are believed to clear body heat, lower blood pressure, and lubricate the intestines. Cooked banana sweetened with sugar is a traditional remedy recommended for coughs.

Fresh Lemon Sponge Cake

The Cantonese make a lovely steamed brown-sugar sponge cake called *ma la gao*. I often vary the recipe, adding orange and lemon peel. This is my lemon-flavored version of this venerable classic. It's delicious with tea.

TEN SERVINGS

2 tablespoons unsalted butter, softened
2 1/2 cups all-purpose flour
2 teaspoons baking powder
1/2 teaspoon baking soda
1 teaspoon salt
5 large eggs, at room temperature
1 1/2 cups tightly packed light-brown sugar

1 cup nonfat yogurt
2 teaspoons vanilla extract
3 1/2 tablespoons finely minced lemon zest, blanched in boiling water for 10 seconds
Juice of 1 lemon
Confectioners' sugar for dusting

1. Generously grease a 10-inch tube pan with softened butter, making certain it is thoroughly coated. Sift together the flour, baking powder, baking soda, and salt.

2. Break the eggs into a large bowl. Beat vigorously with an electric mixer at high speed about 5 minutes, until the eggs are light and lemon-colored and have tripled in volume. Add the brown sugar and beat for 3 minutes. Separately add the yogurt, vanilla extract, lemon zest, and lemon juice, beating well after each addition. Fold in the dry ingredients. Pour the batter into the greased pan.

3. Fill a wok or a large pot with enough water for steaming and heat until boiling. Place the cake pan in a steamer tray over the boiling water or balance it on a trivet or a tunafish can with ends removed in the center of the pan. Cover and steam over high heat for 1 hour, or until the cake is springy to the touch; check the water level after 30 minutes and add more boiling water if necessary. Remove from the steamer and let the cake cool. Unmold it onto a platter, dust with confectioners' sugar, cut into slices, and serve warm or at room temperature with tea.

> ☯ Lemons produce and nourish fluids in the body, clear summer heat, and quench thirst. They also are believed to cleanse the blood, improve digestion, and lower blood pressure. A tea made by brewing lemon peel and boiling water for 20 minutes will temper bad breath.

Orange Madeleines

I was first introduced to madeleines many years ago, when I was studying cooking in Paris. I was totally captivated, and they have become one of my favorite sweets to serve with green or black tea. Most madeleines are very buttery. This version is spongier, with less butter, but still rich and delicious, with a fresh orange flavor.

MAKES FORTY-EIGHT
MADELEINES

1/2 cup unsalted butter, cut into 8
   tablespoon-size pieces
1 cup sugar
4 large egg yolks
1/4 teaspoon salt
1/4 teaspoon baking powder
Peel of 1 orange, finely chopped

Juice of 1 orange
1 tablespoon vanilla extract
1 1/2 cups all-purpose flour
4 egg whites
1/4 teaspoon cream of tartar
Confectioners' sugar (optional)

☯ Orange peel is a popular Chinese flavoring. It stimulates *qi* and is particularly beneficial in aiding digestion. The oil is sometimes recommended for treating indigestion and colic in children. Orange oil is massaged into the skin to remove stretch marks after childbirth. Orange tea, made by steeping the peel in boiling water, is a traditional remedy drunk to relieve stagnant *qi* and remove mucus from the throat or lungs.

1. Preheat the oven to 350°F. Spray madeleine molds lightly with a vegetable oil spray or brush with 2 tablespoons melted butter.

2. In an electric mixer, at low speed, cream the butter and sugar until light and lemon-colored, about 5 minutes. Add the egg yolks one at a time, beating after each addition. Add the salt, baking powder, orange peel, orange juice, and vanilla extract. Beat until smooth.

3. Slowly add the flour, beating, and mix until the batter is even. In another bowl, beat the egg whites with the cream of tartar until stiff. Mix about 1 cup of the batter into the egg whites, then fold the remaining egg whites into the batter. Drop tablespoons of the batter into the molds. (They should be three quarters full.) Bake about 10 minutes, until the madeleines are golden at the edges and firm in the center. Sharply tap the edge of the madeleine molds to dislodge the madeleines onto a cooling rack. Repeat for the remaining batter. After the madeleines are cool, dust them lightly, if desired, with confectioners' sugar. Serve with tea.

泰安参茸药行有限公司
Ginseng Medical Hall
Private Limited

Thye On
泰安

泰安参茸药行有限公司

The Kitchen Clinic
and Herbal Tonics

The Kitchen Clinic, Herbal Tonics, and Daniel Reid

I went to Chiangmai, Thailand, a picturesque city nestled in the mountains north of Bangkok, just to meet Daniel Reid. Although Reid is American, he is considered a noted authority on Chinese medicine and he has written a number of books on the subject, including *The Tao of Health, Sex & Longevity: A Modern Practical Guide to the Ancient Way* (Simon & Schuster, 1989), *The Complete Book of Chinese Health and Healing* (Shambhala, 1994), and *Chinese Herbal Medicine* (Shambhala, 1986).

Years earlier I had talked to Daniel Reid by phone when I interviewed him for a *New York Times* article on food as medicine. His vibrant enthusiasm for the subject was evident even through the telephone line. Reid lives with his wife, Yuki, who is a Chinese-Japanese herbalist and healer. Although he speaks and reads Mandarin fluently, she helps him translate some of the more difficult Chinese medical texts for his books.

Many would consider their life to be rather idyllic: Each morning, they rise at 7:30 and practice 2 hours of *qi gong,* the form of meditative exercise that is believed to control and enhance the body's *qi,* or energy. They then meditate and sip a special oolong tea that they import from Taiwan. Their spartan breakfast consists of pureed tofu spread on toasted wholegrain bread. The rest of the day is spent writing and studying. It's a leisurely existence that has served Reid well; he is forty-eight, but he looks to be in his mid-thirties.

Reid first became involved with Chinese medicine in Taiwan in the early 1970s. After receiving a master's degree in Chinese language and literature from the University of California at Berkeley, he traveled to Taiwan for further study. Once there, he ended up working in restaurants and writing a Chinese cookbook with Jacki Passmore, an Asian food authority.

A recurring sports injury led him to a Chinese physician, who miraculously cured him with acupuncture and herbs. The experience so impressed Reid that he began studying with a doctor. For the next ten years he continued his studies with a number of distinguished doctors in Taiwan before writing his first acclaimed book, *Chinese Herbal Medicine,* in 1986.

Reid's early interest in Chinese food became very useful once he began studying Chinese medicine and herbs. "In Chinese cuisine, as well as in Chinese herbal medicine, there is no clearly defined line between food and medicine," he says. "Traditional Chinese kitchens are always well stocked with a variety of medicinal foods, like ginseng, wolfberry, and jujubes, which are used in cooking to enhance and balance the therapeutic properties of food, while Chinese herbal pharmacies carry seasonings such as cinnamon, ginger, black mushrooms, and cardamom—more food than medicine per se."

Reid suggests that classic Chinese cuisine evolved as an offshoot of Traditional Chinese Medicine, which, he claims, is why virtually all food cooked the Chinese way contains at least one of several medicinally active aromatics and seasonings, such as ginger and garlic. He maintains that in the imperial palaces and wealthy households of ancient China, professional herbalists—not cooks—were hired to take charge of the kitchens, supervising the purchase and preparation of all the foods. The cooks simply acted as their assistants, following the herbalists' instructions in the cooking.

According to Reid, one reason traditional Chinese cuisine sits so well on the stomach, or you "feel hungry again an hour later," is that rich, heavy ingredients such as meat and fish are always cooked with aromatics that balance their pharmacodynamic properties, facilitating their harmonious digestion.

Historically, medicinal herbs were used in cooking to prevent disease, not to "cure" it. Two types of herbal formulas were developed: "constitutional" formu-

las, which were specifically blended to balance inherent and acquired deficiencies in particular individuals, and "tonic" formulas, which boost immunity, enhance vitality, nurture health, slow aging, and prolong life. Whereas curative formulas employ powerful bioactive and occasionally semitoxic herbs, constitutional formulas utilize gentler, more nourishing herbs that balance yin and yang and harmonize the body's energies.

Besides cooking tasty dishes, the family cook traditionally prepares foods that will balance the prevailing energies of the season and the local climate, and that will tone the vital organs, enhancing their functions. Everything is planned according to the principles of yin and yang as well as the basic tenets of Traditional Chinese Medicine.

Furthermore, according to Reid, in traditional Chinese households people consume constitutional herbal formulas cooked into their daily meals for many of the same chronic conditions people in modern Western households take powerful, often addictive pharmaceutical drugs for.

"While the lady of the house sips her chicken with angelica [*dang gui*] soup to regulate her menses," Reid explained, "the lord of the manor might lunch on chicken stew liberally laced with ginseng, wolfberry, and cardamom to compensate for the deficiency in his kidney and adrenal system."

On the following pages are some of Reid's favorite and most useful constitutional and tonic formulas. All Chinese herbs are available at Asian herbal stores.

Ginger-Scallion Root Tea

This is a curative formula traditionally used in Chinese households as a specific remedy for curing colds, flu, and other bronchial ailments of the "cold type." (This phrase denotes those bronchial ailments accompanied by chills rather than fever. Since the tea is a warming yang formula, it should not be used for colds accompanied by fever.) It is also an effective therapy for "stomach colds" accompanied by diarrhea, for nausea and motion sickness, and for chronically cold hands and feet.

6 to 8 thin slices fresh ginger with peel, about the size of a quarter, smashed lightly with the side of a knife 6 to 8 scallions, white part only	2 to 3 teaspoons raw sugar (such as Demerara), honey, or maple syrup, according to taste 1/4 teaspoon sea salt 2 cups spring water

Put the ginger slices and scallions in a small pot (preferably glass or ceramic) and add the sweetener, sea salt, and water. Bring to boil, stir well, lower the heat, and simmer for 10 minutes. Strain and serve hot.

Lotus Root Cooler

This formula is very good for detoxifying the liver and balancing excess "fire energy" from an overheated liver. It cools the blood, calms the nerves, and "refrigerates" the system in excessively hot weather.

1 large fresh lotus root (available at Asian markets) Raw sugar (such as Demerara) or barley	malt (not honey, which would counteract the effects of the root), according to taste 4 cups spring water

Cut the lotus root into 1-inch lengths. Put the lotus root sections and sweetener in a saucepan and add boiling water to cover. Cover with a lid and let steep for 10 minutes. Strain and drink it throughout the day.

Ginseng Licorice Tea

This is an overall blood and energy tonic that also helps to detoxify the whole system. It has specific tonifying effects on the lungs and digestive system. The natural sweetness of licorice precludes the need for any additional sweetener. The white ginseng rootlets from Panax ginseng are sold separately from the roots and are not expensive.

1 handful small tendril rootlets of white ginseng roots	人參（人参）	*(ren shen)*
10 long thin slices of licorice root (Glycyrrhiza uralensis or G. glabra)	甘草	*(gan cao)*

Put the ginseng and licorice together in a thermos or a large teapot and add 4 cups boiling water. Steep for 20 minutes, then pour off the liquid into a separate container. Add 4 more cups boiling water to the ginseng and licorice and steep 20 minutes more. You may repeat this process with the same roots up to 5 times. Strain the tea and drink it throughout the day.

Ten Complete Great Tonic

This is one of the most popular tonic formulas in Chinese medicine, perfectly blended to enhance energy, nourish blood, and balance yin and yang. It strengthens immunity and resistance, regulates vital functions, and prolongs life.

8 grams	Panax ginseng	人参（人參）	(ren shen)
8 grams	White atractylodes rhizome	白术	(bai zhu)
8 grams	Poria	茯苓	(fu ling)
8 grams	Licorice	甘草	(gan cao)
8 grams	Rehmannia root	熟地黄	(shu di huang)
8 grams	Ligusticum	川芎	(chuang xiong)
8 grams	Angelica sinensis	当归	(dang gui)
8 grams	White peony root	白芍药（白芍藥）	(bai shao yao)
4 grams	Cinnamomum	肉桂	(rou gui)
4 grams	Astragalus	黄芪（黄耆）	(huang qi)

Put the herbs in a glass or ceramic heatproof vessel with 4 cups spring water. Bring to a boil, lower the heat, and simmer until the liquid is reduced by half. Strain the broth and reserve. Add 2 more cups spring water to the herbs, boil, and simmer again until reduced by half. Strain the broth, add it to the first brew, and discard the herbs. Divide the broth into 3 equal doses and drink warm on an empty stomach in the early morning, in the afternoon, and at bedtime.

Longevity Tonic

This longevity formula enhances both physical and mental energy. It is also a specific tonic for the liver and kidneys, and may be used for prolonged periods without any side effects.

8 grams	Panax ginseng	人参（人參）	*(ren shen)*
8 grams	Polygonum	何首乌	*(he shou wu)*
8 grams	Lycium	枸杞子	*(gou qi zi)*
8 grams	Schizandra fruit	五味子	*(wu wei zi)*
8 grams	Asparagus	天门冬	*(tian men dong)*

Put the herbs in a glass or ceramic heatproof vessel with 4 cups spring water. Bring to a boil, lower the heat, and simmer until the liquid is reduced by half. Strain the broth. Add 2 more cups spring water to the herbs, boil, and simmer again until reduced by half. Strain the broth, add it to the first brew, and discard the herbs. Divide the broth into 3 equal doses and drink warm on an empty stomach in the early morning, in the afternoon, and at bedtime.

The herbs may also be steeped in 1 liter of vodka, brandy, or other spirits for 3 to 6 months. Strain the spirits, discard the herbs, and drink 1 to 2 ounces daily on an empty stomach.

Female Balance Tonic

This is an excellent blood tonic for women and may be used to balance female hormonal reactions and regulate menstrual cycles. For PMS, take the tonic for one full week prior to the anticipated onset of menses.

8 grams	Angelica sinensis	当归	(dang gui)
8 grams	Rehmannia root	熟地黄	(shu di huang)
8 grams	White peony root	白芍药（白芍藥）	(bai shao yao)
8 grams	Astragalus	黄芪（黄耆）	(huang qi)
8 grams	Poria	茯苓	(fu ling)
8 grams	Licorice root	甘草	(gan cao)
8 grams	Codonopsis root	党参（黨參）	(dang shen)
8 grams	Ligusticum	川芎	(chuan xiong)

Put the herbs in a glass or ceramic heatproof vessel with 4 cups spring water. Bring to a boil, lower the heat, and simmer until the liquid is reduced by half. Strain the broth. Add 2 more cups spring water to the herbs, boil, and simmer again until reduced by half. Strain the broth, add to the first brew, and discard the herbs. Divide the broth into 3 equal doses and drink warm on an empty stomach in the early morning, in the afternoon, and at bedtime. The herbs may also be steeped in 1 liter vodka, brandy, or other spirits for 3 to 6 months. Strain the spirits, discard the herbs, and drink 1 to 2 ounces daily on an empty stomach.

For Common Cold and Flu

A general remedy for colds of the "wind-heat" type. The most common symptoms are cough, headache, and dizziness.

3 grams	(6 months to 2 years)	Dryopteris crassirhizoma 贯众	*(guan zhong)*
5 grams	(3 to 6 years)		
7 grams	(7 to 10 years)		
10 grams	(over 10 years)		

Place the herb in a glass or ceramic heatproof vessel with 4 cups spring water. Bring to a boil, reduce the heat, and simmer until reduced by half. Strain, discard the herb, sweeten to taste with honey, and drink throughout the day.

For High Blood Pressure

This tonic effectively lowers high blood pressure without causing any undesirable side effects.

30 grams	Lonicera japonica	金银花	(jin yin hua)
30 grams	Chrysanthemum flower	菊花	(ju hua)
12 grams	Mulberry leaf	桑叶（桑葉）	(sang ye)
20 grams	Crataegus	山楂	(shan zha)
20 grams	Cirsium japonicum	大蓟	(da ji)

Place the herbs in a glass or ceramic heatproof vessel with 5 cups spring water. Bring to a boil, lower the heat, and let simmer until the liquid is reduced to 3 cups. Strain the liquid and discard the herbs. Divide the liquid into 2 to 3 equal doses and drink two or three times during the day on an empty stomach.

For Constipation

This formula relieves constipation of the "full-hot" type, with accompanying symptoms of a bloated abdomen, foul breath, flatulence, excess body heat, and a headache.

10 grams	Immature bitter orange fruit	枳实（枳實）	*(zhi shi)*
10 grams	Mirabilite	芒硝	*(mang xiao)*
6 grams	Rhubarb root	大黄	*(da huang)*
10 grams	Magnolia officinalis	厚朴（厚樸）	*(hou po)*

Put the Bitter orange fruit and Mirabilite in a glass or ceramic heatproof vessel with 3 cups spring water. Bring to a boil, lower the heat, and simmer until the liquid is reduced by half. Add the Rhubarb and simmer 15 more minutes. Add the Magnolia, stir for 1 minute, then turn off the heat. Strain the liquid and discard the herbs. Divide the broth into 3 equal doses and drink on an empty stomach in the early morning, in the after-noon, and at bedtime.

For Acne or Pimples

This formula helps to eliminate toxins and neutralize the acids that cause skin eruptions. It is important to avoid eating pungent, spicy foods, deep-fried foods, or meats.

8 grams	Schizonepeta	荆芥	(jing jie)
8 grams	Ledebouriella root	防风	(fang feng)
8 grams	Bupleurum root	柴胡	(chai hu)
8 grams	Gardenia jasminoides	栀子（枝子）	(zhi zi)
8 grams	Paeonia lactiflora	白芍	(bai shao yao)
8 grams	Forsythia suspensa	连翘	(lian qiao)
8 grams	Scutellaria baicalensis	黄芩	(huang qin)
8 grams	Poncirus trifoliata	枳实	(zhi shi)
8 grams	Ligusticum	川芎	(chuan xiong)
8 grams	Platycodon root	桔梗	(jie geng)
8 grams	Angelica sinensis	当归	(dang gui)
8 grams	Glycyrrhiza uralensis	甘草	(gan cao)

In a glass or ceramic heatproof vessel bring the herbs and 5 cups spring water to a boil, then simmer until the liquid is reduced to 3 cups. Strain and discard the herbs. Divide the broth into 2 to 3 equal doses and drink on an empty stomach during the day.

For Toothache

20 grams	Gypsum fibrosum	石膏	*(shi gao)*
3 grams	Asarum	细辛	*(xi xin)*
10 grams	Gardenia jasminoides	栀子（枝子）	*(zhi zi)*
6 grams	Paeonia lactiflora	白芍	*(bai shao yao)*
10 grams	Scrophularia root	玄参	*(xuan shen)*
3 grams	Prunus mume	绿萼梅	*(wu mei)*
5 grams	Rheum	大黄	*(da huang)*

Put the Gypsum in a glass or ceramic heatproof vessel with 4 cups spring water. Bring to a boil, lower the heat, and let simmer for 30 minutes. Add all the other ingredients except the Rheum, bring to a boil, and let simmer again until reduced to about 1½ cups liquid. Then add the Rheum and simmer 15 more minutes. Strain the broth and discard the herbs. Let cool and drink in a single dose on an empty stomach.

For Indigestion

This formula relieves indigestion caused by the excess consumption of red meats and animal fats.

15 grams	Crataegus pinnatifida	山楂	*(shan zha)*
6 grams	Citrus reticulata	桔络（橘絡）	*(ju luo)*
8 grams	Poncirus trifoliata	枳实（枳實）	*(liu chen pi)*
4 grams	Coptis chinensis	黄连	*(huang lian)*

Place the herbs in a glass or ceramic heatproof vessel with 3 cups spring water. Bring to a boil, lower the heat, and let simmer until the liquid is reduced to 1 cup. Strain the broth and discard the herbs. Drink warm in a single dose 1 hour after a meal.

For Hangovers

This formula should be prepared and taken in the morning after a night of excessive drinking.

20 grams	Hovenia dulcis	枳椇	*(zhi ju)*
10 grams	Pueraria/kudzu root	葛根	*(ge gen)*
10 grams	Pueraria flowers	葛花	*(ge hua)*

Place the herbs in a glass or ceramic heatproof vessel with 4 cups spring water. Bring to a boil, lower the heat, and simmer until the liquid is reduced to 2 cups. Strain the broth and discard the herbs. Divide into 2 equal doses, and drink the first dose immediately on an empty stomach. Take a second dose about 2 hours later.

ร้านอาหารไผ่ดำบ้านเรา
Golden Bamboo Restaurant My House
ฮะบุญเลขที่ 4109 ถ.เด็กญชัยวรโกระ 21-5791

O·B·B PURE GHEE

A great tradition
of natural taste

MOHAMED MEERA SAHIB (M) SDN. BHD.

TEL: 04-2613664/2622181
FAX: 604-2630379

BEE'S BRAND BIRDS NEST & HEALTH PRODUCTS CENTRE 01-60/62

SRI GANGA FANCY STORE

THAM NONG LA

COME — ENJOY

LAO FOODS

TRADITIONAL

LAO DANCE

DAILY

FOOD FOR THE STOMA

FOOD FOR THE EY

直接進口 德盛行 参茸燕窩藥材海味食品中

公司周年大酬賓 益顧客 一律以成本價大平賣 只限周年酬

中國華佗

保健套餐 $6 起
Healthy Set Meals from $6.0

任选二种加选一种甜品或龟苓
Set meal include any of the following 2 items, plus a dessert or herbal jell

香港生炒糯米饭 Hong Kong Style Fried Glutinous Ric
华佗竽头糕 Hua Tuo Yam Cake
八宝肠粉 Eight Treasures Cheong Fun
神仙粥 Herbal Porridge

$6.00 $7.50 $9.00

Bibliography

Cai, Jingfing. *Eating Your Way to Health: Dietotherapy in Traditional Chinese Medicine.* Beijing: Foreign Language Press, 1988.

Castleman, Michael. *The Healing Herbs: The Ultimate Guide to the Curative Power of Nature's Medicines.* Emmaus, Pa.: Rodale Press, 1991.

Chevallier, Andrew. *The Encyclopedia of Medicinal Plants.* London: Dorling Kindersley, 1996.

Chin, Wee Yeow, and Hsuan Keng. *Chinese Medicinal Herbs.* Singapore: Times Editions, 1990.

Colbin, Annemarie. *Food and Healing.* New York: Ballantine Books, 1996.

Curtis, Susan. *Neal's Yard Remedies: Essential Oils.* Hong Kong: Aurum Press, 1996.

Foster, Steven. *Herbs for Your Health: A Handy Guide for Knowing and Using 50 Common Herbs.* Loveland, Colo.: Interweave Press, 1996.

Haas, Elson. *Staying Healthy with the Seasons.* Berkeley, Calif.: Celestial Arts, 1981.

Hadady, Letha. *Asian Health Secrets.* New York: Crown Publishers, 1996.

Hobbs, Christopher. *Foundation of Health: Healing with Herbs & Foods.* Capitola, Calif.: Botanica Press, 1994.

——. *Medicinal Mushrooms: An Exploration of Tradition, Healing & Culture.* Santa Cruz, Calif.: Botanica Press, 1995.

International College of Traditional Chinese Medicine of Vancouver. *A Professional Career in Traditional Chinese Medicine.* Vancouver: Academy of Oriental Heritage, 1995.

Johari, Harish. *The Healing Cuisine: India's Art of Ayurvedic Cooking.* Rochester, Vt.: Healing Arts Press, 1994.

Lai, T. C. *At the Chinese Table.* Hong Kong: Oxford University Press, 1984.

——. *Chinese Food for Thought.* Hong Kong: Hong Kong Book Centre, 1978.

Leung, Albert Y. *Better Health with (Mostly) Chinese Herbs and Foods.* Glen Rock, N.J.: AYSL Corporation, 1995.

———. *Chinese Healing Foods and Herbs.* New York: AYSL Corporation, 1984.

———. *Chinese Herbal Remedies.* New York: Universe Books, 1984.

Lianming, Zhang, Li Siusong, Xiong Sizhi, and Qiu Pangtong. *Chinese Family Feast Dishes.* Jinan, China: Shandong Science and Technology Press, 1993.

Liebenstein, Marge. *The Edible Mushroom.* New York: Fawcett Books, 1986.

Lieberman, Shari, and Ken Babal. *Maitake: King of Mushrooms.* New Canaan, Conn.: Keats Publishing, 1997.

Lu, Henry. *Chinese Herbs with Common Foods.* New York: Kodansha International, 1997.

———. *Chinese System of Food Cures.* New York: Sterling Publishing, 1986.

———. *Chinese System of Natural Cures.* New York: Sterling Publishing, 1994.

———. *The Chinese System of Using Foods to Stay Young.* New York: Sterling Publishing, 1996.

———. *Doctor's Manual of Chinese Food Cures and Western Nutrition.* 2 vols. Vancouver: Academy of Oriental Heritage, 1995.

Marks, Copeland. *The Korean Kitchen: Classic Recipes from the Land of the Morning Calm.* San Francisco: Chronicle Books, 1993.

Mindell, Earl. *Earl Mindell's Food as Medicine.* New York: Fireside Books, 1994.

Mori, Kisaku. *Mushrooms as Health Foods.* Tokyo: Japan Publications, 1974.

Muying, Zhao. *Chinese Diet Therapy.* Translated by Wen Jingen. Beijing: China Esperanto Press, 1996.

Ng, Siong Mui. *The Chinese Pregnancy and Confinement Cookbook.* Singapore: Landmark Books, 1990.

———. *Nutritious Chinese Food for Infants, Children and Youth.* Singapore: Landmark Books, 1991.

———. *Secrets of Nutritional Chinese Cookery.* Singapore: Landmark Books, 1988.

Ni, Maoshing, and Cathy McNease. *The Tao of Nutrition.* Santa Monica, Calif.: SevenStar Communications Group, 1994.

Ody, Penelope. *The Complete Medicinal Herbal.* New York: Dorling Kindersley, 1993.

———. *Home Herbal.* New York: Dorling Kindersley, 1995.

Patnaik, Naveen. *The Garden of Life: An Introduction to the Healing Plants of India.* New York: Bantam Doubleday Dell Publishing Group, 1993.

Pitchford, Paul. *Healing with Whole Foods: Oriental Traditions and Modern Nutrition.* Berkeley, Calif.: North Atlantic Books, 1993.

Polunin, Miriam. *The Book of Healing Foods.* Toronto: Alfred A. Knopf Canada, 1997.

Rasmussen, Oi Heng. *The Chinese Art of Healthy Eating.* Singapore: Times Editions, 1994.

Reid, Daniel. *Chinese Herbal Medicine.* Boston: Shambhala Publications, 1986.

———. *The Complete Book of Chinese Health & Healing.* Boston: Shambhala Publications, 1994.

———. *The Tao of Health, Sex, and Longevity.* New York: Fireside Books, 1989.

Sharon, Michael. *Nutrients A to Z.* Wales: Prion Books, 1998.

Tan, Cecilia. *The Family Herbal Cookbook.* Singapore: Times Books International, 1989.

Tan, Terry. *Cooking with Chinese Herbs.* Singapore: Times Books International, 1983.

Tang, Stephen, and Richard Craze. *Chinese Herbal Medicine.* London: Judith Piatkus, 1995.

Teeguarden, Ron. *Chinese Tonic Herbs.* New York: Japan Publications, 1994.

Van Straten, Michael, and Corinne Hall. *Super Foods.* Singapore: Dorling Kindersley, 1997.

Weijian, Weng. *Chinese Herbal Foods to Enhance Your Health,* vol. 1. Singapore: Guoji Translation & Publishing, 1990.

Wengao, Zhang, Jia Wencheng, Li Shupei, Zhang Jing, Ou Yangbing, and Xu Xuelan. *Chinese Medicated Diet: A Practical English-Chinese Library of Traditional Chinese Medicine.* Shanghai, China: Publishing House of Shanghai College of Traditional Chinese Medicine, 1990.

Yan Sang, Eu. *An Anthology of Chinese Herbs and Medicines.* Singapore: Eu Yan Sang International Holdings, 1995.

Yeoh, Aileen. *Longevity, The Tao of Eating and Healing.* Singapore: Times Editions, 1989.

Index

a

Academy of Oriental Heritage (Vancouver), 96
Academy of Traditional Chinese Medicine (Beijing), 218
acne, tonic for, 295
acupuncture, 95–6
adolescence, 17
adulthood, 17
aging, 18, 30, 49
allergies, 193
almond(s), 261, 266, 276
  crisps, 276
  pears steamed with honey and, 260
  soy jelly with litchees and melon, 266
Ambila chicken, 100–3
anemia, 258
angelica, 18
  clear-steamed chicken soup with dates and, 28
anticoagulants, 41
antioxidants, 275
aphrodisiacs, 30, 69
appetite, improving, 37, 48, 92, 110, 188, 189, 208, 257, 263, 273
apple(s), 263
  baked with honey, cinnamon, and jujubes, 262
  congee, 273
apricot kernels, 260, 261
arthritis, 77, 110, 149
Asian holistic philosophy, 4–6, 20
asparagus, 127
  congee, 233, 234
  roasted, with sesame vinaigrette, 175
asthma, 266, 276

b

At the Chinese Table (Lai), 68
autumn, diet for, 14
AYSL company, 193
Ayurvedic medicine, 153, 163, 176, 266

babies, 16, 220
bad breath, 190, 279
bai shao (dried white peony), 18
banana, 278
  cake, steamed, 278
  -coconut pudding, 267
barley, 236
  soup, with cinnamon, 48
  turkey congee with, 236
basil, 190
  chicken stir-fried with, 114
  clams with garlic and, 85
  tempeh stir-fried with, 214
basmati rice, 220
bean curd, *see* tofu
beans
  Chinese long, chicken with, 102–3
  see also black beans; soybeans
bean sprouts
  chicken with
    lo mein, 246–7
    noodle soup, 38
    saté, 118–19
  flash-cooked, 161
  garlic bean curd noodles with, 200
  ginger beef with, 148
  in pad thai, 245
  in rainbow salad with spicy peanut dressing, 199

bean sprouts *(cont.)*
    in shrimp and vegetable salad, 190
    soybean, and leeks in hot chile sauce, 198
bean threads, chicken soup with Chinese
        cabbage and, 33
beef, 132
    barbecued, Korean, 150
    garlic
        with broccoli, 144–5
        with golden noodles, 250–1
    ginger, flash-cooked, 148
    grilled, with Thai spices, 146–7
    red-cooked, with sweet potatoes, 152
    soup
        cinnamon barley, Chinese, 48
        with mint, Thai, 49
    stew, curried Malay, 149
berries
    coconut rice pudding with, 272
    congee, 273
beta carotene, 186
Better Health with (Mostly) Chinese Herbs
        and Foods (Leung), 190, 193, 275
bitter (fire) foods, 5
black bean(s), 75, 194, 231
    acorn squash with, 179
    brown rice with chicken and, 231
    halibut with, 71
    shrimp baked with, 75
    tofu with, Cantonese-style, 206–7
blackberries, coconut rice pudding with, 272
black teas, 274
bleeding, 171, 174
bloating, 188
blood pressure, high, *see* high blood pressure
blood tonics, 96
blueberries, coconut rice pudding with, 272
body types, yin and yang, 8
bok choy, 64
    hot and sour salmon with, 64
    pork braised with, 143
    steamed hot and sour hearts of, 172
bone marrow, 32

bones
    fractured, 90
    pain in, 92
Book of Songs, 219
broccoli
    curried tofu with, 210
    garlic, with pine nuts, 162
    garlic beef with, 144–5
    kung pao with peanuts and, 208
    scallops with, grilled hoisin, 83
    with soy-lemon dressing, 173
broth
    chicken, 27
    see also dashi
bu (invigorating foods), 68–9
buns, steamed, 239
burns, 179, 180, 231

C

cabbage, Chinese (Napa), 157, 175, 186
    mu shu pork with, 136
    mu shu vegetables with, 170
    seafood rice casserole with, 222
    slaw, hot and sour, 186
    soup with
        chicken, 33
        kimchee, 35
        stuffed cabbage pot, 46–7
    in vegetarian roll-ups, 201
caffeine, 275
Cai, Jingfeng, 218
cakes, 254–5
    banana, steamed, 278
    lemon sponge, 279
cancer, 66, 156, 177, 185, 186, 195, 202,
        214, 218, 275
canker sores, 160
capsaicin, 110
caramel pumpkin custard, 271
cardiovascular disease, *see* heart disease
carrot(s), 186
    black mushroom and leek soup with, 51

carrot(s) *(cont.)*
  and cabbage slaw, hot and sour, 186
  chicken saté with, 118–19
  in cinnamon curry rice, 221
  congee, 233
    with pork, 235
  curried beef stew with, 149
  in rainbow salad with spicy peanut
    dressing, 199
  in shrimp and vegetable salad, 190
  in vegetarian roll-ups, 201
cashews, chile chicken with, 112–13
cassia, 221
cauliflower
  curried tofu with, 210
  with soy-lemon dressing, 173
cayenne chiles, 111
celery hearts in sesame dressing, 181
cellophane noodles, chicken soup with
    Chinese cabbage and, 33
Chang, Anne, 176
Chang, Raymond, 176–7
Changhai Hospital (Shanghai), 218
Chen, Joyce, 170
chicken, 96–7
  Ambila, 100–3
  barbecued, Malay, 98
  brown rice with black beans and, 231
  chile, with cashews, 112–13
  clay-pot, in oyster sauce, 106
  congee, 233
  flash-cooked, with leeks, 115
  garlic, 144
  grilled, lemon grass, 116–17
  lemon, Vietnamese, 99
  lo mein, 246–7
  red-cooked, with sweet potatoes, 152
  salad
    with fresh mint, 122
    smoky, with fresh herb dressing,
      120–1
  saté, 118–19
  scallion-ginger, 104

chicken *(cont.)*
  soup
    broth, classic, 27
    clear-steamed, 28, 30–2
    drunken, 31, 32
    homey, 33
    hot and sour, 40–1
    miso, with snow peas and tofu, 34
    noodle, Vietnamese, 38–9
    with shark's fin, 36–7
  stir-fried
    with basil, 114
    spicy, with fresh vegetables, 108–9
  tandoori, 107
  wings, Chinese, 105
  yakitori, 123
chicken pox, 184
chilblains, 110
children, 16–17, 84, 96, 113, 238, 281
Children's Hospital (Boston), 56
chiles, 77, 110–11
  chicken with
    Ambila, 102
    and cashews, 112–13
  grilled shrimp with, 76–7
  soybean sprouts and leeks with, 198
Chinese Food for Thought (Lai), 68
Chinese Harvest Home Cooking School
    (Singapore), 131
*Chinese Herbal Foods to Enhance Your
    Health* (Weijan), 273
Chinese Herbal Medicine (Reid), 283, 284
Chinese Herbs with Common Foods (Lu), 96
Chinese Medicated Diet, 198
Chinese System of Food Cures, The (Lu), 75,
    95
Ch'ing dynasty, 68
cholera, 275
cholesterol, 78, 110, 171, 177, 178, 212,
    233
Chou period, 219
chowder, corn, 52
chrysanthemum flowers, 187

cilantro, 184, 190
    dressing, 182
    fish with, steamed, 59
    mussels with, steamed, 88
    vinaigrette, 134
cinnamon, 221
    apples baked with honey, jujubes, and,
        262
    barley soup with, 48
    curry rice, 221
    orange slices with honey and, 256
    pears poached with ginger and, 258
    tofu, braised, 211
circulation, 90, 184, 190
clam(s), 85
    with basil and garlic, 85
    soup, with garlic chives, 44
clear-steaming, 28
coconut, 267
    -banana pudding, 267
    green beans, curried, 163
    rice pudding, with berries, 272
    sauce, shrimp sambal with, 82
colds, 67, 72, 149, 190, 206, 212, 221, 260,
        273
    tonics for, 286, 292
collard greens, pork braised with, 143
Complete Book of Health & Healing, The
        (Reid), 56, 283
congee, 232–3
    with garnishes, 234
    Japanese, with shiitake mushrooms, 237
    pear, 273
    rainbow, 235
conjunctivitis, 163, 187
constipation, 175, 186, 187, 265, 269, 276
    tonic for, 294
convolvulus (water spinach), flash-cooked,
        with garlic, 159
cookies, almond, 276
cordyceps, 217–18
    drunken chicken soup with, 32
coriander, 163

corn
    chowder, 52
    and roasted bell pepper salad, 189
Cornell, China, and Oxford Project on
        Nutrition, Health, and Environment,
        218–19
Cornish game hens, roasted Malaysian, 128
cough, 84, 149, 169, 172, 186, 190, 221,
        233, 258, 261, 273, 276, 278
crab(s), 89
    salad with garlic pea shoots, 89
    steamed, with ginger dipping sauce, 90
cucumber, 157
    in rainbow salad with spicy peanut
        dressing, 199
    sweet and sour, 185
cumin, 82, 153, 163
curried
    beef stew, Malay, 149
    coconut green beans, 163
    pumpkin or squash, 180
    rice, cinnamon, 221
    tofu, 210
custard, 254
    pumpkin caramel, 270

d

dang gui (angelica), 18, 30
dashi, 243
    silken tofu with, 197
    udon with shrimp in, 244
    wild mushrooms with soba in, 243
dates
    Chinese, *see* jujube(s)
    clear-steamed chicken soup with angelica
        and, 38
de arbol peppers, 111
depression, 75, 160, 263
diabetes, 218, 236, 271
diarrhea, 163, 174, 215, 221, 229, 233, 275,
        286
dietotherapy, 217, 218

digestion, improving, 41, 48, 49, 66, 71, 73, 78, 82, 84, 110, 114, 120, 134, 187, 190, 194, 206, 233, 236, 256, 258, 265, 275, 279
  tonics for, 288, 297
diphtheria, 275
diuretics, 149, 175, 185, 233
double-boiling, 28
drunken chicken soup, 31
  with cordyceps, 32
duck, 97
  braised, with tangerine peel and sweet potatoes, 126–7
dysentery, 208, 275

e

eczema, 272
egg drop soup, vegetarian, 50
eggplant
  with black beans, 179
  braised, 169
Encyclopedia of Common Natural Ingredients Used in Food, Drugs and Cosmetics, 193
energy tonics, 96
eritadenine, 156
essence, 56
eye cysts, 256
eye inflammations, 162, 173

f

Family Herbal Cookbook, The (Tan), 30
female balance tonic, 291
fennel, 188
  ginger, 188
  pork tenderloin with leeks and, 138–9
fever, 261, 271, 273
fish
  baked, with wild mushroom sauce, 62–3
  braised, with garlic, 72
  grilled, with miso, 66

fish *(cont.)*
  halibut, pan-seared with garlicky black bean sauce, 71
  salmon, hot and sour, with greens, 64
  soup
    hot and sour, 42–3
    with pea shoots, 45
  steamed, 70
    with black mushrooms and prosciutto, 60–1
    with cilantro sauce, 59
    with ginger and scallions, 58
  stew, spicy, 73
  tuna, grilled ginger teriyaki, 67
five-element theory, 132
five-spice, 134
  pork roll-ups, 134–5
  scallops, 84
  tofu, 195
flatulence, 233, 275
flower buns, steamed, 239
flower teas, 274–5
flu, 67, 72, 212
  tonics for, 286, 292
folic acid, 160
fractures, 90
fried rice, 224–5
  shrimp, 228
  wild mushroom, 226
frostbite, 110, 168
fruit, 254, 255
  apples, 263
    baked with honey, cinnamon, and jujubes, 262
  banana-coconut pudding, 267
  cinnamon-honey orange slices, 256
  coconut rice pudding with berries, 272
  litchees and melon, almond soy jelly with, 266
  mangoes and silver tree ears in syrup, 264
  pears, 261
    Asian, steamed with honey and almonds, 260

fruit *(cont.)*
    congee, 273
    poached in cinnamon-ginger syrup, 258
    strawberries and melon in plum wine,
      257

g

garlic
  beef
    with broccoli, 144–5
    with noodles, 250–1
  broccoli, with pine nuts, 162
  clams with basil and, 85
  crab salad with pea shoots and, 89
  dressing
    bean curd noodles with, 200
    grilled leeks with, 174
    wilted greens with, 160
  fish fillets braised with, 72
  greens with, flash-cooked, 159
  halibut with black bean sauce with, 71
garlic chives
  bean sprouts flash-cooked with, 161
  clampot with, 44
  mu shu vegetables, 170
  shrimp stir-fried with, 77
gastritis, 275
genistein, 194
ginger, 67, 133
  beef, flash-cooked, 148
  chicken with
    and scallions, 104
    clear-steamed chicken soup, 28
  congee, 233
  dipping sauce, steamed crab with, 90
  fennel, 188
  fish fillets steamed with, 58
  lobster with
    saucy, 92
    and scallions, 91
  pears poached with cinnamon and, 258
  rice with, and scallions, 227

ginger *(cont.)*
  -scallion root tea, 286
  shrimp steamed with, 74
  teriyaki tempeh, 215
  tuna with, grilled teriyaki, 67
ginseng
  clear-steamed chicken soup with, 28
  licorice tea, 288
goiter, 85, 88
grains, 218–19
  barley, 236
    soup, with cinnamon, 48
    turkey congee with, 236
  wheat, 219, 238
    cream of, walnut-jujube, 270
  see also rice
green beans
  chicken with, 102–3
  curried coconut, 163
greens
  flash-cooked, with garlic, 159
  grilled squid with, 86–7
  hot and sour salmon with, 64
  pork braised with, 143
  wilted
    grilled scallops and bell peppers over,
      in cilantro dressing, 182–4
    with spicy garlic dressing, 160
green teas, 274
growing years, *see* children
gynecological disorders, 30

h

halibut, pan-seared, with garlicky black bean
    sauce, 71
ham, *see* prosciutto
Han dynasty, 194
hangover, 44, 160, 275
  tonic for, 298
Harvard University, 56
hawthorn, 78
  sauce, shrimp with, 78–80

Healing with Whole Foods (Pitchford), 219, 257
heart, 219
heartburn, 49, 186
heart disease, 66, 161, 177, 214, 218, 275
hemorrhoids, 41, 85, 160, 169, 267
hepatitis B, 176
herbal medicine, 4
herbal tonics, *see* tonics
high blood pressure, 73, 78, 83, 127, 181, 208, 218, 221, 278, 279
    tonic for, 293
HIV virus, 156
hoisin sauce
    grilled scallops with, 83
    grilled squid with, 86–7
holistic philosophy, 4–6, 20
honey, 254
    apples baked with cinnamon, jujubes, and, 262
    Asian pears steamed with almonds and, 260
    orange slices with cinnamon and, 256
Hong Kong, University of, 68
hormones, 30, 177, 212, 291
hot and sour
    cabbage slaw, 186
    hearts of bok choy, 172
    salmon, with greens, 64
    soup
        chicken, 40–1
        seafood, 42–3
hypertension, *see* high blood pressure

i

immune system, 6, 156, 166, 176, 178, 194, 212, 226, 233, 265
    tonic for, 289
Imperial Herbal restaurant (Singapore), 23–6, 78
impotence, 77, 92
insomnia, 238

Institute of East-West Medicine (New York), 176
Interferon, 176

j

jasmine rice, 220
jiang (sweet bean sauce), 81
jujube(s), 263, 270
    apples baked with honey, cinnamon, and, 262
    -walnut cream, 270

k

Kashmiri chiles, 111
kidneys, 52, 56, 74, 77, 88, 92, 132, 163, 175, 219, 272
    tonic for, 290
Korean chiles, 111
kung pao with broccoli and peanuts, 208

l

lactation, 233
Lai, T. C., 68–70
lamb, 132
    congee, 233
    red-cooked, with sweet potatoes, 152
    vindaloo, 153
Lao Zi, 4
laryngitis, 157, 185
late summer, diet for, 13
laxatives, 185
leeks, 115
    in barbecued pork brown rice, 230
    chicken with
        flash-cooked, 115
        lo mein, 246–7
    in cinnamon curry rice, 221
    garlic bean curd noodles with, 200
    grilled, in garlic-soy dressing, 174
    pork with
        and fennel, 138–9
        mu shu, 136

leeks *(cont.)*

    in soup

        with black mushrooms, 51

        hot and sour, 40

    and soybean sprouts in hot chile sauce, 198

    in vegetarian roll-ups, 201

Legal Seafood restaurant (Boston), 55

LEM (lentinus edodes mycelium), 156

lemon(s), 84, 279

    sauce, five-spice scallops with, 84

    -soy dressing, 173

    sponge cake, 279

lemon grass, 99

    chicken with

        grilled, 116–17

        Vietnamese, 99

lentinan, 156

lettuce

    chicken saté with, 118–19

    leaves

        barbecued beef wrapped in, 150

        ground turkey wrapped in, 124

    in shrimp and vegetable salad, 190

Leung, Albert, 161, 190, 193–4, 206, 231, 249, 275

Li Lian Xing, 23

licorice ginseng tea, 288

life passages, 16–20

Lin, Dr., 3–4

litchees, 266

    almond soy jelly with melon and, 266

liver, 73, 88, 132, 198, 272

    tonics for, 287, 290

lobster

    ginger-scallion, 91

    saucy garlic, 92

lo mein, chicken, 246–7

longevity tonic, 290

lotus root cooler, 287

Lu, Henry, 75, 92, 95–7, 127, 194

Luis, Katy, 100–3, 153

Luis, Steve, 100, 101

lungs, 71, 175, 194, 206, 208, 254, 265, 266, 269, 273, 276, 281, 288

m

madeleines, orange, 280

malaria, 208

malnutrition, 157

mangoes and silver tree ears in syrup, 264

measles, 184

meat, 131–3

    lamb, 132

        congee, 233

        red-cooked, with sweet potatoes, 152

        vindaloo, 153

    pork, 132

        barbecued, brown rice with, 230

        braised home-style, 143

        congee with vegetables and, 235

        kimchee soup with, 35

        mu shu, healthy, 136–7

        roll-ups, five-spice, 134–5

        sesame noodles with, 248–9

        spareribs, spicy, in squash or pumpkin, 140–2

        tenderloin, spicy, with leeks and fennel, 138–9

        tofu with, 205

    see also beef

melon(s)

    almond soy jelly with litchees and, 266

    clear-steamed chicken soup with prosciutto in, 30

    and strawberries in plum wine, 257

menopause, 18, 30, 66, 202, 238

menstruation, 181, 193, 258, 272, 291

migraines, 193

millet, 219

Ming dynasty, 155

mint

    chicken salad with, 122

    Thai beef soup with, 49

miso, 66
  chicken soup, with snow peas and tofu, 34
  fish fillets with, grilled, 66
motherhood, 17–18, 28, 89, 96, 171
motion sickness, 286
mucus, excess, 85
mung beans, 161
  see also bean sprouts
mushrooms
  black, 157
    chicken lo mein with, 246–7
    clay-pot chicken in oyster sauce with, 106
    clear-steamed chicken soup with, 30
    in fragrant steamed pearl balls, 202–4
    leek soup with, 51
    mu shu pork with, 136
    steamed fish with prosciutto and, 60–1
    tofu simmered with, 212
  enoki (enokitake), 157, 164
  maitake, 157, 164
  matsutake, 164–5
  oyster, 157, 165
    chicken stir-fried with vegetables and, 108–9
  reishi, 176–7
  seafood rice casserole with, 222
  shiitake, 155–6, 165
    braised garlic fish fillets with, 72
    Japanese congee with, 237
    mu shu vegetables with, 170
  wild, 164–5
    baked fish packages with sauce of, 62
    congee, 233, 234
    fried rice, 226
    grilled, with teriyaki dressing, 178
    with soba, 243
    stir-fried with snap peas in oyster sauce, 166
    and wilted spinach salad, 187

mu shu
  pork, healthy, 136–7
  vegetable rolls, 170–1
mussels, 88
  steamed with cilantro, 88
mutton, 132

n

National Cancer Institute, 193, 194
nausea, 229, 233, 265, 286
nearsightedness, 162, 173
Nei Jing, see Yellow Emperor's Classic of Internal Medicine
Ng Siong Mui, 131–3, 134
Nonya cuisine, 268
noodles, 245
  bean curd, spicy garlic, 200
  chicken lo mein, 246–7
  chicken soup with
    and Chinese cabbage, 33
    Vietnamese, 38–9
  garlic beef with, 250–1
  sesame, 248–9
  shrimp and vegetable salad with, 190
  soba, Japanese wild mushrooms with, 243
  udon, with shrimp, 244
  vegetarian pad thai, 245
nuts, 112
  almond(s), 261, 266, 276
    crisps, 276
    pears steamed with honey and, 260
    soy jelly with litchees and melon, 266
  cashews, chile chicken with, 112–13
  peanut(s), 113
    dressing, spicy, 199
    kung pao with broccoli and, 208
  pine nuts
    garlic broccoli with, 162
    steamed rice with, 220
  walnut(s), 270
    -jujube cream, 270

o

olive kernels, 260
onions, ginger teriyaki tempeh with, 215
oolong teas, 274
orange, 281
    madeleines, 280
    slices, cinnamon-honey, 256
osteoporosis, 194
oyster sauce
    clay-pot chicken in, 106
    garlic beef with noodles with, 250–1
    wild mushrooms stir-fried with snap peas
        in, 166

p

pad thai, vegetarian, 245
pancakes, scallion, 240–2
pancreas, 149, 180, 229
parsnips, 149
    curried beef stew with, 149
Passmore, Jacki, 284
pastries, 254–5
    almond, 276
    Malaysian, 268
    orange madeleines, 280
    see also cakes
peach congee, 273
peanut(s), 118
    dressing, spicy, 199
    kung pao with broccoli and, 208
pear(s), 261
    Asian, steamed with honey and almonds,
        260
    congee, 233, 273
    poached in cinnamon-ginger syrup,
        258
pearl balls, fragrant steamed, 202–4
peas
    in cinnamon curry rice, 221
    congee with, 235
    curried tofu with, 210
    see also snap peas; snow peas

pea shoots
    crab salad with garlic and, 87
    fish fillet soup with, 45
    flash-cooked, with garlic, 159
    wilted, grilled scallops and bell peppers
        over, in cilantro dressing,
        182–4
peppers
    chicken and
        brown rice with black beans, 231
        stir-fried with mushrooms, snow peas,
            and, 108–9
        yakitori, 123
    fish stew with, 73
    and grilled scallops over wilted greens in
        cilantro dressing, 182–4
    hot, *see* chiles
    in rainbow salad with spicy peanut
        dressing, 199
    roasted, and corn salad, 189
    stir-fried shrimp with, 81
    tempeh and
        ginger teriyaki, 215
        with sweet and sour sauce, 213
pequín chiles, 111
phytoestrogens, 18, 194, 202
pimples, tonic for, 295
pine nuts
    garlic broccoli with, 162
    steamed rice with, 220
pineapple, tempeh and, with sweet and sour
    sauce, 213
Pitchford, Paul, 210, 257
plum wine, strawberries and melon in, 257
PMS, 30
    tonic for, 291
poison ivy or oak, 275
pork, 132
    barbecued, brown rice with, 230
    braised home-style, 143
    congee with vegetables and, 235
    kimchee soup with, 35
    mu shu, healthy, 136–7
    roll-ups, five-spice, 134–5

pork *(cont.)*
    sesame noodles with, 248–9
    spareribs, spicy, in squash or pumpkin,
        140–2
    tenderloin, spicy, with leeks and fennel,
        138–9
    tofu with, 205
porridge, rice, *see* congee
potatoes, curried beef stew with, 149
poultry
    Cornish game hens, roasted Malaysian,
        128
    duck, 97
        braised, with tangerine peel and sweet
            potatoes, 126–7
    turkey
        cabbage stuffed with, in soup, 46–7
        congee, with barley, 236
        cutlets, garlic, 144
        saucy, wrapped in lettuce leaves, 124
    see also chicken
prawns, 77
pregnancy, 17–18, 84, 89, 258
prosciutto
    clear-steamed chicken soup with, in
        melons, 30
    steamed fish with black mushrooms and,
        60–1
prostate, enlarged, 265
pudding, 254
    banana-coconut, 267
    coconut rice, with berries, 272
    two-spice vanilla tapioca, 269
pumpkin, 157, 271
    caramel custard, 271
    curried, 180
    spicy spareribs in, 140–2
pungent (metal) foods, 5

q

qi (energy), 9, 32, 37, 56, 59, 88, 184, 198,
    218, 229, 263, 265, 266, 276, 281,
    283

Quarterly Review of Biology, 110

r

raspberries, 272
    coconut rice pudding with, 272
red teas, 274
Reid, Daniel, 56, 283–5
Reid, Yuki, 283
rempeh, 100
rheumatism, 77, 110, 149, 221
rice, 218–19
    brown
        barbecued pork, 230
        basic cooked, 229
        chicken–black bean, 231
    cinnamon curry, 221
    congee, 232–3
        with garnishes, 234
        Japanese, with shiitake mushrooms,
            237
        pear, 273
        rainbow, 235
    cream of, walnut-jujube, 270
    fragrant steamed pearl balls, 202
    fried, 224–5
        shrimp, 228
        wild mushroom, 226
    pudding, coconut, with berries, 272
    scallion-ginger, 227
    seafood casserole, 222–3
    steamed, with roasted pine nuts, 220
    white, basic cooked, 220
rice wine
    chicken soup with, 31
    crab steeped in, 90
Richards, Debby, 278

s

sago, 269
Saitama Cancer Research Institute, 275
salad
    chicken, smoky, with fresh herb dressing,
        120–1

salad (cont.)
   chicken, with fresh mint, 122
   corn and roasted bell pepper, 189
   crab, with garlic pea shoots, 89
   rainbow, with spicy peanut dressing,
      199
   shrimp and vegetable, with fresh herb
      dressing, 190–1
   wilted spinach and mushroom, 187
salmon, hot and sour, with greens, 64
salty (water) foods, 5
sambal, shrimp, 82
saté, chicken, 118–19
scallion(s)
   and ginger
      chicken with, 104
      lobster with, 91
      rice with, 227
      tea, 286
   ground turkey with, wrapped in lettuce
      leaves, 124
   pancakes, 240–2
scallops
   dried, 83
   five-spice, with lemon sauce, 84
   grilled
      hoisin, 83
      and rainbow peppers over wilted
         greens in cilantro dressing, 182–4
   hot and sour soup with, 42
seafood, 55–92
   rice casserole, 222
   soup
      clampot with garlic chives, 44
      hot and sour, 42–3
   squid, grilled, with warm greens, 86–7
   see also fish; shellfish
seasonal diet, 10–15
sesame, 80, 249
   congee, 233
   noodles, 248–9
   shrimp with, 78–80
Shanghai College of Traditional Medicine,
   217

Shanghai Restaurant (Singapore), 268
shark's fin soup with chicken, 36–7
shellfish
   clams
      with basil and garlic, 85
      soup, with garlic chives, 44
   crabs
      salad with garlic pea shoots, 89
      steamed with ginger dipping sauce,
         90
   hot and sour soup with, 42
   lobster
      ginger-scallion, 91
      saucy garlic, 92
   mussels, steamed with cilantro, 88
   see also scallops; shrimp
Shen Nong, Emperor, 4, 274
Sherman, Paul, 110
shrimp
   baked with black beans, 75
   fried rice, 229
   grilled, with chile dressing, 76–7
   hot and sour soup with, 42
   sambal, 82
   seafood rice casserole with, 222
   steamed, 70
      with ginger, 74
   stir-fried
      with garlic chives, 77
      saucy, 81
   udon with, 244
   and vegetable salad with fresh herb
      dressing, 190–1
   yin-yang, with hawthorn dipping sauce,
      78–80
sinuses, 110
snap peas
   chicken stir-fried with mushrooms, bell
      peppers and, 108–9
   garlic beef with, 144
      with noodles, 250–1
   wild mushrooms stir-fried with, in oyster
      sauce, 166
snow fungus, see tree ears, silver

snow peas, 184
  in barbecued pork brown rice, 230
  chicken and
    black bean brown rice, 231
    stir-fried with mushrooms and bell
      peppers, 108–9
  garlic beef with, 144
  shoots, *see* pea shoots
  shrimp sambal with, 82
  soup with
    hot and sour seafood, 42
    miso chicken, with tofu, 34
    vegetarian egg drop, 50
  tempeh and, with sweet and sour sauce,
    213
  udon with shrimp and, 244
soba with wild mushrooms, 243
sore throat, 157, 172, 185, 221, 233, 257,
  260
sorghum, 219
soups, 23–52
  beef with mint, Thai, 49
  black mushroom and leek, 51
  cabbage, stuffed, 46–7
  chicken
    broth, classic, 27
    clear-steamed, 28, 30–2
    drunken, 31, 32
    homey, 33
    hot and sour, 40
    miso, with snow peas and tofu, 34
    noodle, Vietnamese, 38–9
    and shark's fin, 36–7
  cinnamon barley, Chinese, 48
  clampot with garlic chives, Korean, 44
  corn chowder, 52
  egg drop, vegetarian, 50
  fish fillet and pea shoot, 45
  hot and sour, 40–1
    seafood, 42–3
  kimchee, spicy, 35
  shark's fin, 36–7
  sweet, 253
sour (wood) foods, 5

soy
  -garlic dressing, 174
  -lemon dressing, 173
soybeans, 194–6, 202
  black, *see* black beans
  fermented, 71
  see also miso; tofu
soy milk, 269
  almond jelly with litchees and melon,
    266
  pudding
    two-spice vanilla tapioca, 269
    coconut rice, with berries, 272
spinach, 160
  congee, 233
  crab salad with garlic and, 87
  fish fillet soup with, 45
  flash-cooked, with garlic, 159
  grilled squid with, 86–7
  pork braised with, 143
  red-cooked lamb with sweet potatoes and,
    152
  tofu braised with cinnamon and, 211
  wilted
    grilled scallops and bell peppers over,
      in cilantro dressing, 182–4
    salad with mushrooms, 187
    with spicy garlic dressing, 160
spleen, 56, 149, 163, 184, 194, 197, 219,
  229, 245
sponge cake, lemon, 279
spring, diet for, 11
squash
  with black beans, 179
  curried, 180
  spicy spareribs in, 140–2
squid, grilled, with warm greens, 86–7
staples, 218–19
  see also noodles; rice; breads; grains
star anise, 120
stew
  beef, curried, 149
  fish, 73
stir-frying, 20

stomach, 59, 73, 82, 149, 153, 160, 194,
        197, 219, 261, 263
    see also appetite; digestion
strawberries and melon in plum wine, 257
stress, 75, 243, 263
stroke, 275
sugar, 254, 265
summer, diet for, 12
Sung dynasty, 274
Sweet 'N' Tart Cafe (New York), 253–4
sweet (earth) foods, 5
sweet bean sauce, stir-fried shrimp with, 81
sweet and sour dressing/sauce
    cucumbers with, 185
    fried tempeh with, 213
    shrimp and vegetable salad with, 190–1
sweet potatoes
    with black beans, 179
    congee with, 235
    duck braised with tangerine peel and,
        126–7
    red-cooked lamb with, 152
    stir-fried, spicy, 168

t

Tan, Cecilia, 30
Tan, Kok Kheng, 155–6
tandoori chicken, 107
tangerine peel, duck braised with sweet
        potatoes and, 126–7
tannin, 275
Tao of Health, Sex, and Longevity, The
        (Reid), 283
Taoism, 4, 156–7
tapioca, 269
    pudding, two-spice vanilla, 269
tea, 274–5
    ginger-scallion root, 286
    ginseng licorice, 288
    pastries and cakes with, 254–5
tea-smoking, 120
tempeh, 195
    fried, with sweet and sour sauce, 213

tempeh *(cont.)*
    ginger teriyaki, 215
    stir-fried, with basil, 214
ten complete great tonic, 289
teriyaki
    ginger tempeh, 215
    tuna, 67
    wild mushrooms, 178
Thai chiles, 111
thirst, excessive, 112, 163
Three Kingdoms period, 274
thyroid, 85, 88
Tianqiao Hospital (Beijing), 55
toddlers, 16
tofu, 194, 195, 197, 199
    in black bean sauce, Cantonese-style,
        206–7
    braised, with cinnamon, 211
    curried, 210
    fragrant steamed pearl balls, 202–4
    kung pao with broccoli and peanuts, 208–9
    ma po, 205
    miso chicken soup with snow peas and, 34
    noodles, spicy garlic, 200
    pad thai, 245
    in rainbow salad with spicy peanut
        dressing, 199
    rolls, with vegetables, 200
    silken, Japanese-style, 197
    simmered with black mushrooms, 212
tomatoes, 73
    curried tofu with, 210
    egg drop soup with, 50
    fish stew with, 73
tong shui, 253–54
tonics, 96–7, 283–98
    acne, 295
    cold and flu, 292
    constipation, 294
    female balance, 291
    ginger-scallion root tea, 286
    ginseng licorice tea, 288
    hangover, 298
    high blood pressure, 293

tonics *(cont.)*
    indigestion, 297
    longevity, 290
    lotus root cooler, 287
    ten complete great, 289
    toothache, 296
toothache, tonic for, 296
traumatic injuries, 90
tree ears, silver, 265
    and mangoes in syrup, 264
tuna, grilled ginger teriyaki, 67
turkey
    congee, with barley, 236
    cutlets, garlic, 144
    ground
        cabbage stuffed with, in soup, 46–7
        saucy, wrapped in lettuce leaves, 124
turmeric, 103, 108
turnips, cinnamon curry rice with, 221

U

ulcers, 64, 110, 157, 166, 243, 261
urinary problems, 166, 189, 257, 269

V

vanilla tapioca pudding, two-spice, 269
vegetable(s), 155–8
    asparagus, 127
        congee, 233, 234
        roasted, with sesame vinaigrette, 175
    beans
        Chinese long, chicken with, 102–3
        see also black beans; soybeans
    bok choy, 64
        hot and sour salmon with, 64
        pork braised with, 143
        steamed hot and sour hearts of, 172
    broccoli
        curried tofu with, 210
        garlic, with pine nuts, 162
        garlic beef with, 144–5
        kung pao with peanuts and, 208
        scallops with, grilled hoisin, 83

vegetable(s) *(cont.)*
    with soy-lemon dressing, 173
    carrot(s), 186
        black mushroom and leek soup with, 51
        and cabbage slaw, hot and sour, 186
        chicken saté with, 118–19
        congee, 233, 235
        in rainbow salad with spicy peanut dressing, 199
    cauliflower
        curried tofu with, 210
        with soy-lemon dressing, 173
    celery hearts in sesame dressing, 181
    chicken stir-fried with, 108–9
        with basil, 114
    cinnamon curry rice with, 221
    corn
        chowder, 52
        and roasted bell pepper salad, 189
    cucumber, 157
        in rainbow salad with spicy peanut dressing, 199
        sweet and sour, 185
    curried beef stew with, 149
    eggplant
        with black beans, 179
        braised, 169
    fennel, 188
        ginger, 188
        pork tenderloin with leeks and, 138–9
    lettuce
        barbecued beef wrapped in, 150
        chicken saté with, 118–19
        ground turkey wrapped in, 124
    meat with, 133
    mu shu, 170–1
    peas
        congee with, 235
        curried tofu with, 210
    pea shoots
        crab salad with garlic and, 87
        fish fillet soup with, 45
        flash-cooked, with garlic, 159

vegetable(s) *(cont.)*
    wilted, grilled scallops and bell peppers over, in cilantro dressing, 182–4
    roll-ups, with tofu, 201
    and shrimp salad with fresh herb dressing, 190–1
    snap peas
        chicken stir-fried with mushrooms, bell peppers and, 108–9
        beef with noodles and, 250–1
        garlic beef with, 144
        wild mushrooms stir-fried with, in oyster sauce, 166
    squash
        with black beans, 179
        curried, 180
        spicy spareribs in, 140–2
    sweet potatoes
        with black beans, 179
        congee with, 235
        duck braised with tangerine peel and, 126–7
        red-cooked lamb with, 152
        stir-fried, spicy, 168
    tomatoes, 73
        curried tofu with, 210
        egg drop soup with, 50
        fish stew with, 73
    see also bean sprouts; cabbage; greens; leeks; peppers; snow peas; spinach
vegetarian egg drop soup, 50
vinaigrette, 120
    cilantro, 134
    sesame, 175
vindaloo, lamb, 153

W

walnut(s), 270
    -jujube cream, 270
Wang-Lee Tee Eng, Mrs., 25–6
water chestnuts, 21
    in fragrant steamed pearl balls, 202–4

water chestnuts *(cont.)*
    ground turkey with, wrapped in lettuce leaves, 124
    in kung pao with broccoli and peanuts, 208–9
watercress, 159
    fish fillet soup with, 45
    flash-cooked, with garlic, 159
    grilled squid with, 86–7
    wilted, with spicy garlic dressing, 160
Weijian, Weng, 232, 273
wheat, 219, 238
    cream of, walnut-jujube, 270
whooping cough, 84, 186
winter, diet for, 15
wood ears, 41, 165, 171
    mu shu pork with, 136
    mu shu vegetables with, 170–1
Wu Rui, 155

X

Xi, Yuan Zeng, 218
xue (damaging foods), 69

Y

yakitori chicken, 123
yang tonics, 96, 97
yeast dough, Chinese, 238
Yellow Emperor's Classic of Internal Medicine, 4–5, 95, 156
yin tonics, 96, 97
yin and yang, 3–5, 8–9, 24
Yu, Xue Re, 217–18
Yuan Mei, 68, 69

Z

Zhu, Chun-Han, 8, 55–6, 185
Ziment, Irwin, 110
zucchini, 179

A Note About the Author

At the age of nineteen Nina Simonds traveled to Taiwan, where she studied for three and a half years under the direction of Chinese master chefs and became fluent in Mandarin Chinese. Simonds also apprenticed and studied for a year at La Varenne, École de Cuisine, in Paris, and received a Grand Diplôme in classic French cuisine. For the past thirty-five years, she has taught classes in cooking schools across the United States and Europe, and she travels annually throughout Southeast Asia. She and her family lived recently for two years in London.

Simonds is a member of the Nutrition Roundtable at the Harvard School of Public Health. She hosted a food/health/lifestyle special, *A Spoonful of Ginger: Food as Medicine,* for public television, which received a James Beard Award.

Simonds is an Asian correspondent for *Gourmet* magazine and a regular contributor to *The New York Times* travel section. Her articles have appeared in the *Los Angeles Times*, *The Washington Post, Health,* and *Cooking Light*, among others. Her books have received numerous awards; *A Spoonful of Ginger* won both the IACP Cookbook Award and the James Beard Award. Her children's book, *Moonbeams, Dumplings & Dragon Boats: A Treasury of Chinese Holiday Tales, Activities & Recipes* was given a Parents' Choice Award and a Chapman Award for Best Classroom Read-Aloud. She lives in Salem, Massachusetts.

A Note on the Type

The text of this book was set in FF Meta Plus and Sabon.

Heralded as the Helvetica of the nineties, the definitive sans serif face FF Meta was originally commissioned for the German Post Office (Bundespost) in 1984. Although the project was eventually canceled by the Bundepost in favor of staying with Helvetica, Erik Spiekermann completed the design as a digital font in 1989, and it was published in 1991 by FontShop International as part of their FontFont type library. Since that time, the family has been expanded to its current comprehensive state of twenty weights and has been warmly embraced by the international design market.

Sabon is a typeface designed by Jan Tschichold (1902–1974), the well-known German typographer. Based loosely on the original designs by Claude Garamond (c. 1480–1561), Sabon is unique in that it was explicitly designed for hot-metal composition on both Monotype and Linotype machines as well as for filmsetting. Designed in 1966 in Frankfurt, Sabon was named for the famous Lyons punch cutter Jacques Sabon, who is thought to have brought some of Garamond's matrices to Frankfurt.

Composed by North Market Street Graphics, Lancaster, Pennsylvania
Black-and-white prints by Nardulli Inc., Hollywood, California
Printed and bound by Tien Wah Press, Singapore
Designed by Ph.D, Santa Monica, California